D1477116

THE MOTORBUS IN
LONDON COUNTRY

KENNETH WARREN

LONDON

IAN ALLAN LTD

Some Definitions

London country in the text refers to a geographical area, the outer zone where the term was first used by the LGOC. *London Country* (capital C) refers to the company of that name, usually indicated by the initials LCBS, ie London Country Bus Services Ltd. *Country buses* (capital C) is an LPTB term used for the green vehicles plying in the *Country area* (another definition), to distinguish them from the *Central buses* (red) at work in the *Central area*. *London Transport* is a generic term introduced by the LPTB to indicate all the activities carried on by that organisation, including Country buses, Central buses, railways, trams, trolleybuses and coaches; the term lasted throughout the LTE and LTB periods and is still employed by the GLC enterprise.

Some Initials:

AEC — Associated Equipment Company (latterly of Southall, which supplied the majority of London Transport's vehicles during its best days)

BET — British Electric Traction (a holding company with an interest in many bus companies, including Thames Valley)

GLC — Greater London Council

LCBS — London Country Bus Services Ltd

LGCS — London General Country Services Ltd

LGOC — London General Omnibus Company Ltd (also known as General)

LPTB — London Passenger Transport Board

LTB — London Transport Board

LTE — London Transport Executive

MAP — Market Analysis Project

NBC — National Bus Company Ltd

OMO — One-man-operated; in view of the Sex Discrimination Act and the fact that LCBS employs women drivers, this really ought to be OPO or one-person-operated, but the old term has tended to survive.

First published 1984

ISBN 0 7110 1360 8

Published by Ian Allan Ltd, Shepperton, Surrey; and printed by Ian Allan Printing Ltd at their works at Coombelands in Runnymede, England.

Previous page:
RT3442 waits for departure time at Hertford bus station; buses of this type worked the 310 route for many years. This vehicle is in early London Country livery and boasts the logo on the offside rear panel. *Edward Shirras*

Contents

The Tillingbourne Bus Co has had a long history of activity in the Guildford area right through the London Transport era and into London Country times. Here new Dennis Lancet with Wadham bodywork is seen at

Guildford's Friary bus station on arrival from Horsham via Cranleigh and Gomshall. LCBS bus RP36, turned out for the 408A to Merrow, Bushey Hill, looks somewhat ponderous and dated by comparison. *M. J. Dryhurst*

Preface

This book reflects many years' interest in buses, an interest started in the 1930s when I first read the Dartford local timetable; the interest was extended when I discovered reference to routes in Sevenoaks that proved there was life beyond Dartford after all. It is written at a time when there are no longer certainties about bus services; the financial position of bus companies has become a matter of economic consideration and political debate. London Country Bus Services Ltd was established by a political decision to hand over much of the former London Transport empire to the Greater London Council on 1 January 1970, and politicians have seen no reason to keep away since. Bus services in the London Country area are still substantial in terms of the numbers of buses deployed, staff engaged and passengers carried, though there have been withdrawals and reductions in service where passenger loadings have dwindled. Unlike railways, bus services when closed leave nothing behind them except photographs, records and memories; an aim of this book has been to record the past, to jog memories, as well as to survey the present.

I have been grateful to a number of people for help with this book. First I would thank Mr Frank Jones not only for providing access to his unique collection of photographs, but also for his guidance on early vehicles. The late Albert McCall patiently reviewed the 'Buses on the Roads' section and provided much detail for this and other parts of the book. I have drawn on Mr George Robbins's exceptional knowledge of the East Surrey Traction Co and the London General Omnibus Co, especially in the early sections. Mr Dick Turnbull has proved a kindly critic and provided insights into 'How It Happened' by drawing on his experience of London Transport over

50 years. Mr Reg Westgate kindly loaned me some early timetables when they proved impossible to get from any other source. I have had generous help from, and interesting discussions with, Mr Stephen Morris and Mr Alan Butcher of Ian Allan Ltd; the company's photographic collection was opened up for me and I have included many pictures from it. I have also drawn on the London Transport collection and from the work of Reverend Edward Shirras. Mr John Parke kindly gave the text a final reading. London Country Bus Services Ltd has been most supportive in providing information and photographs, though I must emphasise that this book is in no way an official publication. All the views expressed are my own, as is the responsibility for any errors there may be.

I have adopted the convention in the book of working, where the narrative required it, in a clockwise direction starting from Gravesend and coming round to Grays and Tilbury on the opposite bank of the Thames. I hope this allows me to keep a mass of material in some sort of order. I have been unable to include reference to every route and to every bus that has ever run in London country but I hope that there is enough here to interest all those who work or travel on the buses and the historians and enthusiasts. Finally, printing deadlines mean that I have had to stop somewhere, so I have taken events up to March 1984 and 'current' in the text refers to that date. Doubtless by the time the book appears there will have been changes, though I hope they will not be significant enough to alter the main drift of the argument

Kenneth Warren

1
How it Happened

'London country' currently forms an outer ring of bus operations, with London Transport (the responsibility of the Greater London Council), providing services in an inner zone defined for the most part by the GLC boundaries. London Country Bus Services Ltd (LCBS) is a commercial concern, part of the National Bus Co (NBC), and has been at work only since 1 January 1970; however, the concept of London country goes back a long way and the concept and the term may be attributed to the London General Omnibus Co. It was first used formally in agreements signed with the East Surrey Traction Co Ltd and the National Omnibus & Transport Co Ltd in 1921 on 7 and 21 July respectively. The purpose of the agreements (a third on somewhat similar terms was worked out with the Thames Valley Traction Co Ltd) was to define and make provision for working an outer area that the London General Omnibus Co (LGOC) had not the immediate capability or intention of developing itself. The company preferred to use others as agents, working — under fairly tight rein — 'for and on account of General'. The companies selected as agents had more experience of working inter-urban and rural routes than LGOC whose central activity was bus work in London itself; also, and perhaps significantly, the agents were able to operate more cheaply than the larger firm.

In 1921 bus networks throughout the country were at a significant point of development and beginning a decade of dramatic expansion. The seeds of this advance were sown before 1914, many of the firms which became household names in the 1920s and 1930s beginning operations with motor (or steam) vehicles in the early years of the century. World War 1 interrupted progress so far as developing services was concerned, but at the same time brought technical improvements in motor vehicle design, power and reliability. Additionally, a large number of men gained experience with motor vehicles, both driving and maintenance, which was easily convertible to peacetime use. The problems caused by wartime restrictions on the infant motorbus industry took some time to sort out, but by 1921 vehicles were becoming available, there was a vast reserve of expertise to work them, and the social climate of the time encouraged a much greater mobility in the population than had been thought acceptable before 1914. In the social changes in town and country in the 1920s the motorbus had a most significant part to play.

The historical survey which forms the basis of this part of the book goes on to consider the trend towards monopoly of bus operation achieved partially by the LGOC — and expressed in the 'London General Country Services' title adopted for the buses in the outer zone — and almost completely by the London Passenger Transport Board in the years immediately after 1933. The LPTB was succeeded by the London Transport Executive in 1948, in turn replaced by the London Transport Board in 1962; the fortunes of bus work in the Country area reached their peak in the early 1950s and then began a steady decline. The political decision to hand over responsibility for London's public transport (except of course for the British Rail lines) to the GLC posed the problem of management of the buses in London country and of the Green Line coaches; thus London Country Bus Services Ltd was set up to take over those parts of the former London Transport empire and succeeded to a doubtful inheritance on 1 January 1970.

This part of the book includes a consideration of Green Line, the history of which has been tightly interwoven with that of the Country buses throughout almost the entire period; it ends with a survey of the independents who were innovatory and active in the early years — some of them have shown an almost astonishing tenacity in surviving to the present day.

For and On Account of General

The London General Omnibus Company

The LGOC dates back to 17 December 1855 when the 'Compagnie des Omnibus de Londres', with a head office in Paris and a *branch* office in the Strand, acquired most of the 810 horsebuses then running in London. Shortly after, on 11 January 1856, the French title was dropped in favour of the familiar London General Omnibus Co — the term General was included because of the provisional registration of another company, the London Omnibus Co, which came to nothing. In the first year of operation some 450 buses were working daily, each bus travelling an average of 54 miles in service over a period of 12-15hr. The crews worked throughout this tour of duty, but the horses were changed every 3hr after hauling a bus some 12 miles. Each horse consumed 16lb of oats daily, together with 10lb of hay — feeding the 5,800 horses was in fact the most expensive part of the enterprise.

Although the largest operator on the London streets, at no time did the LGOC secure a monopoly. Experiments with new forms of traction, initially electric in the 1890s, then steam (1899) and petrol (also 1899), were made by the smaller companies. However, increased competition from tramway systems and the newly-electrified underground railways stirred the LGOC to order 100 motorbuses (50 German Bussing and 50 De Dion) in 1905. A 'Superintendent of the motor department' was appointed to work alongside the splendidly titled Superintendent of Horses, and no more horsebuses were ordered. Amalgamation with the Vanguard Motorbus Co in 1908 — by which year the LGOC were using the fleetname 'General', first adopted in 1905 — brought with it an engineering plant at Blackhorse Lane, Walthamstow (the predecessor of AEC) and General introduced its own design of bus, the X class, in 1909. Further development work produced the famous B class in October 1910 and 2,500 of these sturdy, reliable vehicles had been built by the end of 1913; the build ceased at B2826 after the outbreak of war. The last horsebus in LGOC service ran on 25 October 1911 and an age quietly departed.

The Underground group of companies acquired financial control of the LGOC which was reconstituted on 27 July 1912 so that all its capital was held by the Underground Electric Railway Co of London Ltd with headquarters at Electric Railway House, the forerunner of 55 Broadway. These changes brought into the London bus scene two men who were to have lasting influence — Albert Stanley, later Lord Ashfield, and Frank Pick; a remarkable management team widely regarded as the architects of London Transport. With secure finances, ambitious management and a reliable motorbus in operation, the London bus scene was set for dramatic change. Hitherto services had operated only to the fringe of the countryside, but in 1912 it was possible to run much further afield. On Sunday 14 July three routes were initiated:

45: Houslow (Bell) to Staines (daily)
61: Brixton to Whyteleafe (Sundays only)
62: Hounslow (Bell) to Windsor Castle (Sundays only)

In August the Windsor route became a daily service and was renumbered 81; it was joined by a new 89 from Hounslow to Burnham Beeches. The B type buses employed proved eminently suitable for this kind of work and in the summer of 1913 a new batch of routes was opened: Golders Green to Hatfield (109), Hounslow Barracks station to Maidenhead (110), Finsbury Park to Hoddesdon (113), Clapham Common to Lower Kingswood (115) and Stockwell to Redhill (116). Two daily services started at this time were 84: Golders Green to St Albans and 95: Bromley to Westerham Hill. When reinstated in 1914 the Sundays only routes were all renumbered in a new series between 151 and 178 and Reigate and Dorking were added to the destinations served. National began running its steam buses to Hampton Court and to Bexley in 1912. All these services were, of course, intended primarily to bring people from inner London out to the leafy country, and the distinction in those days must have been particularly sharp. The outbreak of war brought development of these excursions to a halt, though a few lingered on for a time. Later the requisition of buses for army transport and the general shortage of serviceable vehicles made many of these lengthy journeys out of the question.

East Surrey Traction Co Ltd

The arrival of LGOC buses at Redhill on the Sundays only Route 116 from Stockwell on 20 July 1913 brought that company into contact with the East Surrey Traction Co Ltd whose protests were instrumental in compelling the LGOC to withdraw to Merstham, The Feathers. The LGOC had planned to work to Reigate which was the very centre of East Surrey operations — and has remained the centre of

Above:
This is a very early, probably 1914, photograph of the station forecourt at Golders Green with a B type on the left about to start for St Albans on Route 84. It appears well-loaded, even to the exclusion of some intending passengers; it is probably a Sunday when a trip into the country on Route 84 was a more exciting prospect than the long trip to Oxford Circus and Victoria about to be undertaken by the bus on Route 2 on the right. Golders Green Hippodrome looks impressively new. *D. W. K. Jones*

Right:
This splendid Straker Squire bus on the Harvey & Burrows route to Hertford waits at Waltham Cross. The firm, trading as Hertford & District Motor Omnibus Services, was taken over by the LGOC in June 1924 and the whole operation, including the garage in Ware, was passed to National management. Operated briefly as N25, the Waltham Cross route became 310 under the Bassom scheme. There were six Straker Squires in the Harvey & Burrows fleet and they were used by National until 1927 when they were sold. *D. W. K. Jones*

Right:
Neither driver nor conductor looks particularly cheerful at the prospect of a journey to St Albans on N51 some time in the 1920s after the service had been taken over from Road Motors in 1925. This bus was an AEC Y type with a body built by the National Omnibus & Transport Co Ltd — it therefore differs in appearance from the standard B type to which it was related. The vehicle was new in 1919. Exceptionally, although working a Watford and North London area service (when an LGOC-owned vehicle would have been expected) the bus is owned by National. The splendid departure boards are of note; if the inspector is responsible for keeping them up to time he has a demanding task — and how did he reach the topmost clocks? *George Robbins collection*

bus operations in London country right through their history. The East Surrey Traction Co Ltd was the brainchild of Arthur Henry Hawkins, an employee of Tamplin & Makovski, Electrical Engineers of 57 Bell Street, Reigate. Having explored the possibilities, Hawkins, supported by Albery Waterlow Makovski, established the company and the first service, using two 30hp Leyland buses each licensed to carry 25 passengers, began running between Reigate and Redhill, alternately via the Main Road and Blackborough Road, on 23 May 1911. Expansion of operations was rapid; the original route was extended to Merstham and Meadvale on 12 December 1911; Horley was reached on 15 March 1913, Dorking on 7 April 1914, Riverhead on 11 April 1914; Beare Green (31 May), Sevenoaks (17 June) and Caterham (also 17 June) were other destinations attained in the same year. In the summer of 1914 12 vehicles were at work. By this time Arthur Hawkins had met Albert Stanley and Frank Pick, initially over the proposed LGOC Sunday service to Reigate, which Reigate Council approved following Hawkins' support for it. (It began as Route 160 on 12 April 1914 and ran via Wray Common.) A formal 'area agreement' was signed by the two companies on 26 January 1914 by which the Valley Road (now the A25) from Guildford to Sevenoaks was to be the boundary between the two companies' operations, except where approved for turning and where existing East Surrey services, for example to Kingswood and Caterham, already existed. East Surrey also agreed to buy some buses manufactured by the AEC (but marketed by Daimler). Thus was forged the alliance of Arthur Hawkins, Albert Stanley and Frank Pick, an association that was to prove of vast importance of the whole history of buses in London country.

By 1914, apart from the General's routes from the central zone, East Surrey was the most significant operator in the whole of what came to be termed London country. Bus activity elsewhere was limited to the services of provincial companies penetrating the area — these included the Aldershot & District service opened (by Guildford & District) from Guildford to Dorking on 2 February 1914, subsequently extended to Leatherhead; the Maidstone & District service from Maidstone to Sevenoaks, opened 8 April 1914, and the North Kent Motor Services' Gravesend to Dartford route which had begun the previous year. The redoubtable W. P. Allen had been active between Dartford and Farningham since 19 July 1913 — this road had seen several operators even earlier. Elsewhere, the Great Western Railway had an extensive group of services based at Slough; these had started on 1 March 1904 and therefore rank as the earliest motorbus operations anywhere in London country. The London & North Western Railway (LNWR) had initiated services in the Watford area on 23 April 1906 and developed an extensive network including routes to Boxmoor and Hemel Hempstead, between Croxley Green and Garston, between Tring and Tring station, and to Harrow, Roxeth and Pinner. Away from these centres were large areas with considerable population without any motorised public transport; the field was wide open, but the coming of war in 1914 delayed the development of services by nearly a decade.

National
At the end of the war, bus companies set about the task of restoring their services, renewing their fleets and extending their spheres of interest. The LGOC resumed its 'Summer Sunday' services on 13 April 1919 and Route 81 ran through from Hounslow to Slough and Windsor, among other facilities restored. The company also aimed to establish itself at Watford, and proceeded by agreement with the LNWR to take over its services, opening a garage at Leavesden Road on 25 August 1920. Three routes transferred from Cricklewood — the 140 from Watford to Stanmore and South Harrow, Route 141 to South Harrow and Route 142 to Kilburn Park — were worked by crews paid the 'London rate'; three others — 143 (Croxley Green to Garston), 145 (Bushey station to Boxmoor) and 147 (Bushey station to Hemel Hempstead) — were regarded as 'country routes' and the crews paid accordingly. The differential rates of pay provoked strike action and LGOC passed the Watford garage and Services 143, 145 and 147 to the National Omnibus & Transport Co which started work on 25 May 1921; this decision by the LGOC formalised the distinction between 'Central' and 'Country area' pay agreements which has lasted, in different forms, to the present day.

The National Omnibus & Transport Co Ltd (especially in its former guise as the National Steam Car Co Ltd) with its base in Chelmsford, had had considerable experience of operating buses in London alongside General. Starting in 1909 with a Shepherds Bush-Oxford Circus-Lambeth service, on which the company placed four vehicles in white livery, National had some 100 buses working daily in London by 1912. By agreement with the LGOC, the London routes were withdrawn on 18 January 1919, National receiving in the process the garage and services that General had acquired in Bedford in 1913. Clearly, National was interested in developing its activities, already well-established in Chelmsford and about to start in Colchester, though limited by an agreed policy not to operate within the Metropolitan Police District (or within 15 miles of Charing Cross, wherever the Police boundary was less than this distance). By 1920 the company had opened services from Hitchin to Stevenage and Welwyn, from Dunstable to St Albans and between Bishops Stortford and Epping. The decision of the LGOC to hand over the

Watford services was thus a major benefit to the National company, which, interestingly, had as its chief executive W. J. Iden, who had been in charge of the Walthamstow Vanguard Works during the development of the X type motorbus, the forerunner of the famous B.

For and On Account of General

There was clearly a need to formalise policy in order to secure the LGOC operating territory and to expand into the London hinterland. To this end, agreements were drawn up between the LGOC and East Surrey (signed 7 July 1921) and National (21 July). The agreement with East Surrey defined three areas: the 'London' area (which had the Metropolitan Police District boundary), East Surrey's area, and the 'London country' area (between the two). General had the exclusive right to work in the London area and into the London country area 'as they thought fit'; East Surrey had the right to work in its own, delineated area, and was given authority 'to run and work motor omnibus routes and services for and on account of the General company on such routes wholly within the "London country" area as may be agreed in writing between the parties'. Additionally, East Surrey undertook 'to work such motor omnibus services on such routes to the best advantage and to use their best endeavours to develop the traffic of the London country area'. The company could operate its own services into the London country area from its own area only by agreement with the LGOC, though the well-established services north of the Valley Road were clearly secure.

Further, General agreed to provide 'all the motor omnibuses required to furnish the motor omnibus services to be worked by the Traction Company wholly within the "London country" or the London area'. The LGOC would also 'provide all garages, sheds and equipment necessary for the purpose of housing and maintaining the said motor omnibuses', though the LGOC reserved the right to inspect its own property. The financial details of the scheme were complicated, but the LGOC was to receive a payment from East Surrey monthly. The agreement was intended to last 15 years and was signed by D. Duff (Director) and J. C. Mitchell (Secretary) for the LGOC, and by Temple Newell and Albert W. Makovski (Directors) and Arthur H. Hawkins (Secretary) for East Surrey. Thus were the positions of the LGOC and East Surrey secured, to the evident benefit of both parties.

A similar agreement with National was signed a fortnight later, the same definitions of area being used, ie the London area, the National company's area and the London country area. However, National was not in quite as strong a position as East Surrey which had a soundly-based business already in being in (or near) the London country area; hence

National was not allowed to work into the General or London country areas except to provide services designated 'for and on account of General', though there might be agreed services into the London country area deemed to be 'joint services'. (In fact, there was only one, No 40: Grays to Romford.) Thus all National activity, developed in the 'Watford and North London area', was prompted and controlled by the LGOC, and some former National services — Bishops Stortford to Epping, for example — were changed in status and worked 'for and on behalf of General'. While the relationship between the LGOC and East Surrey appeared to be a co-operative one, National's position vis-a-vis General seems somewhat subservient. Throughout the life of the Watford and North London area, it appeared that the LGOC provided National with only the very minimum number of vehicles to maintain the services, and expected operations to be conducted with the utmost economy. East Surrey was, or seemed, well-provided for, both by the LGOC and from its own resources.

A third agreement was concluded with the Thames Valley Traction Co Ltd — a British Electric

Traction (BET) company based on Reading — and signed on 20 April 1922. Thames Valley agreed 'to run and work motorbus services and routes to the best advantage and use its best endeavours to develop traffic on behalf of the LGOC'. No vehicles were to be provided by General and the financial arrangements therefore differed from those in the agreements signed with East Surrey and National; however, a base was provided: this was the garage at Uxbridge, completed by the LGOC in 1921. Thames Valley took over operation of two LGOC routes on 7 June 1922, No 95 from Uxbridge to High Wycombe, started with a single B type bus sent out from Acton on 16 March 1921 and subsequently extended to West Wycombe (Swan), and No 93 from Hounslow to Uxbridge, started 20 July 1921. Additionally Thames Valley was instructed to initiate services from Uxbridge to Great Missenden via Gerrards Cross, The Chalfonts and Amersham; to Windsor via Cowley, Iver, Langley and Slough; and to Rickmansworth and Watford via Denham, West Hyde and Maple Cross. Some smaller buses were allocated to the new routes, which Thames Valley had got on to the road by the summer of 1922; the West Wycombe service came to be graced with open-top JB type 50-seat Thornycroft double-deckers, some of which were sold to Thames Valley by the LGOC after acquisition from Cambrian. Not all the newly-initiated routes proved profitable and the road via West Hyde was abandoned by January 1923, by which date the Great Missenden route was

cut back to Amersham. The agreement between the LGOC and Thames Valley was due to terminate on 31 December 1928, though a clause allowed for annual renewal thereafter; as will be seen, this option was not taken up.

These three agreements established clearly-defined principles of working, and all participants set to to develop their respective and mutual interests. The first sign of change to the public was the numbering of services; buses operated by East Surrey for and on account of General carried (or sometimes carried — East Surrey was not very meticulous about indicators) numbers prefixed with an S; all routes run by National in the Watford and North London area were prefixed N, while the Uxbridge-based routes operated by Thames Valley were allocated numbers W20 to W23. However, Thames Valley did not use route numbers on its vehicles so these were never carried, though they did appear in timetable books. The system was introduced on 6 August 1921 (later for Thames Valley) and would appear to be the first outward sign of a move towards co-ordinating the whole system in the London country area.

East Surrey Traction Co in the 1920s

The East Surrey Traction Co and the LGOC had in fact anticipated the formal agreement, East Surrey opening a Redhill to Epsom service on 5 June 1920 and taking over the Farnborough-Sevenoaks section of the Autocar route to Tunbridge Wells on 26 May 1921; on the latter service some B type vehicles were provided by General. The main impact of the agreement however came with the setting up of a series of routes from Bromley and West Croydon. Thus three routes began working from West Croydon on 16 August 1921: S3 to Sevenoaks, S4 to Edenbridge, and S5 to Redhill (Market Place). The Sevenoaks-Farnborough service was put through to Bromley North on 6 August 1921, and S10, from Bromley North to Westerham, Godstone and Reigate, began operation on 3 June 1922. S9: West Croydon to Godstone and East Grinstead, was worked alternately through to Hartfield and Chelwood Gate — this also began on 3 June 1922. By this point the LGOC had provided East Surrey with some 29 B type buses, 14 AEC YC double-deck vehicles and six single-deck Tylor-engined buses — a total of 49; by August 1923 East Surrey was working 64 LGOC vehicles alongside 31 of its own! East Surrey began allocating S prefixes to its own routes on 14 April 1922, from which date the company livery changed from blue to the LGOC red — an appropriate economy. Thus it was possible to see obviously London-type buses, in traditional General colours, working 'country' routes and bearing the East Surrey fleetname; the LGOC vehicles were subject to some interchange, though East Surrey allocations were usually kept together, being replaced in groups as the buses became outdated. The B type thus gave way to the K, the PS and the NS, the latter type working well into the 1930s.

The agreement included reference to garages and five were constructed — all owned by the LGOC but leased to East Surrey. These were Dunton Green (opened April 1922), Chelsham and Godstone (both opened 20 January 1925), Leatherhead (1 June 1925) and Swanley (21 October 1925); with East Surrey's own premises at Reigate, the geographical spread of bases was about as good as it could have been. The use of 'out-stations' continued, usually in inn yards, but unfortunate experiences in trying to start the engines in the early morning tended to encourage the policy of putting buses under cover where appropriate expertise was at hand!

The London Traffic Act of 1924 resulted in all bus routes operating into or within the Metropolitan Police District being numbered. This was the Bassom scheme, so-called after the Acting Chief Constable of that name; routes in the northern area were placed in a 300 series, in the south 400, and in the west (from Uxbridge), 500. The scheme was operative from 1 December 1924 and gave rise to route numbers that are familiar today — 301 and 303 in the north, 403 and 410 in the south, among many others. The licensing of bus routes, crews and vehicles within the Metropolitan Police District was in the hands of the Metropolitan Police Public Carriage Office which operated with strict efficiency. Outside the Metropolitan area, however, there was no larger control than the local authority; licensing thus depended on the Town Police Clauses Acts of 1847 and 1889 and the Stage Carriage Act of 1832. The Town Police Clauses Acts were permissive so that not all local authorities had them, and those that did interpreted their powers very differently. Bus operators therefore had to obtain licences to run from each town or borough council whose bounds they proposed entering, and buses on long routes carried a number of licence plates affixed to the vehicle, usually at the rear. The lack of area control in licensing meant, of course, that new operators could seek licences and begin services in direct competition with existing facilities and such control as existed followed from negotiations among the operators themselves. East Surrey throughout its time kept very careful control of its territory — venturesome operators were quickly bought out or allowed to fail; Arthur Hawkin's judgement on these matters was very shrewd. In the north, however, National control was never so complete in its wide, somewhat rural area, nor were its operating bases so well placed. Thus sizeable independents set up business both in direct competition to National, in St Albans, Watford and elsewhere, or where there were obvious gaps in the National network. Smaller operators also abounded. National's policy was to run alongside other operators by agreement where the competitors could not be bought out by the

Above:
This little Thornycroft, seen here in portrait before registration, bears its 'Woking & District' fleetname with some pride. When the bus was taken over on 4 January 1931, the bus passed to East Surrey which continued to use it on the routes from Woking to Guildford and to Windsor. The spare wheel is accessible and very necessary in the early days of pneumatic tyres. *D. W. K. Jones*

LGOC; it is interesting that as late as 1928 the People's Motor Services could begin in Hertford and develop rapidly into an important concern, surviving until taken over by the LPTB in 1933! The real organisational chaos existed in industrial areas at the fringes of the system, especially in Windsor and Slough and in the Grays area where National's own routes had a struggle to survive. Buses running between Windsor and Slough became legion, while it was said that on the road from Grays to Purfleet it was impossible *not* to see a bus!

Throughout the 1920s East Surrey went on maintaining the joint services and developing and extending its own; while use of East Surrey and LGOC-owned vehicles did not become entirely indiscriminate, both companies' buses were put to work on most routes. With the implementation of the Bassom numbering scheme, the S prefix was eventually discarded in 1927. Services were strengthened, especially in the East Grinstead area, and a small garage was opened there in 1925 and another in Crawley in 1929, the only garages other than Reigate that East Surrey actually owned. Following the acquisition by Aldershot & District of the Surrey Hills Motor Services (owned by G. Readings of Ewhurst) on 10 January 1926, an important agreement signed by the LGOC, Aldershot & District and East Surrey (as an interested party) on 27 September 1927 clarified the position in the Dorking and Guildford area and a number of roads were designated 'joint roads'; these were from Shere and Gomshall to

Horsham via Ewhurst, from Guildford to Dorking via Shalford and Gomshall, and from Guildford to Silent Pool via Merrow. Joint East Surrey and Aldershot & District operations between Dorking and Guildford began on 29 February 1928 on Route 25 (now 425!) and East Surrey buses worked between Guildford and Peaslake.

The final years of the 1920s were much taken up by financial manoeuvre as the larger companies (including the railways) sought to secure, and if possible extend, their interests. In February 1928 East Surrey, with the backing of the LGOC, secured control of Autocar Services Ltd of Tunbridge Wells, a purchase completed on 5 April 1928; Arthur Hawkins and Albert Makovski served on the Autocar board. This firm had nearly 100 vehicles at work in a wide area of West Kent and East Sussex and had recently come to terms with its rival Redcar; these operations were kept discrete, though Autocar buses continued to appear in Sevenoaks and on the road between Tunbridge Wells and Reigate (on Route 24). A new category of operation was designated by the LGOC and East Surrey as 'joint areas' — these included the jointly-run East Surrey and Aldershot & District routes in the west and the whole of the Autocar area; while LGOC and East Surrey had equal rights of running in the joint areas, East Surrey was to work the routes 'in joint account'.

An even more dramatic, if expected, financial move came on 12 June 1929 when the LGOC secured control of East Surrey and its subsidiary Autocar. This move was prompted by the increasing threat to the whole LGOC/East Surrey enterprise by the acquisition by the Southern Railway of rights in the bus field under the 1928 Transport Acts. The railway companies found it more convenient to buy into existing companies rather than operate buses themselves, a policy which meant the ultimate disappearance of the railway buses then running in various parts of the country, including Slough, Boxmoor and Tring. Having secured an interest in Maidstone & District, Southdown and Aldershot & District, the Southern Railway had only to purchase shares in East Surrey to set up its intended Southern General Omnibus Co Ltd. This grand plan, which would have established a very significant operating group across Kent, Surrey, Sussex and Hampshire, was frustrated by the LGOC; and East Surrey (and Autocar) became formally part of the Underground group, thus allying at least the southern part of London country with London rather than provincial operators. Arthur Hawkins survived this change and continued in office as managing director.

At this point, East Surrey was operating a fleet of 169 buses of which 103 were owned by the LGOC. There were 126 double-deck vehicles — K, PS and NS types — including 85 LGOC-owned; there were 18 single-deck buses owned by the LGOC and 25 owned by East Surrey in its own right. The company

was working 33 routes of which only seven were entirely its property — the others coming under the joint working arrangement with or on behalf of General. Despite the change in status of the company, both East Surrey and Autocar Services retained their identity and the travelling public were probably unaware of the alteration of ownership; the vehicles were still legally owned by the respective companies. However, the common ownership — and the financial interest acquired by the LGOC in Amersham & District in August 1929 — were helpful in setting up what became the Green Line network from 1929 onwards. The close association of the companies also encouraged the LGOC to go ahead with the acquisition of other operators, including the Woking & District firm of J. R. Fox which was purchased by Aldershot & District on 14 January 1931, with the LGOC providing 74% of the finance. Certain routes, including important ones from Woking and West Byfleet to Staines and Windsor, and from Woking to Guildford and Ripley, were passed to East Surrey together with 15 vehicles and garage premises in Woking. The LGOC also passed three of its own routes to East Surrey on 1 April 1931; these were 70D: Morden station to Dorking, 99C: Erith to Dartford via Crayford and 199A: Erith to Dartford via Crayford and Burnham Road. Five double-deck buses were supplied to work 70D, and five single-deckers the Erith routes; Crayford garage was also handed over. Additionally East Surrey was commissioned to begin Route 422 from Orpington to Chislehurst and Eltham which started on 7 October 1931. This service could conveniently have been worked from the LGOC's own Sidcup garage at Foots Cray, but doubtless there were financial reasons for putting the route into the hands of the subsidiary company. It is interesting to note that in the Watford and North London area the LGOC had acted in a totally different way; thus on 23 May 1928 General took over operation of former National Route N20: Havering-Romford-Dagenham-Aveley, and the Romford-Brentwood section of N50; these ultimately became Routes 103 and 247 respectively. The following year, 306B: Waltham Cross-Waltham Abbey-Epping Forest (Volunteer) became an LGOC route in the summer timetable. The joint working on G40 (Grays-Ockendon-Romford) between National and General continued. National always retained the N designation on services operated for and on behalf of General — a badge which East Surrey had been allowed to discard. (Thames Valley never did carry the prefix W or route numbers on its buses, though this was not necessarily a gesture of independence.)

Thames and Chilterns

Meanwhile, Thames Valley continued to work the group of routes based on Uxbridge garage though there have been suggestions that the company did not market the services or develop them with the vigour that the LGOC had hoped for. Thames Valley had established some services on its own account within or near London country; these included a route from Maidenhead via Holyport and Clewer to Windsor, thence to Englefield Green, Egham and Staines, latterly identified as Route 21, and Route 28 from High Wycombe to Hazlemere, thence alternately to Holmer Green and Penn; some buses ran on to Amersham and Beaconsfield. There was also, from November 1926, a two-hourly service from Windsor to Chalfont St Peter via Stoke Common. The LGOC allowed the agreement with Thames Valley to lapse at the earliest possible point on 31 December 1928 and took possession of Uxbridge garage and the routes operated from there on the following day. Apart from the possible criticism of Thames Valley on the grounds of lack of commitment, General's move was partly financial — Thames Valley as a BET company could not, or would not, be influenced by LGOC money — and partly operational as the LGOC now had a garage in Langley Road, Slough and had found another ally in the form of the Amersham & District Motor Bus & Haulage Co. The Amersham company dated from 15 September 1919 when a local doctor and his friends purchased three vehicles and a garage in Amersham Broadway; services were started to Chesham, High Wycombe and Windsor and the concern had built up a fleet of 30 vehicles by 1929. Amersham & District worked in a compact area and maintained its independence and isolation until the LGOC purchased a substantial interest on 26 August 1929. The Uxbridge to Windsor buses were worked from Langley from 1 January 1929 and the High Wycombe and Amersham routes were subsequently worked by Amersham & District by agreement. The LGOC concentrated its efforts on the rapidly growing area of suburbia east and south of Uxbridge, and the garage there became — and has remained — identified with Central buses, ceasing its connection with London country altogether.

Watford and North London

National worked steadily through the 1920s in the Watford and North London area, a rather more rural and scattered region than Surrey; travel habits were perhaps not so ready for change as in the more affluent southern counties. Away from the towns (and only Watford, St Albans and Hertford were of any size) the area was — in places, still is — surprisingly rural. National's services for and on account of General, with the exception of those between the main centres, were always rather more tenuous than East Surrey's in the south, and in any case motorbus operation in much of Hertfordshire came some 10 years after the East Surrey start in Reigate. As has been indicated earlier, National had sought or was seeking to develop services at locations all over the

country, from Cornwall to East Anglia, and perhaps looked on its role in the Watford and North London area as a caretaker exercise without any real security of tenure. The company was not asked to, nor did it, commit any resources of its own to the exercise and throughout was wholly dependent on vehicles and facilities supplied (one suspects not very generously) by the LGOC.

However, services were developed with some drive and on 6 August 1921 the St Albans-Hatfield-Welwyn route (N5) was started, and a week later N6 was working between Watford and Chesham, via Rickmansworth. National vehicles reached Hertford on 12 August, and on 14 December Route N11: Hertford to Bishops Stortford was opened — thus there was now a line of route right across Hertfordshire. By the end of 1922 buses were running from Watford to Barnet (N13), to Uxbridge (jointly with

Below:

An unusual vehicle for East Surrey, this Renault was acquired when the Rural Omnibus Service owned by L. S. Chell was taken over on 4 January 1928. Mr Chell worked an interesting route from Cobham to Guildford via Downside, Effingham and Merrow. The bus was seen operating Route 22 from Sutton (Volunteer) to Dorking North; it was provided with 20 seats, though it looks larger. It proved not entirely satisfactory and was sold in 1931. *George Robbins collection*

Thames Valley as N24), Bedmond (N15) and Bovingdon (N17); other important routes opened were Hertford to Watton and Hitchin (N12), and from St Albans to Hemel Hempstead (N14). A garage built by the LGOC at Hatfield came into use during the year. The Leavesden Road garage proved inadequate by 1925 and a new garage in Watford High Street was opened to accommodate 60 vehicles and the headquarters staff for the Watford and North London area. Meanwhile National had been set up in a small base in the yard of the White Hart Hotel in Romford; this served to develop N20 from Romford to Dagenham and Aveley which started in August 1923, and later a route from Romford to Warley, Brentwood and Ongar which became N50.

An important acquisition by the LGOC was that of Harvey & Burrows of Hertford which took place in July 1924 by which time this vigorous little company was running to Stevenage, Puckeridge, Buntingford and Royston; the most important route however was that between Hertford and Waltham Cross, the forerunner of the 310. National was made responsible for the services which were numbered between N25 and N31 and for management of the garage behind the Town Hall in Ware. On 16 April 1925 another thriving enterprise, Road Motors Ltd of Luton, was purchased by National; this firm, started by T. R. Attree in 1910, operated a number of services in and around Luton as well as some in Weymouth, which made the business especially attractive to National. Luton was on the southern edge of National's own area and only four of the Road Motors routes worked into the London country area; they ran from Luton to St Albans, Markyate, Caddington and Wheathampstead. These were sold to the LGOC but operated by National for and on account of General from 1 January 1927. They do not appear to have carried the N prefix, exceptionally; though the list of routes in the timetable books gives each of these routes an 'N', the timetable itself does not. Another operator in the Luton area, F. C. H. Motor Haulage & Engineering Co, was purchased in April 1926 and this added two routes from Luton — to Ley Green and Hitchin, and to Tea Green — to the network. National found it expedient to work with other operators and allied itself with Aston; the Chiltern Bus Co (E. Prentice & Son), the Aylesbury Bus Co and West Herts on Routes 301 and 302 from Watford to Aylesbury and Hemel Hempstead; the co-ordinated timetable came into force in February 1929. Similarly, No 51 (Luton to St Albans) was worked with Comfy Cars and Express, all journeys by each operator being indicated in the timetable.

National was allocated the standard LGOC vehicles of the time; initially they were painted white but by 1923 were kept in red livery with the National fleetname. In 1931 there were 50 double-deck vehicles at work, 31 NS type (dating back to 1924) and 19 new ST type vehicles, a contrast indeed. Single-deck buses comprised 13 S type (new in 1922), 55 Associated Daimler 416s (1927), six Guys (1927) and five Reliances (1929). These vehicles were worked hard, averaging 40,000 miles per year in 1929; this was nearly twice the mileage of most buses in provincial service.

The financial structure of the National Omnibus & Transport Co Ltd was greatly changed by the interest taken by the railway companies — the widely scattered nature of the company's operations and its relatively under-resourced provision made it a natural focus of speculation and investment. The LGOC had been able to forestall railway ambitions in the southern area of London country, and the northern area was almost as secure — the LGOC strictness of its dealings with National in the matter of acquisitions, licences and operations in the Watford and North London area is thus explained. National was only an agent, the LGOC remained the principal; whatever happened to National would not affect the ownership of routes or rights of road. All operations within the strictly defined area were entirely 'for and on account of General'; when Harvey & Burrows had been acquired its sphere of operations had been designated a 'General extended area'. The Railway (Road Traffic) Acts became law on 3 August 1928 and following negotiations with the railway companies National was split into separate operating companies — Eastern, Southern and Western — which became operational in 1929, ultimately becoming part of the Tilling group in 1931. The National Omnibus & Transport Co, however, retained its identity in the Watford and North London area. The appropriate solution to the problems of securing LGOC territory lay in either creating a new subsidiary company or in extending the interests of an existing one, and the latter course was adopted. However, 'East Surrey' would hardly have been an appropriate fleetname to appear on buses running in Buckinghamshire, Hertfordshire and Essex, so the decision was taken to change the historic name of East Surrey Traction Co Ltd to London General Country Services Ltd; the new company was registered on 25 January 1932 and the Watford and North London area operations were taken over on 1 March. For the first time the identity of a single operator in the great arc encircling London was affirmed. It is also important to note that this operator was a wholly-owned subsidiary of the LGOC.

London General Country Services

The advent of London General Country Services Ltd marked the end of an important, perhaps the most important, phase of development of bus work in London country. Between 1920 and 1932 the LGOC, at a time when there was considerable dissatisfaction with its services in the inner zone and great competition with independent operators, nevertheless sought to develop the hinterland. It used the East Surrey company, National and — on a slightly different basis, Thames Valley — to develop services as economically as possible, as it had to maintain its capability in the central area. During this time most of the foundations of the present system were laid, subsequent changes being organisational rather than fundamentally creative. The entire bus industry was in any case now subject to regulation by statute — the 1930 Road Traffic Act; Traffic Commissioners were now responsible for licensing vehicles and crews, fares and services. Much energy was now deployed to secure continuation of those services that were operating and appearances in the traffic courts were added to the experience of transport managers. In outcome, the Traffic Commissioners tended to favour the large, established operators, many of the smaller ones disqualifying themselves by their poorly-maintained vehicles. Even so, the granting of licences was generous enough to provide a plethora of bus firms in London country and further legislation was needed to sort out the tangle. Meanwhile, the newly-established London General Country Services Ltd set about taking stock of its empire and, with the LGOC, moved steadily towards an integrated system.

With the cancellation of the agreement between the LGOC and the National Omnibus & Transport Co Ltd, it was decided that East Surrey should formally take over the vehicles and spare parts that National had used in the Watford and North London area, though the LGOC would retain the freeholds of the garages there. East Surrey, in its new guise as London General Country Services Ltd (LGCS), took over operation of the services north of London on 1 March 1932; National's procedures differed considerably from the East Surrey pattern and Arthur Hawkins had to familiarise himself with an area he hardly knew, with many services running at irregular intervals, or on certain days only, in contrast to his established preference for regular-headway daily services. For convenience of operation LGCS was divided into two divisions, southern (formerly East

Surrey) and northern (formerly National), each with a traffic manager. Additional head office accommodation was planned and new building started at Bell Street, Reigate. The new fleetname was based on the word 'General' in gold with red pointing on a silver grey panel, with 'Country Services' in gold on a red background underneath. All former LGOC buses on loan to East Surrey and to National were sold to the LGCS on 7 April 1932; these numbered 143 and 129 respectively and when added to East Surrey's own fleet of 76 made a total of 348. Shortly after, on 11 May, all Green Line coaches came under LGCS management and the new company was therefore responsible for operating nearly 800 vehicles.

The LGCS initially continued to operate the former East Surrey and National buses in red livery with the 'General' fleetname. However, in the drive for a new identity, the colour of the uniform of platform staff was changed to green which was an appropriate colour for country services. The change

Below:
This bus, an ADC416 type, started life as an LGOC coach in 1928, but two years later exchanged bodies with a Reliance. Allocated to National in 1930, it became one of 53 vehicles of its class operated in the Watford and North London area; it is seen here in LGCS livery at Borehamwood station on the 304. It is perhaps curious that at this late stage the bus should not have a windscreen; apart from this deficiency the styling is quite modern.
D. W. K. Jones

to green effectively allied country bus staff with Green Line coach crews now based at LGCS garages, and also allowed ready interchange in case of need, in operating duplicate vehicles for example.

Some consolidation of activity was achieved when LGCS took over the Great Western Railway routes in Slough on 10 April 1932. This acquisition included 14 vehicles working several routes from Slough station to Beaconsfield, with spurs to Hedgerley Village and, in the summer, to Burnham Beeches via Salt Hill or Stoke Common. A planned interchange of services between LGOC and LGCS in the Banstead area, due to take place on 1 June 1932, foundered in the face of union opposition at Sutton garage. The services involved were 80 and 180, Morden station to Lower Kingswood and Walton-on-the-hill respectively, and the Sundays only 228 from Morden station to Lower Kingswood via Epsom. These services were duly passed to London Country Bus Services on 24 April 1982, after a long wait of 50 years. This failure left LGCS with some specially ordered Bluebird ST type buses on its hands which had to be deployed elsewhere. The small firm of A. E. Gilbert, running between Hertford and Essendon, did not prove so difficult and was acquired on 27 December 1932. On 1 March 1933 there were considerable changes, successfully implemented, which transferred the two services from Uxbridge to Windsor (503 and 507) and two local LGOC services in Windsor (short workings of 81) to the LGCS, including the garage at Langley Road, Slough. Route 117D (Slough to Staines) and the long-established Route 162B (Slough to Staines and Leatherhead) were also transferred on that day, becoming 417 and 462 respectively. Eight new Bluebird STs and two six-wheeled single-deck LT buses were allocated for this opera-

tion. In exchange the LGOC took over the working of two former East Surrey routes in the Orpington area, the 411 and 422, with six NS buses; in the 1934 renumbering these became the familiar 51 and 61.

The London, Midland & Scottish Railway bus services from Boxmoor to Hemel Hempstead and Harpenden, and a recently-started service to Whipsnade, together with the Tring Town to Tring station service, were taken over by the LGCS on 28 April 1933; seven Leyland Lions and one Albion in crimson livery were acquired. The purchase of C. Aston of Watford and the Chiltern Bus Service at Tring on 9 and 10 May respectively brought more services under LGCS control, and on 26 June the Watford Omnibus Co Ltd, with 10 buses, was formally acquired by the LGOC. Another acquisition during the LGCS period was of 'full rights of road' between Windsor and Staines Bridge from the Thames Valley company on 10 June; two double-deck Leyland Titans were included in the deal. Associated takeovers during this period were of Chesham & District Bus Co Ltd by Amersham & District on 8 December 1932, and of the Aylesbury Motorbus Co by Eastern National on 11 May 1933;

An independent vigorously at work throughout the early 1930s was People's Motor Services Ltd with a network of routes radiating from Ware and Hertford. This bus, a Gilford 1660T with a body by Duple for 32 passengers, was remarkable as being the only vehicle in the 19-strong fleet *not* given coachwork by the proprietor, Mr W. Thurgood. New in 1929, the vehicle lasted until December 1937; in the LPTB classification it became GF169. *J. F. Higham*

both these changes had implications for the London country network.

The LGCS era lasted less than 18 months, and was something of an interim arrangement, not without interest in itself. The minutes of the managing directors' meetings 'on matters relating to Green Line Coaches Ltd and London General Country Services Ltd' record that these were usually small affairs attended by Arthur Hawkins and either Lord Ashfield or Frank Pick — when Lord Ashfield turned up he was always noted as 'in the chair' which suggests that for the most part the meetings were fairly informal in his absence. Occasionally other directors would attend. There were several pre-occupations including the siting of garages — thus LGCS undertook the preliminary planning of the present Hertford and St Albans garages, though

plans for premises in Chertsey and Tonbridge came to nothing — in Tonbridge anyway the land was said to be too expensive. The construction of Windsor garage illustrates the emphasis on economy; the building estimate of £32,618 was pared down to £30,000 before authorisation. The subject of heating in the engineering areas of the existing garages was raised by the Factory Inspectorate but no action was taken; when the union requested the fitting of windscreens in the older types of bus it was agreed not to do so on the grounds that the vehicles had no more than two or three years to run. Interestingly the private car business at Reigate made a loss and Hawkins was instructed to dispose of this activity promptly. There was also a resolution that: 'Steps be taken at an early date to standardise wages throughout LGCS on the basis of the wages formerly paid by the East Surrey company, it being noted that this decision would involve certain reductions of wages paid to staff employed in the Northern Area transferred from the National company.'

The financial tightness of LGCS, inherited from the good business practice of East Surrey, inspired later theories among busmen that Country services saved money for the Central area to waste. Towards the end of the LGCS more and more decisions were deferred until the advent of the new administration, and on 1 July 1933 the much debated and oft heralded London Passenger Transport Board came into being. That event opened another chapter in London country history.

The London Passenger Transport Board

The discussions and manoeuvres leading to the setting up of the London Passenger Transport Board (LPTB) were lengthy. Political opinion was divided — those to the left saw the possibilities of a publicly-owned industry, those on the right preferred private enterprise. Arguments within the bus industry itself were more concerned with boundary maintenance; some of the more ambitious definitions of the Board's area were altered when, in June 1931, those companies with area agreements with the LGOC were able to keep them in being. (The exception here was the Dartford and Gravesend area.) On vesting day, Saturday 1 July 1933, the new Board found itself responsible for bus, tram, trolleybus, coach and train operations over a large area. From the point of view of London country, London General Country Services Ltd and Green Line Coaches Ltd became the Country Bus & Coach Department of the LPTB; Arthur Hawkins remained in office as general manager. (He was not the only survivor — Albert Stanley, now Lord Ashfield, and Frank Pick were respectively chairman and vice-chairman of the Board.)

The task of the new Board was essentially to co-ordinate existing facilities. The second report (dated 30 June 1935) refers to 'a mass of unrelated and often conflicting services in the country areas'; 'the Board have attempted to build a co-ordinated and regular system. In doing so they have sought to preserve every necessary facility and to anticipate, to some extent, the future requirements of the travelling public'. Wasteful competition was to be eliminated! A later report (1938) indicates that the 'country area inheritance' included 66 independent operators

Below:
After the formation of the LPTB, red Central buses continued to operate well into London country. This is Tilling ST No 1016 on a Route 146 journey from Westerham Hill to Lewisham. The stop is at Biggin Hill, and the conductor is in the process of inserting his time-card into the machine that was once a feature of bus activity in many parts of London. These splendid buses, new in 1931, were at a discount when the LPTB standard types arrived, and so were relegated to reserve duties quite early in their careers. This vehicle was on loan to Crosville for five years during the war (from January 1942 to December 1946); after a brief spell at its old garage, TL — Tilling's Lewisham — the bus was withdrawn and scrapped in 1947. *London Transport*

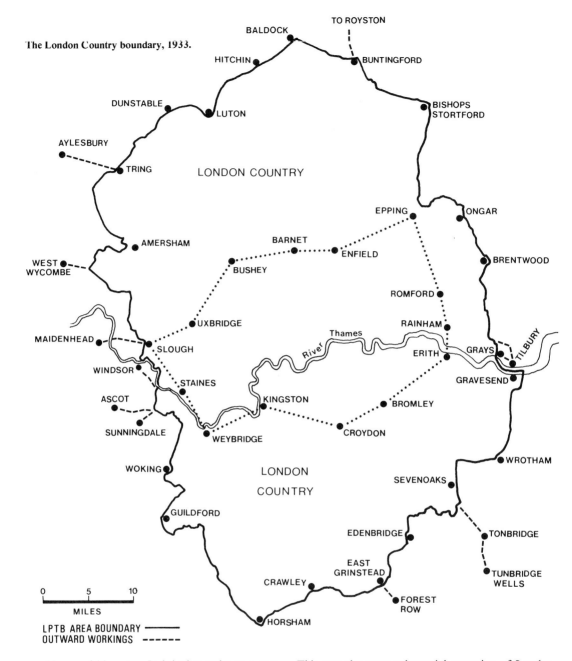

The London Country boundary, 1933.

TO ROYSTON

BALDOCK

HITCHIN • • BUNTINGFORD

DUNSTABLE • BISHOPS STORTFORD

• LUTON

AYLESBURY

• TRING

LONDON COUNTRY

EPPING • ONGAR

• AMERSHAM BARNET • ENFIELD BRENTWOOD

WEST WYCOMBE BUSHEY

ROMFORD

• UXBRIDGE RAINHAM

MAIDENHEAD Thames TILBURY

SLOUGH River ERITH GRAYS

WINDSOR GRAVESEND

• STAINES

ASCOT KINGSTON • BROMLEY

SUNNINGDALE WEYBRIDGE CROYDON

WOKING LONDON WROTHAM

COUNTRY SEVENOAKS

GUILDFORD

EDENBRIDGE TONBRIDGE

EAST GRINSTEAD TUNBRIDGE WELLS

CRAWLEY

FOREST ROW

HORSHAM

0   5   10

MILES

LPTB AREA BOUNDARY ————
OUTWARD WORKINGS   ------

working on 246 routes. In bringing order to a confused situation the Board undoubtedly raised standards of provision and the prestige of public transport; however, in striking a mean some of the very best practice as well as much doubtful working was lost.

On 1 July Maidstone & District surrendered its Dartford and Gravesend local routes to the LPTB, together with 55 vehicles — mainly double-deck Leylands, dating from 1928 onwards — and two garages, that at Priory Road, Dartford, and the former tram sheds in Old Dover Road, Northfleet.

This was the most substantial extension of London country interest, but it was counterbalanced by the hiving off of Autocar whose operating area lay outside the LPTB sphere. Maidstone & District took over management of this concern, an appropriate recompense. Autocar's share of services between Sevenoaks and Tonbridge were taken over by the Board, journeys via the main road becoming 402A and the whole operation via the Weald 454. Operations that now lay outside the LPTB boundary included the road from Forest Row to Tunbridge Wells on Route 24 — this became an Autocar preserve; the Forest Row to Uckfield section of 409 and the Crawley to Handcross section of 26 were sold to the Southern Railway which immediately passed them to Southdown Motor Services Ltd for operation. On 1 August the joint working with Aldershot & District on Route 25 ceased and the LPTB became sole operator between Dorking and Guildford. The Board took over the former Aldershot & District times to Newlands Corner and Ewhurst, together with six buses and the small garage at Ewhurst. A month later, on 1 September, Eastern National surrendered some routes in the Grays area, including its interest in G40 to Romford and Route 36 to Rainham and Romford. All these companies, of course, had had area agreements with the LGOC or its partners.

There can seldom have been a time when planners have had such exciting work to do. For the next two years independent companies that had been operating in London country were acquired either by compulsory purchase (if working in the Board's special area) or as a result of the Board's refusal of consent to operate, or by persuasion and agreement. There were 21 acquisitions of bus operators in the country area in 1933, including the Lewis Omnibus Co of Watford, with 25 buses (a Metropolitan Railway interest) (1 October 1933), Amersham & District, with 48 vehicles (24 November), and People's Motor Services of Ware with 19 vehicles (30 November). There were 40 takeovers in 1934, though these numbers are higher if the coach firms acquired during the same period are added. Eight more purchases were made before the end of 1939, the last being West Kent Motor Services Ltd on 3 October 1939; this company had approached LGCS at least once with a view to sale in 1932. Apart from the larger concerns like the Lewis Omnibus Co Ltd of Watford, the firms acquired were usually small; the following table will indicate the scale of the exercise:

No of independent firms acquired	No of buses purchased from each
3	0
12	1
14	2
9	3
12	4
4	5
1	6
1	7
2	8

The number of buses acquired was not an exact indication of fleet size as in some cases only part of the stock was taken over. The Board's first report listed the undertakings acquired up to June 1934. In the Slough and Windsor area these comprised Bell's Bus Service, F. Berry, F. Bowler (who worked in Beaconsfield), Lucas & Son, Clarke's Blue Bus

Service, the Nippy Bus Service, F. C. Owen, the Royal Blue Motor Bus (only one, a Ford), E. A. Shand, the Speedwell Bus Service and the TT Bus Service. A. E. Warwick, who ran two Bedfords to Farnham Common, was listed as 'pending' — he survived until 26 October 1934. The Watford group included Biggerstaffs' Bus Service based at Sarratt, the Elite Bus Co, the Pioneer Omnibus Co (which worked a solitary Chevrolet on routes from Hemel Hempstead) and YS Coaches (responsible for a local route in Watford to Leggatts Rise). Eleven operators were acquired in Grays, with three more pending; five were acquired in Romford, with two pending. There were considerable lists under Gravesend (six), St Albans (nine) and Staines (seven); in the Hertford area four operators were purchased.

For some time until they were repainted or discarded, acquired buses ran with 'General' applied to the sides but in their former liveries; the legal ownership and address, 'London Passenger Transport Board, Bell Street, Reigate', was in its customary place. London Transport as a fleetname dates from 1934; when Chiswick overhauls were instituted in February 1935 the legal owner's address was changed to 55 Broadway, SW1.

Following acquisition of local firms, the next step was to produce area schemes; these were introduced as follows:

> 31 January 1934 — Watford and Hemel Hempstead
> 16 May 1934 — Dartford, Swanley and Gravesend
> 18 July 1934 — Grays
> 5 September 1934 — Epping
> 10 October 1934 — Knockholt and District
> 5 December 1934 — St Albans
> 5 June 1935 — Grays (again!)
> 14 August 1935 — Hertford
> 18 March 1936 — Slough and Windsor
> 13 May 1936 — Amersham

There were no major alterations to route structures in the former East Surrey area — these had been effectively and efficiently planned already and only a handful of independent firms had survived in any case. The Amersham & District network was similarly well planned and established and lasted virtually unaltered until 1936. The position was very different in areas where independents abounded, most notably St Albans, Watford, Windsor and Slough, and Grays. While the new routes were rationally evolved, it cannot be said that the LPTB was much thanked for its efforts. Almost all schemes changed existing services, usually reducing frequency of operation. Passengers who had become used to buses serving their roads every few minutes were not pleased by 10min services, even if they were regular. The larger vehicles employed by the Board and the

Hemel Hempstead garage in October 1935 presents a view characteristic of the early years of the LPTB. The buses are an interesting and varied lot. Facing the camera, from left to right, the are a Reliance with a new Weymann 30-seat body; a Bluebird Regent, ST1074; GF21, a Gilford, new in 1929 with a Wilton body — it was originally a 28-seater coach belonging to Regent Motor Service and ran between Hertford and Oxford Circus; another Gilford, GF158, acquired from Maidstone & District on 1 July 1933; another Gilford; and three NS double-deckers are parked in the corner. The indicator of the fourth bus described shows 'Two Waters Garage' by which the premises were first known. *London Transport*

Centre left:

Dorking garage, 1936. The only two six-wheeled 'Scooters' which worked in the Country area are shown here — officially Renowns or LT class, they are LT1247 and LT1248; they ran for many years on the 425 to Guildford. The rear of the vehicle on the left is that of Q83, new in October 1935. The Birmingham Railway Carriage & Wagon Co body initially seated 37 passengers, though two seats were lost when the driver's cab was fully partitioned across the front of the vehicle. Such privacy was considered essential by the drivers who were distracted by the lively young or the garrulous elderly who always occupied these front seats. The radiator grille of the engine at the side can be plainly seen. This bus was withdrawn in March 1953. *London Transport*

Bottom left:

In this early postwar view of Sevenoaks bus station the vehicles are the products of the LPTB's standardisation policy. On the left is STL1475, a Weymann-bodied front-entrance Regent new in 1936; of note are the restricted rear blind display and the white disc painted on the lower panel to assist sighting of the bus in the blackout. T662 is ready for a Green Line journey to Windsor on 705, a route introduced on 29 May 1946; another of the distinguished 10T10 class, T691, also began life as a Green Line coach but has been put to bus work and painted accordingly. Route 421, of course, derived from West Kent Motor Services. The photo must have been taken at about 4pm at the end of a schoolday. *London Transport*

more formal crewing arrangements implied the end of the many liveried 12- and 14-seaters and of the familiar drivers who would cheekily stop anywhere, deviate from routes if need arose or wait until latecoming regular passengers arrived. The local press of the time does not make happy reading as passengers endeavoured to cope with change. Another cause of some sourness was the fact that the Board did not find employment for all bus crews in the firms acquired. A further source of annoyance was the ending of many cross-town facilities where the Board's boundary ran through the centre of a town. Thus east-west journeys were severed in Grays and in Slough; although the legislation allowed the Board 'unrestricted running' to Maidenhead, this

road was never used and operations in the area were rigidly divided by the LPTB and Thames Valley.

However, the Country Bus & Coach Department under Arthur Hawkins pursued the Board's objectives. (It has been suggested that Hawkins never found the satisfaction in a large organisation that he had experienced in building up East Surrey. He was particularly annoyed when one of his drivers who had said 'Good morning Arthur' for 20 years one day addressed him as 'Mr Hawkins'.) There was enormous investment by the new Board; new buses appeared in large numbers, notably front-entrance STLs, a large fleet of single-deck Qs and the Leyland Cubs for rural routes. Most of the acquired stock had gone by 1936, all of it by 1938. New garages were put up at Amersham (replacing the former Amersham & District premises), Grays, Hemel Hempstead, Hertford and Epping; Northfleet was built to replace the former tram sheds in the Old Dover Road. Bus shelters began to appear at points all over London Country, some of the Charles Holden T-shape design, others — equally well-designed — of wood. Timetable boards became ubiquitous, bus stop signs were placed at main stops (not everywhere yet — they did not become compulsory until the war). Timetable booklets assumed the form of 'local timetables', available throughout the London country area from inquiry offices and newsagents, price 2d (1p). Publicity was undoubtedly good. New bus stations were built at Sevenoaks, Dorking, Windsor and Hertford and poster displays were always attractive. The smart green uniforms much enhanced the appearance of drivers and conductors. The buses ran well — there were always sufficient crews and vehicles, and the vehicles were very reliable; a bus missed from the timetable almost merited an item in the local newspaper. Buses were now appearing in a new livery officially described as mid-green with apple-green window frames, black lining, silver roof and orange wheels. This was undoubtedly a good time for the busman to be alive, with traffic growing year by year.

The Country Bus & Coach Department had the benefit of central services built up by the LPTB which included engineering, accounting, publicity and uniforms. After 4 February 1935 the overhaul of all the more modern types of bus and coach was transferred from Reigate to Chiswick to take full advantage of standardisation of the fleet. This is the point, perhaps, to note the relationship of Country buses and Green Line coaches; coaches were worked from country garages by separately designated crews — the pay scales were different. However, buses were made available as substitutes or duplicates, and many of these were needed on summer Sundays; bus crews would then work into London termini. The close relationship between the country bus and coach was emphasised by coaches working with bus fare scales between Farningham and Wrotham (Route B, from 16 May 1934), Bishops Stortford and Epping (Route V, 5 September 1934), and over several other sections. On these journeys the coaches would carry a small slip-board indicating '1d ($\frac{1}{2}$p) fares on this coach'. The ticket system on buses and coaches was the Bell Punch, a feature that lasted until the 1950s; other companies were experimenting with Willebrew and Setright systems at this time, and the conservatism of the LPTB in respect of fare systems is surprising.

Immediately before the outbreak of World War 2, in fact on 1 September 1939, buses had to be substituted for the Green Line coaches (withdrawn to serve as ambulances) over roads where bus fares had been charged. The enforcement of the blackout regulations made operating conditions difficult at night; shaded headlamps were in use and only a minimum amount of light was allowed inside vehicles; later the windows were covered by sealed-on netting which afforded a view through a small aperture in each sheet. Staffing became difficult, though recruitment of women conductors eased this and there appear to have been fewer problems than in later years. The vehicles operated by the Country Bus & Coach Department contained a good proportion which were new in the mid-1930s, the oldest buses at work being the 1930 ST and T types, so the serviceability of vehicles never presented many problems either; in fact the Country fleet benefited from the drafting of some rear-entrance STLs from the Central fleet for Green Line work in 1940 — on the withdrawal of Green Line (for the second time) on 29 September 1942, these buses were retained at Country garages. The most acute engineering problem probably arose from the government-inspired experiments with 'producer gas'; 18 STs in Grays — a fortuitously flat area — for a time in 1942 towed small, interestingly black trolleys. Another 82 buses (including some single-deckers) were converted similarly, but performance was poor and reliability suspect.

As the war went on services were withdrawn in the evenings after 19.00 except for special factory journeys, with the introduction of summer schedules on 5 May 1943; in the same programme most Sunday morning journeys disappeared. Dramatic incidents were fortunately few, though Northfleet garage received a direct hit from an anti-aircraft shell in 1940, Swanley was damaged twice and Epping was blasted by a flying bomb. Seating arrangements in some single-deck buses were altered to a perimeter style, some vehicles working from Addlestone garage were painted grey (for journeys to the Vickers aircraft factory at Weybridge) and destination blind displays were much reduced. The services were maintained in an almost exemplary fashion and in fact improved to accommodate the remarkable increase in passenger numbers in the Country area. The figures are striking: compared with the last

Above:
An independent operator which preserved independence, though somewhat reluctantly, was West Kent Motor Services Ltd which the LPTB bought out in 1939. This bus is a Dennis 30cwt chassis with Short bodywork, new in 1930; it was actually supplied to H. M. Howells of Greenhithe & District Bus Services who sold it to West Kent in 1933, having run it on the company's route from Dartford to Bean. It is seen here shortly after acquisition by the LPTB; though repainted and numbered D202B it was withdrawn after a few months, being replaced by a Leyland Cub as soon as the road had been authorised for 20- instead of 14-seaters. The route became 421: Sevenoaks-Otford-Kemsing-Heverham. *John Parke*

peacetime year, passenger journeys had increased by 46% in 1941 and by 90% in 1945! Car miles run by Country buses increased from 28,586,000 in 1938/39 to 37,680,000 in 1945 — an advance of 32%. Much of the additional accommodation needed was provided by placing double-deck buses on former single-decker routes, though clearly frequency of service was much increased in specific cases. The timetable booklets at the end of the war in fact contained more journeys than in the 1930s, and this happy situation continued into the postwar years. In 1947, the last year of the LPTB, car miles travelled by country buses increased to 44,059,000 — up 92% compared with 1938/39; passengers carried increased from 136,151,000 to 265,578,000 over the same period — and this was a slight reduction on the 274,809,000 carried in 1946. By this time, too, the Green Line coaches were back on the road, though their figures are not included here. The whole of the immediate postwar period was characterised by buoyant traffic.

Arthur Hawkins, who had seen his empire grow from two buses in 1911 to a vast operation encircling London, retired in 1946. In a sense he was privileged to work in an era of expansion; his successors have had to face all the problems of falling traffic and a steadily diminishing share of the travel market.

The London Transport Executive

The London Passenger Transport Board ceased its legal existence on 31 December 1947 and its responsibilities were vested the following day in the British Transport Commission, a vast nationalised conglomerate. Management of London Transport affairs was undertaken by an executive, and as far as Country buses and coaches were concerned there was no outward sign of change. Passenger numbers in London country continued to grow — they reached their highest point in 1952 and again in 1955 at 297,000,000, though there were signs of decline in optional or pleasure travel which were first mentioned in the 1949 report. However, investment proceeded apace and in the early 1950s the RT and the RF were supplied in such numbers as to make them the standard vehicles in the fleet; only the low-bridge buses (labelled RLH) and the Guy Specials (which replaced the Cubs) provided variety of type. A substantial number of Eastern National services in Grays was transferred to the London Transport Executive (LTE) on 30 September 1951, and a major co-ordination scheme introduced on 1 January 1952 restored cross-town running in Grays after nearly 20 years.

A major preoccupation of Country bus management became the provision of services in the new towns which were in process of evolution; these were Crawley, Hemel Hempstead, Welwyn Garden City, Hatfield, Stevenage and Harlow. There were, in addition, the large LCC estates building at Aveley

and Sheerwater, among others. The problems of mounting services were considerable; often there was not a conveniently-placed garage — Harlow had initially to be served from Epping, Stevenage from a very circumscribed Hitchin; passengers were relatively few during offpeak times, yet passenger expectations of frequent services were high. It was noted at Harlow that everyone who travelled seemed to want to do so at the same time (ie by the same bus!) as everyone else. In Crawley the services were much criticised — extreme peak loadings at factory opening and closing times caused people to be left behind, while during the day buses rarely carried a good load. There were also complaints from the staff at the complexity of their operation with 'a lot of route and blind changing'. The choice was between providing a self-contained local service, with buses running almost empty for much of the day, or extending existing trunk routes into the estates and complicating their schedules. Despite much debate and the provision of new garages at Stevenage (1959) and Harlow (1963), the new towns services have only recently been provided on a basis that appears to please both travelling public and the staff.

Away from the new towns, expansion continued and a new garage was opened at Garston in 1952 with space for 150 vehicles, a number it has never housed. A tours programme was initiated with a short experimental list in 1949 with trips to Windsor, Whipsnade and in North Kent; increased to 50 excursions in 1950, the total on offer reached 150 by 1956. The destinations had to be within the old LPTB boundary — a test case at Hitchin in 1948

Left:
This handsome Bristol K type was among some 200 vehicles hired by London Transport in 1949 to make up the fleet numbers — the older classes were losing their certificates of fitness at an alarming rate and there was a serious shortage of buses pending the arrival of the new RTs. They were destined for Tilling companies — which were probably as short of rolling stock as London Transport — but were delivered new to London in their owners' liveries but with the roundels on the radiators, neat destination board identification and the garage and running number brackets. A few came to the Country area, and this one is working from Chesham to Watford — it is a lowbridge type, probably substituting for a life-expired ST. *Ian Allan Library*

Above:
RLH33 is caught at Little Chalfont in 1964. Some 45 of these buses were delivered to Country area garages in 1950 and 1952; they were lowbridge vehicles constructed by Weymann and though related to the RT were obviously different in design and in mechanical specifications. They were handsome vehicles nonetheless and 17 survived to be taken into stock by London Country in 1970, though they were displaced within two years by Merlins and Swifts.
G. Mead

Below:
This view of St Albans garage in 1950 shows two postwar buses, the RTs, among a collection of prewar vehicles, all single-deckers. The RTs are Nos 1013 and 1010, newly delivered to the garage in November 1948; curiously there are two body types, RT1010 being equipped with a roof 'lighthouse' route number box, painted over. From left to right are the rear of TF66, a Green Line coach new in 1939; Q202, delivered in 1936 for Green Line work; and Q81 which also started life as a coach. Alongside the RT is Q223, originally a coach; the rear of Q28; a 10T10 T475, once a coach; and an unidentified rear. All the single-deck buses and coaches were replaced by the RF class from 1951 onwards. *London Transport*

involving the LTE and W. H. Smith over a Hitchin to Weston service legally decided this issue. Derby day at Epsom became the most concentrated sports lift of the year, with buses and crews drawn from garages all over the system. Crowds were still flocking to the Surrey hills — *and* travelling by bus; experiments with the radio direction of buses in the Dorking area and at Epsom Races by mobile inspectors were initiated in 1950 and the system was used later at such events as Biggin Hill air displays. Some new services introduced in 1949 served many villages in thinly-populated rural areas for the first time; Route 479 began working on 15 June between Dartford and Farningham via Darenth, whose residents had never before seen a service bus. Another new venture started on 21 March 1956 was the 803, an express bus running between Uxbridge and Welwyn Garden City via Watford and St Albans, every 30min at peak hours; RTs were used and a journey on this fast route was said to be a memorable experience.

Even so, the problems that were going to beset London Country — and other operators — were beginning to appear. Passenger numbers on 'optional' journeys continued to decline as car ownership rose — in 1952 the summer seasonal services and extensions were reduced compared with the 1951 schedules. Costs were beginning to rise and staff shortages were noted in the latter part of 1950 — the competition for labour in the area of London Airport and in the Watford area was becoming apparent. The British Transport Commission is sometimes charged with having sought to reduce the earnings of London busmen in order to keep a balance with wages paid in its provincial undertakings. Whether this was deliberate policy or not, there was considerable unrest over wages in the mid-1950s that culminated in the strike of 1958 when not a bus left any LTE garage between 5 May and 20 June. The strike had a traumatic effect on Central road services, a less dramatic one on Country routes;

Right:
The years of the London Transport Executive were dominated on the roads by the RT which became the standard double-deck bus in the fleet. Here RT1661 heads out of the Hemel Hempstead industrial area near the Swallowdale roundabout on a wintry day. The 314B was one of the routes later handed over to the Autofare buses of the MBS type, a change of practice which proved very unpopular. RTs worked every kind of service, trunk routes, local routes, special journeys for factories and schools and some were allocated to Green Line. In all these activities they proved eminently reliable. *Edward Shirras*

though passenger numbers were down 21% in 1958 compared with 1957, there was a recovery, but in the long term the decline in numbers was evident. Private cars were usually cited as a menace in LTE reports and by the operating manager, Geoffrey Fernyhough, who added poor summer weather, TV and increased fares to the list of factors involved. It was thought that more comfortable vehicles, a punctual and reliable service, improved frequencies (where justified) and courtesy to the public would win people back to the bus. A particular cause for concern was the viability of single-decker routes — most ran at a loss and an experimental one-man-operation of a full-size single-deck bus (an RF) in 1955 was followed by a series of conversions so that by 1959 some 136 RFs were running OMO and only three single-deck services were crew-operated.

The final year of the LTE, 1962, showed that 238,000,000 passengers were carried and that Country buses ran 43,814,000 miles; this compares with the high points of 297,000,000 passengers and 48,500,000 miles achieved earlier, but the most difficult times were yet to come. The Transport Commission did not inspire great political confidence by this time and it was disestablished in 1962; on 1 January 1963 London's transport came under a London Transport Board, responsible to the Minister of Transport and required to provide an adequate service and to pay its way. Both requirements proved beyond it. However, outwardly the Country buses and coaches, with the RTs and RFs in sterling health, went about their business.

Below:
On a very wet day in Hertford GS14 stands alongside RW3. The GS — Guy Special — was the standard small bus which replaced the Leyland Cubs in 1953/4; it was designed for one-man-operation on such routes as the 308 from Hertford to Newgate Street and Cuffley station. Though the bus is equipped for driver-only working it appears to have a conductor, though of course he may be the driver of the less reputable Reliance; this is engaged on the local route to Bengeo which was probably the best kind of proving ground for experimenting with front-entrance/central-exit vehicles. Introduced in 1960 the three buses of the RW class were never well-liked and were disposed of quite early in their careers. *M. J. Dryhurst*

The London Transport Board

In retrospect the seven years (1963-1969) of London Transport Board (LTB) oversight of bus services in London country were disastrous. Passenger journeys fell each year with increasing steepness, down to 179,000,000 in 1969 — a loss of 25% compared with 1962. Much of this loss was undoubtedly caused by the increased use of the car for business and pleasure travel, and the falling away of traditional expeditions in the evenings and at weekends. Loss of custom on Sundays was particularly frightening. By 1966 Saturday was no longer the heaviest day; though loads in the mornings were still good, traffic fell away sharply in the afternoon; traffic receipts on Fridays were consistently above those of Saturdays. Staff morale was particularly low during this period, and staff shortages endemic; there were periods when overtime and rest day working were banned and services became erratic and unreliable. The Brown-Phelps report resulted in new scales of pay for platform staff from 18 December 1963, but in September 1966 the Country buses and coaches were some 550 short on an establishment of 5,500. Overall this shortage could have been coped with, but the staffing was especially poor in some garages — Garston and Hemel Hempstead were almost perpetually short.

Part of the malaise sprang from uncertainty of the future during a period of comparative boom — these were the years of 'swinging London' after all. Platform staff could see the empty seats in their vehicles and contemplate their futures rather bleakly at the next re-scheduling exercise. Conductors were particularly vulnerable as almost every indication pointed towards one-man-operation. The RT and the RF continued to be the backbones of the fleet, yet one design dated from 1938 and the second from the early 1950s. The system in which they ran tended to look anachronistic, as indeed it was; timetables were trimmed with increasing frequency and the service trundled on. The operating manager, G. Fernyhough, became increasingly and unavoidably adept at finding reasons (or excuses) and his Bulletin, distributed to the staff, makes somewhat dismal reading; perhaps he was as much a prisoner of the traditional concept as anyone. Loss of traffic is frequently ascribed to 'a bad summer and snow at the end of December'. He was realistic enough to state that passengers lost were probably lost for good; he saw the necessity 'to reduce the number of scheduled bus duties a little due to the present serious staff shortage. Otherwise the services become unreliable

and the passengers never know where they are'. He expressed some optimism in February 1965 with the delivery of some new vehicles — 100 RML buses, among others; 'these will give a new look to our fleet and should attract new passengers and "knock" the private car'.

The private car was certainly causing damage to the bus services; increasing congestion in the town centres caused delays to buses and poor time-keeping. There were few bright lights during this period which was very much one of a grimly-determined holding operation in more and more uncertain circumstances. The Dartford Tunnel opened on 18 November 1963 and a bus service was immediately put on between Grays and Dartford; the service was an immediate and undoubted failure as passengers were very few. There was also a bizarre facility provided by a fleet of five Ford buses, based at Dartford, to carry cyclists and their machines through the tunnel — there were seats for 33 people on the upper deck and the lower deck comprised

Above:
The years of the London Transport Board were dominated by the need to reduce costs and the move towards high-capacity, one-man-operated single-deck buses was given impetus by the Reshaping Plan of 1966. Here MBS289 operates a local Hemel Hempstead service and heads away from one of the stops in the centre of the new town. Route 314A was a distant derivative of the former 314 that ran for many years from Hemel to St Albans until the mid-1950s. This vehicle was withdrawn in 1978 and sold the following year. Route 314A has now been incorporated into the H group of routes. *Edward Shirras*

racks for 23 bicycles. Doubtless had the tunnel opened in 1939 or 1940 as intended, there would have been some custom; however, by 1963 the cycle was not a favoured mode of transport. After some weeks of virtual inactivity, the buses were withdrawn and replaced by single Land Rover with a trailer. Fortunately the loss was not borne by the bus operator, but it would be interesting to know what happened to the buses!

Below:

MBS15, alternatively coded XMB, was one of the first of the Merlins; it had a Strachan body and was licensed for 72 passengers, only 31 of them seated. It went the rounds before reaching Tring in the early 1970s and is seen here in London Country livery at Aldbury. The vehicle was the sole representative of its type in the London Country area, though large numbers were at work on various schemes in the Central area; of all the Merlins the Strachan-bodied ones were the least respected. In 1973 London Transport, for some reason, took this one back and provided LCBS with MBS4 in exchange. MBS15 was withdrawn along with 130 others in 1977; MBS4 lasted until 1979. The 387 service really deserved a better vehicle; it dates back to 1 March 1914 when it was started by the London & North Western Railway; passed to the London, Midland & Scottish Railway it was acquired by London General Country Services on 11 April 1933 and was given the number carried today. *London Country*

The publication of the London Bus Reshaping plan in September 1966, with its emphasis on one-man-operation of large single-deck vehicles with front doors for entry and central exists, was not at first thought to have much relevance for Country bus operations. However, there was clear need to try another mode of operation and 9 March 1968 some AEC Merlin vehicles, coded MB, were put to work on Route 447 from Reigate garage. Mr Fernyhough wrote: 'The new buses have been well-received by the public. The drivers' reaction to the new vehicles has also been generally favourable'. In fact the MBs were very unpopular with operating and engineering staff — they were cumbersome and unreliable. They were also intensely cold in winter. However, seven more were drafted to the Uxbridge-High Wycombe road and another 18 were promised. By January 1969 32 of the slightly different MBS class (they seated 25 passengers and allowed 41 standing) were at work from Hatfield, Hemel Hempstead and St Albans. They were not well received by the public and they were to prove a doubtful legacy to London Country. In particular, the Autofare ticket machines into which passengers fed coins were poor substitutes for the (usually) cheerful and helpful conductors, and were certainly more likely to break down. While the decors of the new buses were pleasantly functional, the emphasis on standing room rather than seats did nothing to improve the image of the public service

29

This bus is No 8 in the XF class, the code designating Experimental Daimler Fleetline. The London Transport Board purchased eight of these buses in 1965 and employed five at East Grinstead and three, including this one, on the Blue Arrow routes in Stevenage. XF8 is seen here heading out of East Grinstead after transfer there, having been painted in more staid colours by LCBS. These were the first double-deck vehicles capable of being worked OMO taken into the London Transport fleet, though it was some time before the concept was accepted and put into practice, as here. *Edward Shirras*

vehicle at a time when it was under increasing threat from the private car.

The whole period of the LTB was dominated by problems mainly derived from the awareness that public transport, if provided on the customary scale and using traditional operating methods, was unlikely ever again to pay its way. The Board endeavoured to cut its costs, and solve some of its staffing difficulties at the same time, by moving towards OMO on a much larger scale than that employed hitherto. This change in style of working led to protracted negotiations with the union over job losses and the appropriate payment for the 'driver-operator'. These negotiations eventually required the intervention of the Government-inspired Prices and Incomes Board. The change to OMO also required the development of a new generation of vehicles where the emphasis was on moving the largest

number of people using the minimum number of buses and staff — passenger amenity and comfort were at a discount. The 1968 Transport Act accelerated the process by introducing 'new bus grants' of up to 25% of capital costs (50% from 1972) for vehicle types approved by the Ministry of Transport; the approved types — single or double-deck — were all designed to be operated by the driver only. The new bus grant and fuel tax rebate were paid by Central Government, but the Act also involved local authorities which were empowered to contribute towards bus company revenue, initially at least for the purpose of sustaining rural services. All these moves tended to destabilise the existing situation so that the traditional financial approaches and operating procedures were revolutionised, though the full impact of the changes did not appear until the early 1970s.

As one element in the preliminary negotiations and consultations that led to the 1968 Act, a joint statement by the Ministry of Transport and the leader of the GLC was issued on 15 December 1967 to the effect that the GLC would become the statutory transport planning authority for London, with responsibility for the provision of public transport services. A new London Transport Executive would be formed, its members appointed by the GLC; the GLC itself would control policy, finance and the broad principles of operations, the Executive to be responsible for day-to-day management. The agreement meant that the future of the Country Bus & Coach Department was very much in doubt as the bulk of its operations were patently outside the GLC boundary. There were suggestions that the green bus

This photograph was taken in September 1971, early in the LCBS period; however, the scene at West Croydon is entirely representative of the last days of the London Transport Board. On the left AEC Swift SM533, a Metro-Cammell-Weymann-built vehicle seating 41 passengers, is engaged on Route 403A to Warlingham Park Hospital; next is RT3173, bound for Effingham; DMS139, a Daimler Fleetline with Park Royal coachwork, is just leaving and XA31, an early Atlantean, is working a Croydon local express route on a one-man-operator basis. Of the four vehicles only the RT, new in May 1952, was to have a full life; especially unsatisfactory was XA31 which was shipped to Hong Kong in 1973; perhaps the climate there suited it better. *Stephen J. A. Madden*

Above:
In the last days of the working to Four Elms RF686 is seen in September 1971. This is the point where buses on 413 ran down to Brasted and the stop sign is for that route. The Four Elms service, here diverted by a road closure, derived from a West Kent Motor Services through run to Edenbridge. On acquisition by the LPTB this through facility was severed, but after the war buses ran two-hourly to Four Elms where a connection was made with Maidstone & District for Edenbridge. Very few passengers made the journey through some of the most scenic parts of the North Downs. *Edward Shirras*

services should be absorbed by the adjacent provincial companies — Maidstone & District taking over its former territory in North and West Kent, for example, but in the event the creation of the National Bus Co in the 1968 Act provided the solution in the setting up of a new company, London Country Bus Services Ltd, as a subsidiary of the NBC. The political manoeuvres that culminated in the passing of the London (Transport) Act 1969 and the transfer of Central Bus and Underground operations to the GLC on 1 January 1970 perhaps explain the confusion of policy in which Country buses operated towards the end of the 1960s; it may also explain the lack of investment that was to cause LCBS many problems in its early years.

31

London Country Bus Services Ltd

The Inheritance

By the Transport (London) Act of 1969, the Country Bus & Coach Department of the LTB was to be transferred to 'such company, being a wholly-owned subsidiary of the National Bus Company, as may be designated for that purpose'. Thus London Country Bus Services Ltd, incorporated on 9 October 1968, remained non-operational until vesting day, 1 January 1970, when 'all the property rights and liabilities of the Board's undertakings commonly known as Country Buses and Coaches' were transferred to the designated subsidiary. Itself a newly-constituted body, the National Bus Company (NBC) did not consider its infant health improved by responsibility for LCBS and drew attention to the shaky finances; LTB figures are quoted indicating that the Country Buses & Coaches had run up losses of £988,000 in 1968 and £555,000 in 1969.

On vesting day LCBS began trading with no bank balance and a sum of £2,500 in petty cash floats. There were no depreciation reserves though these had stood in LTB books at £5,500,000; further, the company has alleged that in the years pending the break-up of the LTB the fleet of vehicles and the buildings had been allowed to deteriorate. The new company's problems were at first organisational: the designated head office at Reigate was small and there were no central workshops. In London Transport days a range of some 40 common services had been built up, for example in scheduling, press and public relations, canteen service, traffic audit, accounts and insurance. London Country had to establish its own departments; plans were made to build an extension to the administrative block at Lesbourne Road and this was opened on 27 March 1972 confirming the long primacy of Reigate in London country affairs. It was as well that the new managing director, Cyril Buckley, could say: 'As a new company we have a golden opportunity to build up a good public image' — the task in the circumstances was formidable. Geoffrey Fernyhough survived the changes and was appointed general manager, responsible with the traffic manager, the secretary and accountant, and the chief engineer for day-to-day management. The NBC influence was made manifest by appointment of senior staff from other subsidiary companies; for example, the new traffic manager (North), E. A. Allison, came from Crosville; conversely the assistant district superintendent (South West), W. Wheeler, was appointed a divisional manager with Southdown at Portsmouth. These were the first moves towards eliminating the London Transport image and creating a new identity.

The route networks and schedules inherited from the LTB and its predecessors were instantly recognisable to students of timetable booklets in the 1930s. Change had been largely incremental and without doubt there was need for fundamental reappraisal; there were particular problems with the archaic Green Line operation but that is not to be discussed here. All modifications to bus working in the LTE and LTB period had been additions or alterations to an existing map as though that map were holy writ. It was some time before London Country could reorganise radically services or groups of services but the changes were radical when they came. The methods of working had been inherited from the LPTB although in the 1950s and 1960s considerable progress had been made with the introduction of OMO of single-deck buses — all were so operated by 1 January 1970.

Vehicle Policy

The new company's policy was to implement OMO throughout the fleet as soon as possible, but this was difficult in view of the number of vehicles that could only be worked by two people. Thus the fleet included 488 RT vehicles and 100 RMLs; the RTs — the backbone of the double-decker fleet — were now up to 22 years old; in fact the average age of the vehicles available to London Country is given as 18.5 years, an astonishing figure. The RTs and RFs were really beyond retirement age but they were far more reliable and better liked by passengers and staff than the other LTB legacy, the MB group; though relatively new they were ponderous in operation, not very comfortable for drivers or passengers and subject to crippling defects. London Country brought 563 new vehicles into the fleet in the years 1970-73, but this achievement was not without problems of maintenance of such varied types; NVA (no vehicle available) and NDA (no driver available) came to dominate operations to such an extent that all services appeared to be kept on the road only by a series of improvisations. 'Preferred types' were allocated but buses (and coaches) were put on to routes as available, the only criterion being that they were running. A climax of uncertainty was reached in 1974 when single or double-deck vehicles might appear on routes with Maidstone or Southend Corporation buses hired to fill gaps, deputising for example for the RMLs suffering defects from which

Top:
SM474 stands on the forecourt of Amersham garage prior to departure on Route 362A to High Wycombe, having started from Ley Hill. Ordered in the last days of the London Transport Board, the bus was relatively new, having been delivered to London Country whose logo it boasts in 1971. The Swift at 33ft was some 3ft shorter than the Merlin and more suitable for country roads. RT3615 appears to be relegated to a staff bus and was perhaps one of those displaced on the arrival of the SM class.
Edward Shirras

Above:
In the early days of its existence London Country was compelled to withdraw certain seriously loss-making rural routes. These included the long-standing 452 from Dartford to West Kingsdown which had never been more than a Saturdays and Sundays only operation. Latterly journeys were offered on Saturdays only, and RF207 is seen on the very last day, 13 February 1971. The cement dust lies heavily on the roads and verges of Greenhithe — note the works chimneys in the background — and seems to have settled on the bus as well. *Tom Maddocks*

some never recovered. Through this dismal period the RTs and the RFs soldiered on, often unkempt but reliable. The advent of the Leyland National, of which London Country now has the doubtful distinction of being the largest owner, was marred by the spartan interiors, the noisiness of the engine and — at least initially — by high defect records. Prolonged negotiations with the New Town Commissioner at Crawley culminated in the allocation of a plot for central workshops and Tinsley Green was opened in 1976. Garston garage became, in part, the northern works and individual garages with the necessary equipment and expertise were allocated specific engineering jobs; thus at Guildford gearboxes are overhauled and Grays does the recertification work formerly done at Romford (RE). With the new engineering organisation in being, by 1977 the NVA position had been reduced from an average of 60 vehicles daily to 30. (It is still the expressed opinion of the older garage staff that the RTs were much easier to deal with than the present types; it was said that the RT could be given treatment and put back into service during layover time, but this is by no means true of the Leyland National.)

County Council Revenue Support

Of great importance to London Country (and to other companies, of course) has been the developing relationship with county councils in whose areas it operates. In the latter part of the 1960s it was clear that financial difficulties arising from increased costs and lower ridership, even with increased fares, had put many services, especially rural ones, in jeopardy. The 1968 Transport Act empowered local authorities to subsidise bus services that were considered socially desirable but making heavy losses. These powers were confirmed and extended by the 1972 Local Government Act, by which the current county and district council structure came into being on 1 April 1974. However, much the most comprehensive legislation was that in the Transport Act (1978); the counties became responsible for 'developing policies for public transport provision and co-ordination, and for entering into arrangements with operators to provide services deemed to be socially necessary'. County councils had a duty to prepare public transport plans and to enter into negotiations with bus operators; thus Essex County Council acts through its Public Transport Subcommittee to which the county planner reports. The Essex County Council Transport Plan is published annually in accordance with Section 2 of the Transport Act (1978). The fourth of these documents, that for 1982/3, includes a survey of public transport provision — road, rail and ferry — and the results of investigations. Changes made in the system in consultation with the county are indicated and those services in receipt of grant aid are listed; the T routes in Harlow are among those subsidised. In fact, the sums received from county authorities are considerable; in 1979/80 London Country received £1,869,000 from Surrey, £214,000 from West Sussex, £377,000 from Buckinghamshire as well as grants from Kent, Hertfordshire and the GLC. The policy has arisen that in each area county councils prefer to deal with one operator or — where there are two or more — to put pressure on them to rationalise their services into a coherent local pattern. The Market Analysis Project (MAP) schemes referred to later and the transfers of services between London Country and Eastern National in Grays in 1980 are evidence of this policy at work. The tendency has been to tighten county boundaries — services crossing boundaries cause accounting problems, some of them deriving from the different perceptions of the services in question by two local authorities. Surrey County Council Transportation Committee has encouraged London Country operation and pursued a policy of limiting London Transport workings over the GLC boundary into the county; the view generally expressed is that London Transport operating methods are expensive. Long-established LT services in the Weybridge area and routes to Lower Kingswood and Walton-on-the-Hill

Below:
Experiments which offered a new rapid-transit facility in Stevenage began at the very end of the London Transport Board era on 29 December 1969. This was Blue Arrow, and two Daimler Fleetlines in blue and silver livery linked Chells with the industrial area in the new town. The scheme was adapted by LCBS into Superbus, and Metro-Scania MS2 in yellow and blue livery is seen here in September 1977; it is working alongside Atlantean AN9 which is probably substituting for an MS vehicle as availability of this tye at this time was not high. Further adaptations turned the local service network into StevenageBus, using Atlanteans equipped with fare boxes; the current scheme was introduced on 26 April 1980.
M. J. Dryhurst

Above:
London Country experienced acute vehicle problems in the mid-1970s as older types were crippled by lack of spares (a situation that affected the RMLs particularly) or newer vehicles proved to be chronic invalids. Rolling stock hired in 1976 included coaches from Royal Blue (mainly allocated to Dunton Green) and buses from Maidstone, Bournemouth, Eastbourne and Southend Corporations. So desperate was the position that London Transport lent some Merlins. Here a Southend Transport Leyland, in blue livery, is about to take a Route 397 journey from Harlow; it is a smart and sturdy-looking bus. *P. J. Snell*

Below:
The Watfordwide scheme came into operation on 31 March 1979 and one of its most important aspects was the penetration by the buses into the town centre. It was launched with an intensive publicity campaign and a revised fare structure which standardised fares to and from each residential area. Weekly and monthly travel cards were introduced and a drive to improve staffing had good results. Patronage increased in the first year by about 9%, with an increase in revenue in real terms. Lost mileage through staff shortage was reduced from 10% to less than 3%. SNB239 and SNB455 stand in the Market Place on 25 March 1982. Route W1 ran along Garston Lane to Kingswood and back via North Watford and Harebreaks; W2 worked in the reverse direction. *G. B. Wise*

have thus passed to LCBS. The working of the 1978 Act has led to a great deal of co-ordination of bus networks, especially where two operators are involved, though the pressures local authorities can bring to bear through finance limit to some extent the freedom of operators to solve their problems in their own way. Without much doubt, however, many services now running would have disappeared long ago without grant aid. In 1981 18% of London Country's running costs were provided by county councils, a sum described as critical for balancing the books. The extremely bad weather of 1982 was followed by a spate of unreliability at certain garages, largely the result of vehicle breakdown and staff sickness; one county council sought assurances that there would be a rapid improvement in services or consideration would be given to possible withdrawal of some support — a threat not easy to live with.

Working with county council and other planning authorities, London Country has carried through several experiments. The Stevenage Blue Arrow (actually an unwilling LTB initiative — the Board thought the fares too low) and Superbus schemes provided intensive services from the residential areas to the town centre and to the factories. Blue Arrow buses picked up passengers as near their homes as possible and worked on a flat fare or contract basis. Some Metro-Scanias were allocated, looking most distinctive in yellow and blue livery, though they eventually proved troublesome. Some aspects of the concept were incorporated into the StevenageBus network. There was also an investigation into local services in the Hemel Hempstead area in 1974, as a first move towards the H system of routes implemented later. The Hemel Hempstead services had been built up stage by stage as the new town developed and presented a somewhat incoherent pattern of 30 routes. The aim was to reorganise the provision into a 'rational, comprehensive and regular frequency network' and to avoid such anomalies as

three different routes to the town centre from Bennett's End with different fare scales. Surrey County Council underwrote a modest experiment with local bus services in Oxted from 3 April 1976; a reduction in fares on 464 (Holland via Hurst Green to Oxted and Limpsfield) brought a convincing increase in passenger use from about 325 journeys daily in mid-1976 to about 440 within a year; however, there was an equally convincing loss of revenue of 19%. The second part of the experiment was the introduction of the 465, using the 'spare bus' to run journeys from Oxted station to various destinations at shopping times; this was an interesting initiative, though somewhat expensive. A two-zonal fare system in St Albans was started late in 1981 which had the effect of simplifying the fare structure dramatically.

Boundary Changes
Partly, but not wholly, through county council policy the boundaries of London Country activity have changed very considerably. Exchanges of services with LT have tended to confine that operator's routes within the GLC area and to greatly reduce 'outrunning'. Conversely, the penetration of London Country's bus routes into the former Central area has been limited. Long-established, former Central bus routes have been trimmed — the 21 has not worked east of Swanley for many years, the 81 does not go south-west of Slough, nor the 116/117 beyond Staines. Major changes occurred on 28 January 1978 when 264 (Kingston-Sunbury-Walton-Hersham) and the Sunbury Village to Chertsey section of the 237 were withdrawn; in replacement London Country 459 and 461 worked, initially to Feltham, over some of these roads. A survey of passengers on the new routes revealed

greater satisfaction on the grounds of punctuality and reliability. The outer section of 84 from New Barnet to St Albans became a LCBS working on 24 April 1982, and on the same day the company took over parts of three routes in the Banstead area: the 164 to Epsom, the 80/280 to Lower Kingswood

Major innovations and reorganisations have followed the MAP (Market Analysis Project) surveys in areas to the west of LCBS territory. The Weyfarer scheme was put into operation on 31 August 1980 and involved a high level of co-operation between London Country and Alder Valley. The jointly-issued publicity included press releases, free leaflets and exhibitions. Headed 'Partnership for a better local bus service', this photograph which appeared in the local press briefing shows a green London Country and a red Alder Valley bus sporting the new Wayfarer symbol. The differences in frontal styling between the LCBS vehicle and the older Alder Valley bus are interesting.
Ian Allan Library

Cross-town working in Gravesend by London Country and Maidstone & District began on 30 October 1976 when LCBS routes were extended into Riverview Park and Maidstone & District vehicles worked to Northfleet. In 1978 London Country became the sole local operator in Gravesend and on 1 April Routes 497 and 498 were put on from Pepper Hill Estate to River View park, with some journeys starting from Northfleet (The Plough). Leyland National SNB330 swings out of the one-way system past the clock tower in Gravesend. The clock tower was a terminal point for many years, though in fact buses had to stand in the road opposite. *G. K. Gillberry*

and the 80A/280A to Walton-on-the-Hill. These roads were covered by new Route 418, an altered working of 422 and new 420 respectively. Further inroads into London Transport facilities were made on 29 January 1983 with the withdrawal of Routes 211 (Tolworth-Kingston-West Molesey-Walton-on-Thames) and 219 (Kingston-Weybridge); these were replaced by extensions of London Country Routes 437 and redirection of 461 to Kingston. It is interesting to note that approximately 20% of LCBS service mileage is operated within Greater London by buses and Green Line coaches. Since 1976 these have been worked on a 'Fares and Services' agreement; they attract revenue support from the London Transport Executive which in 1980 amounted to £1.14million.

Boundary changes with other NBC companies included the interchanges with Maidstone & District in Gravesend starting 30 October 1976 by which London Country Routes 480 and 487 extended eastward into Valley Drive while Maidstone & District worked cross-town to Painters Ash and Coldharbour. A more extensive reorganisation took place on 1 January 1978 when the Maidstone & District depot at Overcliffe — a landmark for many years — closed, London Country becoming the main Gravesend town operator, taking over some tours and excursions as well. On 19 July 1980 Maid-

stone & District lost its Kemsing local service to Sevenoaks to London Country. Southdown agreed to pass all its Crawley town services to London Country in April 1971 and closed its own depot in the town; the whole of the northern part of East Sussex has proved poor bus country and former full services to Crawley and East Grinstead have shrunk to minor operations with some replacements by London Country. In the north United Counties is currently operating some former London Country services including the 360 from Luton to Caddington and the 364 (Luton to Kimpton and Codicote), acquired on 4 December 1976 pending the closure of Luton garage (LS). These have been further exchanges of mainly minor services, mostly in the Hitchin and Welwyn areas, London Country becoming responsible for the last remnant of the old Birch 203 from King's Cross to Rushden, latterly United Counties 82, now London Country 314: Hitchin to Welwyn. Agreement with Eastern National has further limited that company's work in Grays; from 1 September 1979 Eastern National 269 (Grays to Brentwood) became London Country 369, while Eastern National took over the Warley-Brentwood-Ongar section of 339, renumbering it — logically — 239. Some changes to local routes confirmed London Country as the town operator in Grays and Tilbury.

Changes in Provision
LCBS has abandoned some routes altogether, of course; they are mainly very rural ones and include the Leatherhead to Esher section of 416 which was passed to Mole Valley on 29 November 1975, the 485: Westerham to Edenbridge, replaced by a limited Maidstone & District offering on 31 December 1981, the 382 between St Albans and Codicote (31 March 1979), and 381 between Epping and Toothill, much earlier in 1971. Of particular interest was the closure of Route 336A: Rickmansworth to the Loudwater Estate; this route was served to the end by buses of the GS class and with the withdrawal of the route on 30 March 1972 the last of these buses was taken out of service. London Country has acquired some independent interests, including the Tillingbourne 451: Horsham to Colgate and Faygate service on 27 January 1979 — this was incorporated into the 434/474 schedule. That same company's once-monthly run to Chichester was worked by London Country from 3 September 1980; with a journey on the first Wednesday of each month this service from Guildford must rank as London Country's smallest commitment. (It was withdrawn after the journey on 1 September 1982.)

Services provided by London Country have been adjusted to cater for the lower levels of use patently obvious in the evenings and on Sundays. Almost every service has a thinned evening timetable; some now cease altogether between about 19.00 and the

last bus of the day at 22.30 — a kind of extended Coronation Street interval — and some have no evening service at all. Thus the 424 Reigate to East Grinstead service is closed by 19.38; there are no evening buses in East Grinstead on Mondays to Fridays after the departure of the 19.22 No 409 for Godstone with the single exception of the 22.36 on 434/438 for Crawley; evening services to Lingfield cease before 18.00. (This last situation is exceptional — there is a good measure of activity in Crawley.) Sunday services have progressively been subject to reductions in frequency, then operated on double-deck routes by single-deck OMO buses, and then withdrawn altogether especially where they parallel Green Line routes. Sunday working is now extremely limited throughout the London Country system — a far cry from the 1930s when every available bus and crew were mustered for the journey home. Hatfield garage currently provides no buses on a Sunday, Dartford puts out two, Guildford three — few garages reach double figures. More recently Green Line services have been adapted to take on bus functions every day and the parallel bus services have been abandoned. Thus 715 serves as a bus between Guildford and Kingston, as do 702 and 712 between Bishops Stortford and Epping — both sections from 2 April 1977. The 706 Tunbridge Wells to Victoria route was diverted to run through Sevenoaks Weald on 22 April 1981, leaving 454 as vestigial remains and replacing 402 altogether, the latter number disappearing after 57 years. In the evenings no buses work on Route 301/302 after the 20.23 departure (weekdays) from Watford for Hemel Hempstead; Green Line 708 covers the road to

Aylesbury after that time and all day on Sunday. All the reductions in service, especially the shrinking of the time services span to about 12hr or less, reduce the 'wheels turning' time that used to be a mark of productivity. In East Surrey and National days the longer the bus was in service on the road the higher its earnings were likely to be. However, in these days of extremely limited use of the services on Sundays and in the evenings, there is little point in carrying rows of empty seats from place to place. The capital investment has now to earn its return over a much shorter period of time — if it can earn a return to all. Reductions of staff and vehicle requirements have led to the closure of garages, several after many years of existence; thus Luton, High Wycombe and Tring all closed in 1977 and, most recently, East Grinstead closed its doors on 29 December 1981.

Reorganisations

However, the position is not entirely gloomy and London Country, once through the traumas of its early years, has made considerable innovative changes to its network, in most cases the first major alterations for 40 years. There have been several localisations of services which have clearly differentiated between town buses and inter-urban buses and given the local routes a separate identity. Thus the S group came into existence in St Albans on 30 October 1976, the H group in Hemel Hempstead (8 January 1977), the C group — a significant reorganisation, this — in Crawley on 1 July 1978, and the Watfordwide system (W routes) started on 31 March 1979. Later StevenageBus (SB) took over from the rather tarnished Superbus image on

Above left:

London Country AN116, an early Atlantean with Metro-Cammell coachwork built in 1972, is seen here in red livery; it is one of four vehicles on contract to London Transport for the Round London tour. Two are open-top and two have roofs; they are garaged at Leatherhead. This bus is seen in Kingston in September 1982 on its way to take up duty. *John Marsh*

Above:

Another LBCS acquisition was of part of the 84 which now runs from St Albans to New Barnet station; red buses thus gave way to green after nearly 60 years. Leyland Olympian LR4, purchased for the conversion, is seen in St Albans shortly after the changeover on 24 April 1982. London Transport allowed 41min to Barnet Church, a time which LCBS cut to 34; however, this proved too tight a timing, especially at peak hours. *G. B. Wise*

26 April 1980 and the TownBus started at Harlow on 30 August in the same year. All these developments are based on perceived passenger needs, a flat fare or zonal system and services running regularly and without deviation throughout the day. C Line, allocated a batch of 24 Atlantean buses, was London Country's biggest service reorganisation ever in one location and the largest publicity campaign was mounted to go with it. The scheme is said to have improved receipts, boosted staff morale and recruitment and completely revitalised the image of the bus

in the area. The randomly numbered services were replaced by eight lettered routes, C1 to C8; there are also three peak hour routes, C15-C17, and one schools route, C21, Crawley, with a population of 75,000, is of course a new town with a large number of people likely to use the buses; as has been noted, its neighbour — East Grinstead — has a very different social structure and a very small base of actual or potential bus-users.

Much the most interesting service reorganisations, all implemented in 1980, followed Market Analysis Projects (MAP) of which there have been three in the London Country area: Chilternlink, covering services in Amersham and High Wycombe (implemented 13 April), Thamesline (Windsor and Slough, planned for 31 May but delayed by a strike) and Weyfarer (Woking and Guildford, started 31 August). The projects and techniques associated with them were developed by the NBC in conjunction with Colin Buchanan & Partners; the purpose of each project was to 'identify precisely the present use being made of the buses (in a given area), together with the detailed requirements of existing and potential users'. The information gathered from surveys was intended to be used 'as a basis for replanning bus networks to match more closely present and anticipated levels of demand'. The surveys covered every Monday to Friday and Sunday journey and a sample of Saturday services; there were also selected household interviews. Thus in Maidenhead and Slough 52,860 on-bus survey forms were completed, and 497 house-based ones. Traffic flows were identified, the characteristics of the passengers analysed in terms of sex, age, car ownership and purpose of journey, and the costs of the existing services were established. Some of the financial analyses tended to be melancholy; in the services operating in Slough only the 441, in a four-week period ending on 3 November 1979, showed a tiny margin of fare income over costs — £44, with running costs at £43,771. The county councils, as providers of grant aid, were interested parties to the MAP investigations and provided assistance, both financial and with personnel. The networks proposed aimed to cater for the bulk of the existing demand, though excessively unremunerative services were recommended for withdrawal. Evening and Sunday services were 'critically reviewed'. It was hoped to maintain 'an acceptable standard of mobility'. A number of new cross-town links was established, London Country and Alder Valley working into each other's territory and co-ordinating services on common roads. The MAP schemes were strongly marketed — there was a great deal of promotional publicity; some fare incentives were advertised; maps and timetable booklets were distributed to households. In Woking and Guildford 'promotional buses' were placed in town centres; there were free balloons for the children and a balloon race —

publicity devices that Frank Pick could never have dreamed of. The emphasis was on schemes that would at least approach viability and require as little county council support as possible; the economies that followed implementation reduced the number of buses needed, and the number of drivers — less so in London Country than in Alder Valley, but significantly even so. It is to be hoped that the new schemes, all with their local fleetnames, will be acceptable to the travelling public over the long term — the changes in route patterns are for the first time based on detailed analysis of passenger journey characteristics in relation to the logistic requirements of the operator.

Future Prospects

Staffing has been a problem for London Country throughout its existence — thus continuing a trend inherited from LTB days and earlier. Acute shortages were noted at Addlestone and Windsor in 1970; there was a shortfall of 320 drivers in 1978, about 13.5% of the establishment. Services were kept going only by a great deal of overtime and rest-day working, both expensive expedients; however, scheduled miles lost were kept to a respectable minimum — the loss in 1978 was 5.3%, but this figure disguises several black spots such as Hemel Hempstead and Watford. Only in 1982 did fully staffed garages become the rule rather than the exception. Among other changes in the environment, the building of bypasses and motorways has benefited London Country operations by siphoning traffic away from the now secondary roads that remain the bus routes. The Tonbridge bypass was opened on 12 July 1971 and at a stroke the congestion in Tonbridge High Street all but vanished; the completion of the Sevenoaks to Godstone section of the M25 in 1980 has cleared the A25 and allowed the buses to keep time for the first time in years. All over the system traffic engineering has helped improve the operating environment, though the pedestrianisation of urban precincts has tended to keep the buses away from the very centres they serve best. However, the opening of Watford centre to buses in the Watfordwide scheme has done much to redress the balance, at least in that town.

In its early days London Country was at least in appearance a close relation of London Transport; the vehicles were former LT buses, with the characteristic interior decors; working methods were LT ones and the casual observer might have thought that nothing had changed. However, a new logo replaced the roundel — this was allegedly intended to represent the green fields around London or a wheel going through the fields; it was quickly dubbed the 'flying polo'. NBC influence became more explicit, especially after the retirement of Geoffrey Fernyhough in October 1972 and NBC liveries were adopted, together with the now familiar 'N' sign.

London Country has looked increasingly like any other NBC company, especially with the influx of the Leyland Nationals and the disappearance of the RF from service in March 1976 — the RT hung on to run in scheduled service until June 1977. Destination displays have been reduced to the single line — a regrettable trend, this — and suffixes to route numbers have almost entirely disappeared; thus Route 303A, after a long existence, became 300 on 16 February 1974, while in other cases such as the 305 all workings were subsumed under the one number. The old LT roundel bus stop signs have almost gone, the company having a statutory duty to change to the standardised national bus stop sign by 1985. While bus work has tended to survive in a somewhat hostile environment, London Country's most imaginative developments have been in the Green Line field; there has been a rapid increase in coach activity, some of it in co-operation with other NBC companies; this semi-fast work may well be the sector that will prove the most promising kind of service that a bus company can provide in the years ahead.

It seems likely that bus traffic will continue to decline in the long term, for a variety of social and other reasons. However, the need for the bus has been stressed by the Bus & Coach Council which in 1982 published a well-devised and illustrated book *The Future of the Bus*. Intended to 'stimulate a debate on the role of the bus in society' the report identifies the passengers' needs and the operators' problems in providing a service that will satisfy them in a period of financial stringency. The steadily reducing grant aid from central and local government has emphasised the vulnerability of bus services, many — if not most — of which cannot be self-supporting. A second report, published in July 1982, was of more immediate interest to London Country; this was *Transport in London*, the report of the House of Commons Transport Committee. Among the proposals was the establishment of a Metropolitan Transport Authority which would assume a supervisory role over the road and rail services of the GLC, main line rail and NBC services within an area that very closely resembles that designated in 1933 for the London Passenger Transport Board. It does not appear that that body will be revived in any form, so there will be no instance here of history rewriting itself. However, the London Transport Operators' Partnership to be established will have oversight of 'timetabling and service integration, interchange investment and planning, creation of common fare structures and marketing of services, but not the general pooling of passenger revenue'. Even if the plan is implemented, it looks as if the operators are assured of a large measure of independence in the way they manage their concerns; London Country looks set to continue its separate existence first won (or granted) in 1970.

Green Line

The development of the Green Line coach network, the system of semi-fast coaches that has been a feature of travel in the London area for many years, is inextricably bound up with the history of the motorbus in London country. However, the idea of a coach running on a frequent service throughout the day and on which it was not necessary to book a seat was really too advanced for the LGOC. The first initiatives were therefore those of independent companies which started services to Central London termini from points outside the Metropolitan Police District; there was no licensing control except that of the local watch committees. The independents frequently represented themselves as — and often were — local men in combat with the giant LGOC and its subsidiaries. It was, of course, the technical development of the coach that made such services possible, together with the availability of money, much of which had been paid by the LGOC to independent operators to buy them off the London streets. Thus in 1927 and 1928 services were established from Tunbridge Wells (Redcar), Luton (R. W. Priest and, later, Strawhatter), Aylesbury (West London Coaches), Bedford (Birch) and Guildford (Skylark) among many others. East Surrey tried out a limited service from Redhill and Reigate (one route via Croydon, a second via Sutton) which started on 7 August 1928, though — at least initially — this required booking; loadings were poor and the routes were withdrawn on 3 March 1929.

The LGOC found itself compelled to participate in the coach business in order to protect its own interests, and so put on a service from Watford (Leavesden Road) to Golders Green on 2 October 1929 using vehicles from its private hire fleet. Withdrawn on 12 November, service was resumed on 18 December 1929 and, additionally, coaches were run through to Charing Cross Embankment. The LGOC then formed an Express Department and started services to Windsor via Slough on 20 April 1930, and via Staines on 10 July in the same year. East Surrey began operations on behalf of the LGOC on 6 June 1930, opening services from Reigate, Redhill and Dorking; Autocar began a service from Tunbridge Wells on the same day. The next step was the setting up of Green Line Coaches Ltd, a wholly-owned subsidiary of the LGOC, on 9 July 1930; from that date development of the coach services was co-ordinated and undertaken by Green Line Coaches itself and by East Surrey and National acting as agents; Amersham & District was

Above:
T122 was one of the first series of coaches built for and allocated to express work in 1930; early deliveries were in LGOC, East Surrey and Autocar liveries but after the formation of Green Line Coaches Ltd on 9 July 1930 they were all painted green. This vehicle had seats for 27 passengers and is seen here on a short working of Y1 from Romford; RE was the code for the former Hillman garage which at one time housed 80 vehicles for the intensive services operated to Aldgate. T122 lasted on Green Line work until it was replaced by the 10T10 type in 1938.
D. W. K. Jones

also involved. The green livery adopted by the new company quickly ousted the red and black colours of the LGOC coaches. Vehicles were put on the road as fast as they were delivered by the AEC — these were T types of two varieties, the earlier batches 27-seaters with a door at the back, the second version seating 30 with a front entrance. A coach station was built at Poland Street, just off Oxford Circus, and this opened for business on Christmas Day 1930. The flurry of activity continued into 1931 with the intention of mounting as many services as possible by 9 February, the date specified in the 1930 Road Traffic Act as a deadline for pleading 'established facility' in seeking licences under the new legislation.

The development of the network proceeded in the next two years by the taking over of independent

operators' services by the LGOC, a process completed by the LPTB after 1 July 1933. After this date independent coach services could only survive in the LPTB area if they started from outside the boundary. The press of vehicles on the Embankment and at Oxford Circus was identified as a major source of congestion, and a Committee of Inquiry into the operation of London motor coach services was set up in 1932 under Lord Amulree. The report of this committee, dated 18 June 1932, would have stifled much of the recent development, but a second report, dated 2 August 1932, was more generous to the operators. From 4 October 1933 most of the Green Line coach routes were worked on a cross-London basis, though largely kept well out of the West End; the services were lettered in a clockwise fashion, starting with A and AA from Gravesend. The outer destinations were, of course, inside the LPTB area, though Tunbridge Wells, Aylesbury and Baldock, among others, were made accessible by special agreements. The coaches ran over roads already served by buses, but a minimum fare on the coach secured the local traffic for the bus. However, where traffic was thin the LPTB embarked on a policy of withdrawing the bus service and transferring the bus fare scale to the coach. By 1939 these stretches of road included Swanley to Wrotham on B, St Albans to Dunstable on H2 and Grays to East Ham on Z1 and Z2. The close association between buses and coaches had been formalised by the LPTB

in setting up the Country Bus & Coach Department, managed by Arthur Hawkins. While vehicles and crews were specially designated for Green Line work, buses — also now in green — were used as reliefs and bus platform staff worked them. Buses and coaches were housed together in the garages, though some premises were concerned solely with either one or the other.

The whole enterprise was brought to a halt on 31 August 1939 when the threat of war activated the plan to convert the coaches into ambulances; over 400 vehicles were so dealt with in 24hr. However, limited Green Line operations were resumed on some routes during the 'phoney war' period in 1939 and 1940; a full-scale restoration was undertaken in two stages on 4 and 18 December 1940 by Government direction — Green Line was seen as a suitably flexible means of getting people into and out of London at a time when bombing had reduced markedly the capacity of the railways. For the first time Green Line routes were numbered, all terminated in Central London, and many were worked by double-deck vehicles, mostly borrowed from the Central fleet. By 1942 the shortages of fuel and rubber resulted in a Government order to withdraw all coach services, and Green Line ceased working on 29 September 1942. Once again buses replaced the coaches on those stretches of road where the coach had provided the only facility.

After the war Green Line came back in a series of

restorations which started on 6 February 1946; by the end of June the system was established and offered a series of cross-London routes plus some, including those from Bishops Stortford, Brentwood and Tilbury, that terminated at Aldgate. An important change was the use of numbers in the 700 range; the familiar yellow blinds date from 29 May 1946, though the design has changed several times. The basic pattern of routes thus established was maintained more or less intact for the next 30 years; additional services were mounted for the new towns, and in 1953 an innovatory peripheral route, 725, was started between Windsor and Gravesend via Croydon. Two more such routes, 724 (Romford to High Wycombe) and 727 (Luton to Crawley) appeared in 1966 and 1967; they were important in making new links, the 727 with London Airport (later served by 724 as well) and, operationally, in being one-man-operated. Through the years the splendid 10T10 coaches gave way to the equally commendable RF coaches which identified the service for much of this period, though on some routes double-deck working was implemented with RT, later RMC and RCL, vehicles. The service ran into disrepute in the late 1960s when timekeeping and reliability became extremely suspect; excessive traffic on the roads caused delays and shortages of staff caused cancellations; worn-out vehicles also became a problem.

London Country Bus Services Ltd inherited a very run-down system which shrank year by year. It is to the great credit of the company that in 1976 a determined effort was started to restore the Green Line image, notably by revising services in accordance with perceived passenger demand, by marketing these new facilities vigorously and by providing new vehicles in distinctive livery, of which the RB and RS coaches were the first. Green Line now reaches far beyond the former confines of the LPTB area and coaches currently offer daily, regular-interval services to Brighton, Oxford, Northampton and Cambridge in association with other companies. The old cross-London workings have been abandoned and all services to and from London terminate at Victoria or Oxford Circus. There is also a whole series of special journeys for shopping or pleasure purposes; commuter journeys are offered on many routes. There is no doubt that Green Line is now the most prestigious activity undertaken by LCBS and includes participation in the National long-distance network. The close relationship with the buses, of course, continues; thus duplicate journeys are operated by buses (often ANs) and on certain routes the coach works as a bus, thus satisfying — if not completely — both local and longer-distance passengers. On Sundays the coaches are the only public service vehicles running on many roads. In 1962 327 vehicles were allocated to Green Line work, including 82 RTs; currently some 210 coaches are deployed on a much more extensive pattern of routes.

Independent Operators

The operations of the major companies in London country have always been supplemented by services provided by independents; before the setting up of the LPTB these independents were, of course, numerous, but it is perhaps surprising to find that over the years many of them not only survived but flourished. Few independent companies were interested in the trunk routes, though in the north several worked alongside National in shared time-tables. Very many small companies became rural explorers, initiating routes from towns into the villages that larger companies were not interested in; these flourished in Hertfordshire where National was under-equipped with small buses that could safely run along narrow roads. A third function of the independent operators was essentially urban — to provide a frequent service along known traffic flows from suburbs to town centres; it was in this kind of activity that the most intense competition appeared.

Frederick Lewis of Watford was an example of the main road operator. Having started a Watford to Rickmansworth service in 1923, by the end of the decade Lewis was working every 30min between Rickmansworth and St Albans, hourly to Chorley-wood and The Swillett (the forerunner of 361) and about every 2hr to The Chalfonts, Gerrards Cross and Windsor (this route became 335). Lewis amalgamated with the North West Land & Transport Co Ltd to form the Lewis Omnibus Co Ltd which was registered on 22 November 1929. The North West Land & Transport Co had been responsible for the former Metropolitan Railway bus service from the somewhat remote Metropolitan Watford station into the town, a service initiated by the Metropolitan on 1 November 1927 but rendered illegal by the failure of the railway in 1928 to secure authority to operate bus services. The new company took over the former railway service and in 1930 added a route to Berkhamsted via Amersham that almost exactly paralleled the National N6.

When taken over by the LPTB on 1 October 1933, the Lewis Omnibus Co Ltd handed over 25 vehicles, including six AEC Regents that had been running on the St Albans road since 1930 and five Albion single-deckers that had been purchased by the Metropolitan Railway and which, until recently, had been running in the splendid teak livery characteristic of the railway stock in use until the 1950s. (Lewis's own livery was maroon and cream.) Two other operators active in the Watford area provided double-deck buses on the 301 to Aylesbury; these

were Aston's Bus Service which sported two Leyland Titans in its fleet and the Chiltern Bus Service that fielded three more. There were several operators in St Albans which competed with and later ran an agreed timetable alongside National. A. R. Blowers (Express Motor Services) ran to Luton, F. J. W. Cobb (Albanian) to Dunstable, and W. J. Flower and C. H. Etches (City Omnibus Services) to Welwyn Garden City, which was also served by Charles Russett and Son (St Albans & District). All these firms were taken over by the LPTB.

West Kent Motor Services Ltd is an excellent example of a modest-sized rural operator. Registered on 24 October 1927, the company started a circular route from Sevenoaks to Otford, Kemsing, Seal and back to Sevenoaks on 30 November of the same year. Following pressure from East Surrey, the direct Sevenoaks to Otford section was withdrawn, but there was considerable expansion in other directions including the mounting of services via Riverhead and Chipstead to Ide Hill and Edenbridge or Brasted. There were services from Sevenoaks to Bayleys Hill and to Fawke Common, and a peak hour operation from Tubs Hill station to Seal. Having survived the early wave of takeovers, the company was acquired by the LPTB on 3 October 1939 and the routes were rearranged; 413 worked from Chipstead to Sevenoaks, Bayleys Hill, Ide Hill and Brasted, 413A deviated to Ide Hill (Scollops Road) — the section to Edenbridge was abandoned, being outside the LT area; 421 became Sevenoaks to Otford, Kemsing and Heverham. Maidstone & District took over the Fawke Common and Tubs Hill services which passed out of the LT area. These routes remained in being, unchanged for many years, though it is interesting that the current 457/467 circulars are nearly identical to the very first route mounted by West Kent in 1927.

An almost exact contemporary of West Kent was the People's Motor Services Ltd of Park Road, Ware, a company registered on 11 June 1928. The founder was Mr W. L. Thurgood, a coachbuilder who was able to build up a system of routes very quickly by identifying gaps in National's provision. Having started with a service from Hertford to Braughing operated by Mr F. Mardell, People's Motor Services buses competed with National on the road to Bishops Stortford via the Hadhams and on the Wormley route except for a deviation through St Margarets. A new service via Sawbridgeworth ran to Bishops Stortford and two routes were run to

Above:
This Thornycroft was delivered to People's Motor Services Ltd in 1931 and given its smart 20-seat body by its owner, Mr W. Thurgood. Acquired by the LPTB on 30 November 1933, the bus became NY9 and was operated by London Transport until 1937 when it was sold; it saw service in Abertillery until 1950. The route to Dane End and Walkern became 384 and is still in the timetable book.
J. F. Higham

Right:
Imperial buses have been a familiar sight in Windsor for nearly 60 years. The proprietors were A. F. and A. J. Moore who suffered the loss of one of their routes to the LPTB on 20 December 1933 — this was the run to Langley. However, the firm continued in business and in the most recent timetable offers a circular service from the Theatre Royal in Windsor to Three Elms, Ruddles Way and Clewer, and back to the town centre; a 20min service is maintained during the day which required three buses. In this 1968 view a Bristol LL5G formerly owned by Thames Valley is going about its business. *M. A. Penn*

Right:
A Willowbrook-bodied Ford of Rover Bus Service heads out of Hemel Hempstead on a peak hour working. Both vehicles and the town have changed dramatically since Mr J. R. Dell's firm began operations in the early 1930s. The main route has always been between Hemel and Chesham, and until 1964 London Transport also worked between the same points alongside Dell; this was Route 316.
Kevin Lane

Baldock. The company was undoubtedly enterprising, had a great deal of local support that recalled the early days of Harvey & Burrows, and owned splendid vehicles with pneumatic tyres that gave a more comfortable ride than the more cumbersome LGOC buses with which National was provided. The LPTB was much more interested in People's Motor

Services than it had been in West Kent and the firm was acquired on 30 November 1933. However, the People's image was kept alive well into 1934 as the buses continued in their former livery and under Mr Thurgood's management until the LPTB effectively took charge. The routes were then numbered; the Buntingford and Royston service was included in 331, the Bishops Stortford via The Hadhams service in 340. Others routes, some of which are still recognisable today were:

- 380: Hertford-Ware-St Margarets-Wormley
- 384: Hertford-Sacombe-Stevenage-Letchworth-Baldock
- 386: Bishops Stortford-Buntingford-Hitchin
- 388: Hertford-Tewin-Welwyn-Hitchin-Baldock
- 389: Hertford-Sawbridgeworth-Bishops Stortford
- 390: Hertford-Roydon-Epping

Nineteen buses, all relatively new, were handed over to the LPTB but they were all out of stock by 1937. Thornycroft was not an LPTB preferred type.

The rural delights of villages by the Lea and the Rib rivers and the Stort Navigation are, of course, far removed from the almost frenzied activities of many urban independents. The plethora of buses on the road from Windsor to Slough has already been noted. Frequent services were offered between Staines Bridge and Englefield Green, notably by B. Dobson's Bluebell Services and A. Howes (Howes' Brown Bus). In Watford the Elite Omnibus Service (A. C. Barton) ran three vehicles between Cassio

Bridge and Bushey Mill Lane — this service became 385; the Watford Omnibus Co Ltd offered services from Harebreaks to Hamper Hill and Oxhey Hall Farm which the LPTB identified as Routes 345 and 346. The Watford Omnibus Co was the direct descendant of the Watford Co-operative Mutual Omnibus & Transport Co Ltd which had been founded in July 1926 by staff whose employment with National ceased because they had participated in the General Strike. However, the venture became insolvent and the company was in the hands of B. and F. W. Holt in 1931. There were intensive town services in St Albans and even more frenetic activity at Grays where Harris, Mrs E. J. Cox (Purfleet Service) and Reliable (J. T. G. Smith and E. Godden)

all worked buses to Purfleet, among others. It is interesting that there were no exactly parallel urban local services operated by independents in the former East Surrey territory. This is probably because the towns south of the Thames did not promote that kind of frequent service and in any case East Surrey kept careful control of its area. It is of note that the first East Surrey service was in fact just such a local route between Reigate and Redhill.

Some independents on the periphery of London country have had long histories. Among these is the Tillingbourne Bus Co which has been in business since the 1920s and is currently working a network of routes on the Guildford-Cranleigh-Horsham axis. The company worked Route 448 from Guildford to Ewhurst jointly with LT before taking over entirely in 1964. The acquisition of the bus services of Tony McCann Coaches Ltd has strengthened Tillingbourne influence in the area. In Windsor, Imperial Bus Services serves the Clewer and Dedworth areas, having survived the amputation of a service a Langley by the LPTB on 20 December 1933. Another long-standing operator is White Bus Services which works from Windsor to Sunninghill across the Great Park. B&B Services (S. J. and A. M. Tate) has run services from Potten End to Berkhamsted, Apsley Mills and Hemel Hempstead for over 50 years, while the Rover Bus Service (J. R. Dell) has had a similarly long spell on the Hemel Hempstead to Chesham road, shared at one time with London Transport. At the very edges of London country are several companies of some antiquity; the Red Rover Omnibus Ltd is a large independent whose buses work urban routes in Aylesbury and other services while the prestigious Cambridge independent, Premier Travel Services Ltd, makes contact at Bishops Stortford and Royston. Biss Brothers, a firm active at one time in central London, runs some rural routes from Bishops Stortford, including one to Furneux Pelham. Smith's of Buntingford Ltd offers journeys from Buntingford to Hitchin on Tuesdays and Saturdays; B. C. Cannon Ltd of Puckeridge has a Thursdays only return facility from Braughing to Bishops Stortford. The Stag Bus Service owned by E. C. W. Halls works five journeys on Thursdays from Sheering via Hatfield Heath (where the Stag public house gives its name to the service) to Bishops Stortford. There is thus very considerable variety of provision in terms of kind of service, types of bus and modes of operation in or near the London country area, a variety that has survived the standardised techniques of the LGOC, its agents and its successors. Several operators have initiated services in recent years in what may be considered unfavourable times for the bus, but they have survived on roads that would not sustain the larger companies. There are now friendly links between LCBS and the small operators whose services form part of the larger pattern.

2

Buses on the Roads

The motorbus has been a familiar part of the town and country scene for nearly 80 years, as long as a long lifetime. In London country people who travelled on the 303 to Hitchin or the 409 to East Grinstead in their youth are now accompanying their grandchildren on buses carrying the same route numbers. The continuity of service on the main bus roads in London country has been questioned only in the past decade when revisions (and withdrawals) have altered facilities that seemingly have always been available. RT and RF buses were on the routes for the better part of a working life and spanned two generations of passengers.

Certain services currently in operation have had the same numerical identification since 1924, others since the LPTB scheme of October 1934; in many instances the origins are even earlier and the histories

of some go back to the early years of the century. The 'route biographies' included in this part of the book survey many decades of activity and change in bus operation; new companies have taken over, new vehicles have superseded old, the lines of routes have been revised to cater for new passenger demands and styles of working have been modified. Finally, of course, diminished passenger loadings have sometimes ended the service altogether. Each route is really a microcosm of the whole system while retaining its own essential characteristics. Each timetable in the current book has an individual history and is the end product of cumulative change. Those who study the pages devoted to the 370 or the 406 are looking at historical documents; those who study further can visualise the early forms if they ponder long enough.

ROUTE 480

Along the Thames

The only part of London country to support tramway systems has been the highly urbanised, highly industrialised Thames-side area dominated by Dartford and Gravesend. The Gravesend & Northfleet Electric Tramways Co Ltd reached Galley Hill, Swanscombe, and the Dartford Council Light Railways extended eastward to Horns Cross, a somewhat bleak settlement even for this rather unfriendly region. Proposals were made on several occasions to

construct lines between Galley Hill and Horns Cross to make through running possible between Dartford and Gravesend but objections by the South Eastern & Chatham Railway brought them to nothing; there were other problems, too, in linking a council line to a BET one. However the motorbus provided the answer and in 1913 North Kent Motor Services a subsidiary of the Gravesend & Northfleet Tramways, began working a useful bus service from

Gravesend to Dartford; the service managed to keep going during the war, though with some interruptions.

The Maidstone & District Motor Services Ltd took over North Kent Motors and assumed responsibility for the Gravesend to Dartford operation on 15 March 1920, working it initially as Route 21; with extension eastward to Chatham and Faversham it became 26. Maidstone & District opened its Overcliffe offices and depot in 1922 and strengthened its hold on Dartford with the building of a garage in Priory Road in 1927; with the withdrawal of trams in Gravesend on 28 February 1929 the company worked the replacement services from the former Old Dover Road tram depot. There was general satisfaction with the Maidstone & District services between Dartford and Gravesend which were on a regular 5min headway, with additional facilities offered as far as Horns Cross by the increasingly antiquated trams, now provided by Bexley Council, and the frequent local bus services from Swanscombe. However, the London Passenger Transport Act brought large-scale changes to this part of North Kent, and the transfer of 43 Leyland buses, the Priory Road garage in Dartford and the Old Dover Road base to the LPTB was the biggest single upheaval in the entire LPTB Country area.

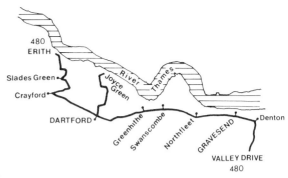

Above:
Route 480, 26 September 1982.

Below:
STL 963, though dressed for Route 487, was one of 17 of its type allocated to Northfleet in February 1935, and spent much of its life on Route 480. Initially the livery, as here, was dark green with light green window surrounds and a silver roof. The great defect of this LPTB-designed body was the intense draught which blew into the saloon and up the stairs whenever the vehicle was driven at any speed. This bus last worked from Dartford before being withdrawn in April 1951; it was then used for training at Hounslow before being scrapped two months later.
Ian Allan Library

Above:
RT3127 became in the fullness of time the last operational RT turned out by Northfleet garage, still looking in good shape some 25 years after delivery in April 1950.
Route 487 is a descendant of the former Gravesend & Northfleet Electric Tramways route which was motorised in 1929 and operated by Maidstone & District with buses in special livery. The number 487 was allocated early in LPTB days. *Edward Shirras*

The service between Westgate Road, Dartford and the Milton Ale Shades at Denton — the Board's eastern boundary — was maintained on a 5min headway, initially by former Maidstone & District buses with 'General' on the sides, as Route 486; the Maidstone Route 26 now started at Overcliffe and retained its identity for over 40 years.

With the reorganisation of services in the North Kent area, from 16 May 1934 Route 486 was withdrawn and a total of 12 buses per hour were scheduled to leave Denton on Routes 401 to Sevenoaks, 407 to Sidcup Station, 477 to Orpington and Chelsfield and 491 to Bexleyheath via Old Bexley. This complex arrangement of services certainly provided a variety of destinations for passengers on the Gravesend to Dartford road, but at a cost of regularity and, from the operating point

of view, of control. Further changes followed the timely withdrawal of the trams in Dartford and their replacement by trolleybus 696 on 20 November 1935; a basic 10min service was provided between Dartford and Denton under the now well-known number 480, a number that had hitherto been used on an obscure works service between Perry Street and Rosherville. The service was supplemented between Dartford and Horns Cross by buses on Routes 407 from Sidcup, 477 from Orpington and a new 492 from Lower Belvedere; all these buses ran through to Gravesend Clock Tower on Saturday and Sunday afternoons, often being red Central area vehicles on temporary transfer.

It will be noted that the former 5min daily through service had been somewhat reduced and that the loss of the trams from Horns Cross had not really been compensated. An additional serious loss was of cross-town facilities in Dartford; eventually the Board accepted the criticisms and on 6 April 1938 Route 480 was extended westwards to Erith (Wheatley Arms) over the former Route 499 road which itself dated back to an LGOC service started in 1916, reaching Dartford on 12 June 1922 and transferring to East Surrey on 1 March 1931. Route 480 thus linked communities all the way along the Thames from Denton to Erith along a switchback road as far as Dartford, then across more level riverside country. Large paper mills, cement works and electrical factories provided a very high level of traffic; the concentration of hospitals in Dartford, together with the leisure and shopping facilities of the

Above:
RML2343 waits opposite the garage in Priory Road, Dartford, to take a 480 departure. Buses of this class had worked the route since 21 November 1965 and this vehicle spent its entire life at Northfleet garage. It was sold back to London Transport in 1979, by which time its appearance was pitiable, but in desperation for some reliable buses London Transport put new life into it. The poster advertising lively London looks like a hangover from the swinging '60s. *Edward Shirras*

area, brought large numbers of passengers to the buses. By this time front-door STLs were working the route and these were supplemented during the war by the rear-door variety transferred from the Central area.

In a revision of services in Dartford starting on 6 February 1946, Routes 407 and 492 were withdrawn, leaving the Dartford to Gravesend road to the 480, with some journeys provided on 477 from Orpington, though these disappeared just over a year later on 4 June 1947. Thus the 480 came into its own as a major trunk route operated almost exclusively by Northfleet garage. RTs arrived in August 1949, a move accompanied by a slight tightening of the running time; 19 vehicles were allocated to the service in 1962 lists. These buses were replaced from 21 November 1965 by the same number of RMLs and Route 480 remained a Routemaster preserve for the next 14 years until the buses almost literally fell to pieces. The 480 timetable continued largely unchanged into the LCBS era, though from 30 August 1975 some journeys were renumbered 482 and sent to Singlewell. However, with the acquisition of Maidstone & District interests in Gravesend Route 482 was withdrawn and from 30 October 1976 the 480 was operated from Valley Drive, MacKenzie Way, well to the east of the former terminus at Denton. New Atlantean buses were allocated to the route, just in time, on and from 19 November 1979, by which date the RMLs and the motley collection of vehicles that supplemented them were in a deplorable visual state, being

battered, patched and generally unkempt. The Atlanteans were worked OMO from 26 April 1980.

The most recent changes on the Thames-side road have been to reduce through journeys; two buses hourly run from Valley Drive to Erith and two to Joyce Green — a timetable change that dates from 5 December 1981. The route is supplemented by local services from Gravesend to Swanscombe and from that point to Dartford. The timetable thus has rather a complicated appearance, though in concept it is not unlike the services provided in the 1920s, though not so frequent of course. Only on Sundays does Route 480 have undisputed mastery of the Gravesend to Dartford road and there is now a half-hourly service (hourly through to Erith) along this quarry-scarred route with its frequent views of a now rather empty river.

Through the Darent Valley

Route 401 between Dartford and Sevenoaks along the Darent Valley is such an archetypal London country route that is is perhaps astonishing that it no longer runs south of Eynsford and only infrequently to that point. East Surrey took over the service from Mr W. P. Allen, trading as Farningham & District, who began working between Dartford (Post Office, later The Bull) and Farningham on 19 July 1913 and extended to Sevenoaks on 5 January 1917. (He was not the first operator of motor buses on the Farningham road, though probably the most persistent.) East Surrey, having reached Sevenoaks, eyed this obvious extension to its activities and the LGOC supplied the company with four B type buses in July 1920 for a Dartford to Sevenoaks service; labelled S1, 12 journeys were offered in the timetable published to start on 30 July 1921. However, Mr Allen kept his service in operation on the grounds that his agreement with the LGOC was to be implemented one year after the end of the war, and there was legal difficulty in stating when this was. Eventually, on 1 September 1922, Route S1 came into being, worked by B types initially, replaced by Ks in 1923; there were buses every 30min between Dartford and Farningham and four journeys worked through to Sevenoaks.

Some journeys were diverted to Horton Kirby for a short while from 10 November 1923 but these were abandoned when S1 was put through to Bexley (War Memorial) across Dartford Heath on 5 May 1924; the service was worked in two overlapping sections: Bexley to Farningham and Dartford to Sevenoaks, each every hour. Four buses were kept in the yard of the Lullingstone Hotel at Swanley and a fifth was sent out from Dunton Green. A further extension brought the route to Bexleyheath Clock Tower on 6 October 1924 and the Bassom scheme identified the route by its time-honoured number, 401. East Surrey did not have matters all its own way and the viability of its service was threatened by C. M. Hever's Darenth Bus which began a Dartford to Eynsford via Horton Kirby run on 15 March 1928; in response East Surrey started a similar service between the same termini three days later as Route 401B. Rivalry on the road ended when C. M. Hever handed over to East Surrey on 27 July 1930, to the regret of villagers who had favoured the 'small man'. At the southern end Sevenoaks Motor Services began working between Sevenoaks and Shoreham Village via Otford and Twitton on 24 November 1929. East Surrey worked a competing service,

initially by way of Shoreham station, later by exactly the same route; under this pressure the Sevenoaks company surrendered in April 1930, the two directors — P. Berry and B. Durrant — becoming drivers at Dunton Green and their two Bean buses passing to the East Surrey fleet.

In LGCS days the main service (Route 401) was worked by NS buses, smaller vehicles being allocated to Routes 401B (the Horton Kirby route) and 401E (Sevenoaks to Shoreham Village). By 1 July 1933 the 401B lost its identity to a new 499: Eynsford-Horton Kirby-Dartford-Erith, running over former LGOC

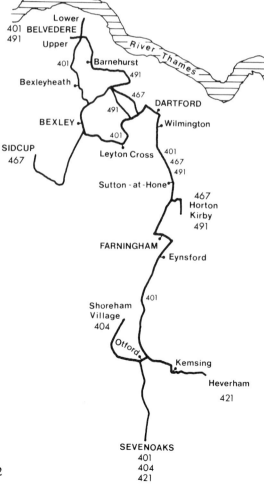

Darent Valley routes, 1 May 1946.

roads to make an extremely unlikely match between rural communities and highly industrialised Thames-side. From being sleepy backwaters, Farningham, Eynsford and Shoreham found themselves in the 1920s and 1930s transformed into well-known resorts; on Sundays and bank holidays crowds of people from London and the industrial towns of North Kent poured into the Darent Valley, much to the evident annoyance of the farmers and many of the villagers. The bridge and ford at Eynsford were photographed time and time again, being used in posters and in the weekend walks columns then featured in the London evening newspapers. There was also good work, business and shopping traffic; in the evenings the cinemas in Dartford attracted custom. These passenger movements sustained a frequent service, up to six buses per hour between Farningham and Dartford, with additional journeys to and from Horton Kirby.

A reorganisation of the Dartford services on 16 May 1934 altered the 401 to work between Sevenoaks and Gravesend (Denton), though the former Sevenoaks to Bexleyheath route was resumed on 20 November 1935 after public pressure, mainly from parents of pupils attending schools in Shepherds Lane, Dartford. By the late 1930s front-entrance STLs were operating 401, Qs were at work on 499 (now truncated to Dartford to Farningham via Horton Kirby), with Cubs on the Shoreham Village service, now Route 404. The acquisition of West Kent Motor Services on 4 October 1939 created a new route from Sevenoaks via Otford to Kemsing and Heverham; this was numbered 421 and was originally a Dennis 30cwt and then a Leyland Cub working.

The exigencies and increased traffic in wartime brought double-deck vehicles to the Dartford-Horton Kirby road but they could not work through to Farningham. After the war there were considerable

Above:
SM493 is seen at Sevenoaks bus station soon after the conversion of 401 to this style of working in July 1971. The vehicle has undoubted London Transport characteristics and is not unpleasing in appearance; however, it did not endear itself to drivers or passengers. Route 401 has not reached Sevenoaks since 1 January 1978, the year in which this bus was withdrawn.
Edward Shirras

revisions; Horton Kirby journeys were projected to Sidcup station (467) and Lower Belvedere (491) on 6 February 1946, and shortly after — on 1 May — Route 401 assumed an urban role by extension from Bexleyheath to Belvedere. RTs arrived for these services in September 1950 (for 467/491) and in February 1951 (for the 401); they were allocated to 421 following the great building boom in the Otford and Kemsing areas, and RFs appeared on 404. An interesting development was the mounting of a rural service between Dartford and Farningham via Darenth Village (which had never before seen a regular bus) and Horton Kirby, restoring buses to the 'back road' that had lost its provision early in the war. Numbered 479, it began on 15 June 1949; initially Cub-worked, a GS was allocated to it later. It had quite high use, especially in the evenings, as the bus passed a large number of inviting public houses and the last bus to Dartford was often full. However, revenue fell and the route was abandoned on 29 October 1958. This withdrawal was an early indication of the shrinking of traffic on the Darent Valley routes and the Saturday and Sunday services were progressively thinned through the 1960s. The 401 developed a spur into Joydens Wood Estate (401A), but otherwise reductions were the keynote of the time. After the advent of London Country, Route 401 become OMO in 1971 using SM vehicles; later Leyland National buses were allocated. Some Eynsford to Dartford journeys were projected to Longfield as Route 400 on 30 August 1975, and all workings from Horton Kirby were sent to Sidcup, by two routes numbered 491 and 492. The abandonment of the Eynsford to Sevenoaks section on 1 January 1978 altered the whole character of 401 as it had existed for so long; a substitute Sunday service, Route 456, was put on to cater for those from Sevenoaks visiting Dartford hospitals, but it was little used and disappeared when grant aid ran out. The only signs of expansion of London Country interest in the area came in 1980 when acquisition of the Maidstone & District Kemsing service on 19 July created a new route pattern from Sevenoaks via Otford as the 457/467.

The current position shows Route 401 reduced to a few journeys; until 1983 these ran from Belvedere to Dartford Shepherds Lane with a handful of journeys sent on to Farningham and Eynsford or Swanley. (In 1866, according to the timetable, W. Holland's omnibuses, the *Vivid* and the *Wonder*, offered four journeys from Dartford to Farningham with two going on to Eynsford — and there were two journeys on Sundays; London Country provision is not significantly greater, and there is no Sunday operation!) From 23 July 1983 the 401 was extended from Belvedere into Thamesmead, thus giving it a highly urban role. The 404 now works, basically hourly on weekdays, from Shoreham Village to Sevenoaks, with some journeys extended to Ide Hill over the former 413. Joydens Wood now enjoys a service of its own, numbered 421, between Thamesmead and Swanley garage. The main operation on the Farningham road is therefore the 492 which, with two buses hourly (on weekdays) is a substantial service with one bus starting at Horton Kirby and the second from South Darenth, both running to Sidcup station. Thus the formerly subsidiary route has assumed the major importance, and only the observant are likely to see Route 401 on destination blinds.

Over the North Downs

Route 402, at one time a half-hourly trunk route between Bromley North station and Sevenoaks with many journeys working through to Tonbridge, has the doubtful distinction of being a major early route that has entirely disappeared from the timetable book. Its origins are an Autocar venture, a service from Tunbridge Wells to Sevenoaks started on 11 August 1919 which was extended to Farnborough (George & Dragon) on 8 November in the same year. At Farnborough it was possible to change to the LGOC Route 47 for travel into London. The section of route north of Sevenoaks was particularly vulnerable to East Surrey attack and was purchased by the LGOC for East Surrey operation before the signing of the agreement between the two companies — it was therefore the very first of the services operated on behalf of General. At first buses from Farnborough made immediate connection at Sevenoaks Market Place with Autocar buses bound for Tonbridge and Tunbridge Wells; in fact the East Surrey vehicles carried 'Tunbridge Wells' on their destination boards as if to prove that the original service was still in being. The route was extended to Bromley North on 6 August 1921, in accordance with the LGOC/East Surrey scheme, and numbered S2 — this became the time-honoured and now lamented 402 on 1 December 1924.

This was almost a classic East Surrey route, working from a lush London suburb, over the North Downs with breath-taking views from Polhill, into a relaxed and distinctive town that became for many years a select resort and centre for walking expeditions to Ide Hill and the Weald. Traffic was good throughout the week and especially heavy on Sundays and Bank Holidays as urban dwellers came out into the Kent countryside; it was also heavy on Saturdays when shopping trips were made into Bromley. Another section of the Autocar service was acquired on 1 July 1933, that between Sevenoaks and Tonbridge station which became LPTB Route 402A starting from Tubs Hill station. Curiously, though connections were maintained at Sevenoaks, through running from Bromley was not scheduled. Route 402A took up the Autocar timings as far as Tonbridge alongside the Redcar service from Sevenoaks to Tunbridge Wells and Uckfield, and the second Autocar route (also acquired on 1 July 1933), that between Sevenoaks and Tonbridge via Sevenoaks Weald, numbered 454 — of this, more later. The first through bus working on the Ton-

bridge road followed the acquisition on 31 July 1935 of the Redcar service, latterly worked by Maidstone & District; again, perhaps surprisingly, this was by the 403 from Westerham and West Croydon rather than by the 402, and Route 403 absorbed both the Redcar and 402A times. Route 402 thus maintained its Bromley North to Sevenoaks identity; numerous short workings between Dunton Green and Sevenoaks Car Park, later called the Bus Station, carried this number — many of these were positioning journeys for buses on other routes. When Green Line coaches were withdrawn (for the second time) during the war, from 30 September 1942 the Sevenoaks to Tonbridge service was strengthened by extending Route 402 — four buses an hour were then scheduled, one on Route 402, two on 403 and one on 454.

The pattern of services over Riverhill persisted and good passenger loadings were a feature of the wartime and postwar years. STLs gave way to RTs

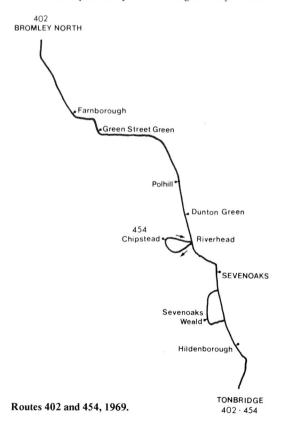

Routes 402 and 454, 1969.

Above:
Dunton Green in July 1922. The four B type buses were all LGOC vehicles, delivered to East Surrey in 1921; they are in the deep blue livery of East Surrey and carry that company's fleetname and address. Two of the buses, and probably the other two as well, are working S2 which by that time had assumed its archetypal form: Bromley North to Sevenoaks. B1214 and B324 were returned to the LGOC later in 1922 being replaced by other B types; when B2126 and B725 were sent back by East Surrey in the following year they were replaced by Ks. When this photograph was taken the garage had been operational only three months; the urgent discussions going on at the doors and the ladder suggest some builders' maintenance problems. *London Transport*

on this trunk route, six vehicles being allocated to the 402 during the 1950s and 1960s. Traffic congestion in Tonbridge High Street was often an operational problem, and timetables carried the information that at times of congestion buses would turn at the Star & Garter at the northern end of the High Street — the inference being that passengers would have to walk the rest of the way. By the mid-1960s the main service was from Bromley North to Sevenoaks, through buses to Tonbridge being operated on Monday to Friday afternoons and on Saturdays; the Sunday service to Tonbridge on this route had by this time disappeared. Since then there has been a progressive reduction of the service. The Tonbridge

workings had disappeared altogether by 1972, by which year the route was worked OMO by RF vehicles, later replaced by Leyland Nationals in 1975. In the timetable introduced on 29 April 1978 there were only six through journeys from Bromley to Sevenoaks on Mondays to Fridays, though an hourly frequency was maintained as far as Pratts Bottom. This was almost the end, and the route was withdrawn altogether on 21 April 1981. There is some consolation that this road was taken over by the formerly prestigious Green Line 706 (earlier 704), and that the number 402 was not immediately used, as planned, for the Bexleyheath to Swanley via Joydens Wood service.

The 454 has at least survived, though in highly tenuous form. With the acquisition of West Kent Motor Services the route was diverted at Riverhead to Chipstead from 3 October 1939 and remained in this form for nearly 40 years. By the late 1970s there were few through journeys to Tonbridge and the routeing was changed in the Riverhead area. However, the timetable changes which withdrew 402 altogether retained Route 454, though only as a vestigial remnant: it is now an AN operation between Sevenoaks and Tonbridge with an extension to and from Knockholt and there are two journeys on Mondays to Fridays. Otherwise, the diversion of Green Line 706 via the Weald apparently suffices for the traffic on offer. It is thus pleasing to think that 454 has a place still in the timetable book, but the skeletal form of the operation does not give much confidence in its long-term health.

Above:
The shortages of standard vehicles in the mid-1970s brought some interesting hired buses into London Country service. This Royal Blue Bristol MW/Eastern Coach Works coach was one of six working from Dunton Green in October 1975; because the doors were manual a conductor had to be carried, which made the operation somewhat expensive. They were worked on Mondays to Fridays only on most of the routes served by Dunton Green, including 402; they were fitted with number and destination blinds, though there does not seem to have been time to find them for this vehicle. All the hired buses and coaches were returned to their owners in 1977.
London Country

Below:
In the last days of the 402, Green Line RB61 works an early journey from Bromley. Turning out coaches for early journeys on bus services has been standard practice since 1962, the vehicles taking up their intended role later in the morning. From 21 April 1981 former Route 402 passengers were accommodated on Green Line 706.
Michael Dryhurst

The Westerham Connection

For many years the timetable for Route 410: Bromley North to Reigate has been prefaced by a note: 'Connections are made at Westerham with buses to and from Sevenoaks'. This is a relic of a direct service from Sevenoaks to Reigate that last ran in 1926; there has never subsequently been a through link along the Valley road, now the A25; it has to be travelled in stages. This Reigate to Sevenoaks service dates back to April 1914. East Surrey started a route from Redhill to Bletchingly, up and over Redstone Hill, on 20 June 1912, one of the first operations beyond the confines of Reigate. It had the distinction of being worked by the first double-decked bus operated by the company, a CC type Daimler with a Dodson body for 34 seats which was on loan in September 1913. On 7 April 1914 the route was extended westwards to Reigate and eastwards as far as Godstone Green, reaching Riverhead four days later, and the Tubs Hill station on 17 April. Finally the Market Place in Sevenoaks

was attained on 17 June. East Surrey became the main operator between Westerham and Sevenoaks as George Humphreys & Co withdrew a motorbus service it had run between those two points since 1908, latterly with a Hallford bus. East Surrey provided a two-hourly service over the whole route, with additional journeys from Reigate to Godstone Green. This route was considered important enough to be worked throughout World War 1, although an experimental economy in out-stationing a bus at Brasted in October 1914 had to be ended when the crews could not start the engine.

The agreement between East Surrey and the LGOC facilitated the opening of S3 from West Croydon to Westerham and Sevenoaks on 16 August 1921; running every 2hr this interworked with the Reigate service over the Westerham to Sevenoaks section, operated under the number S24 from 14 April 1922. The next development came with the opening of S10 from Bromley North station

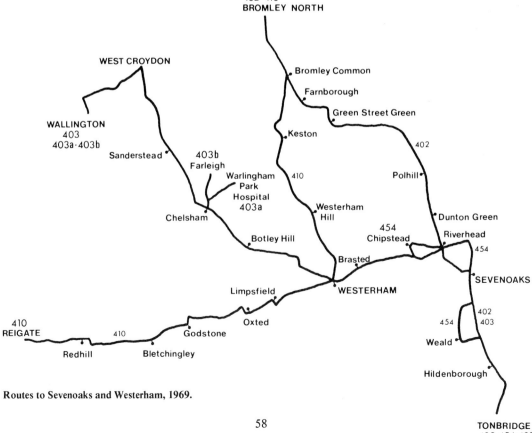

Routes to Sevenoaks and Westerham, 1969.

to Westerham and Reigate which began on 3 June 1922; the LGOC were already working to the top of Westerham Hill but the road beyond, a stiff test for the buses, was new ground. An hourly service was provided to Westerham, two-hourly beyond to Reigate and interworking with the first leg of S24. A proposal to start S10 at Lewisham in 1924 came to nothing. With the Bassom scheme Routes S3 and S10 become 403 and 410, numbers that are still in use. S24 retained that designation until it was withdrawn on 15 June 1926; from the following day 403 and 410 were advertised to connect at the Kings Arms, Westerham, and both services were put on an hourly basis.

Once in being, Routes 403 and 410 had uneventful histories for some time, apart from changes of vehicle allocation and the opening of spurs from Chelsham to Farleigh and Chelsham Mental Hospital (now Warlingham Park), running in 1934 under numbers 415 and 420 respectively. The 410 retained its open-top PS buses some time after other routes had discarded them because a low bridge on line of route in Oxted prevented the use of covered normal-height vehicles; eventually 12 lowbridge STLs, always known as the 'Godstone' STLs, were allocated to the route in April 1934 and they worked it continuously until replaced by the RLH type, another lowbridge variety, in 1950. In 1935 the

LPTB purchase of the Redcar operation between Sevenoaks and Tonbridge, latterly a Maidstone & District working, allowed the extension of Route 403 to Tonbridge station on 31 July; this route was extended westward to Wallington on 2 September 1936 to participate in the very frequent Wallington Green-West Croydon-Chelsham service then operating. Early in the war, from 26 May 1940, Route 410 was severed at Biggin Hill and ran in two sections: Reigate to Biggin Hill (Black Horse) and Leaves Green to Bromley North. There was no service covering the gap until 2 April 1941 when Cuboperated 410B was introduced running along by-roads. Through working was restored on 14 January 1942, though while running across Royal Air Force territory no passengers were allowed to enter or leave the vehicle and a sentry was carried to ensure that this regulation was carried out. With the withdrawal of Green Line services on 29 September

Above:
Vehicle shortages in 1974 and 1975 brought unusual allocations to the 403. Second, third and fourth from the left are Maidstone Corporation Atlanteans in blue livery. The bus on the far left is a former Ribble Leyland in use for driver training. RCL2239 (second right) is in National Bus Co green, while its companion RCL2237 (right) is in the lighter shade initially adopted by LCBS.
Michael Dryhurst

1942 there was a proposal to run the 403 to Tunbridge Wells — an interesting suggestion, but nothing came of it.

Business was brisk on both routes in the postwar period, with Westerham and Sevenoaks as major tourist centres. RTs were allocated to the 403, and to its subsidiary services to Farleigh and Warlingham Park, now numbered 403A and 403B; they eventually appeared on the 410 after that route was circuitously directed away from the offending railway bridge in Oxted on 4 November 1964, giving way to RMLs a few months later. In London Country days the number 403 was given to the Wallington to Chelsham service, the parent route, West Croydon to Tonbridge — now diverted along Selsdon Road and equipped with single-deck vehicles — becoming 403A. This change, together with one-man-operation, was instituted on 3 July 1971; with the advent of three-numeral destination blinds 403A became 483, the number in current use. The 410 became OMO too, being the first major route to receive (double-deck) Leyland Atlantean vehicles for the purpose on 19 February 1972.

Services in the Sevenoaks area have tended to suffer considerable reductions in recent years, partly because of diminishing passenger numbers and partly through diminishing local authority support. The January 1982 timetable for Route 483 shows an hourly working, by ANs, between West Croydon and Sevenoaks with some additional journeys between Westerham and Sevenoaks, some of which date back to the closure of the Westerham branch line from Dunton Green and which were, at least originally, subsidised by British Rail. Tonbridge journeys are limited to one Monday to Friday morning timing, plus an afternoon working on schooldays only. The 410 is still a substantial service with through journeys running every 30min at peak times and supplementary timings between Bromley North and Biggin Hill; at the other end of the route the long-established 411 provides additional journeys between Reigate and Godstone. There is no Sunday service on either route. The 410 and 483, successor to 403, still connect at the Kings Arms, Westerham, buses from all four points arriving at 47 or 48min past each hour so that for 2min or so there are four AN double-deckers standing there. There are many attractions to the tourist in Westerham, but there are those visitors who think this moment the best part of their day. It would be interesting to see how many passengers change from one vehicle to another; an inspector of many years experience cannot recall seeing any. However, the possibility is there and with the opening of the M25 which has drawn away the traffic that used to choke the town and the approach roads to it, the connections are more likely to be made.

Two Routes to East Grinstead

While the 409 service from West Croydon to East Grinstead is justly well-known, it is not often realised that for a short period in the 1920s there was an alternative route between these two points, the 404 which ran via Botley Hill, Oxted and Edenbridge. The 404, started as S4 as one of the LGOC-inspired Croydon routes on 16 August 1921, ran via Limpsfield to The Star at Edenbridge on a two-hourly basis, being extended to The Crown at East Grinstead via Dormansland, Lingfield and Felcourt on 1 August 1924. On the main Eastbourne road, S9 was by this time well-established and AEC YC type double-deckers were running from West Croydon through Purley, Old Coulsdon and Caterham to Godstone and on across rather open country to Lingfield, Felbridge and East Grinstead; beyond this town the buses ran to Forest Row, then alternately to Hartfield (The Dorset Arms) and Chelwood Gate in the heart of Ashdown Forest. East Surrey had offered a service from Reigate to Forest Row and Hartfield from 11 April 1916, but workings beyond Godstone were withdrawn at the end of that year not because of wartime problems but because the East Sussex County Council demanded a road tax on the service of 2d ($1\frac{1}{2}$p) a mile. However, the service was resumed on 14 July 1919 — the tax no longer being legal — and the section south of Godstone was subsumed in the new S9 which began operation from Croydon on 3 June 1922. The Chelwood Gate leg was further extended on 19 October 1922 to Uckfield station, a destination well into Southdown territory and some 32 miles from West Croydon; through running to Hartfield ceased on 3 May 1924, all buses now concentrated on the long through route. S4 and S9 assumed their new identities as Routes 404 and 409 on 1 December 1924.

It is evident that Route 409 quickly became a money-spinner, while the 404 was a much more doubtful proposition. In an endeavour to increase revenue the latter route was diverted through Oxted in 1925, but on 16 June 1926 the West Croydon to Botley Hill section was withdrawn altogether — the only one of the Croydon routes to suffer such a fate — and buses worked from Tatsfield to East Grinstead and, only for the summer of 1926, to Hartfield. In another change of identity, the 404 was

sent beyond East Grinstead to Turners Hill, Crawley Down, Crawley and Ifield over the former S28 road which had been worked since 26 July 1924; the route thus became Oxted to Ifield on 31 October 1928. The number 404 was really inappropriate as this was no longer a route operated on behalf of the LGOC, nor did it come anywhere near the Metropolitan Police District; it was changed on 16 April 1930 when, extended at both ends, it became Route 34: Hurst Green-Oxted-Edenbridge-East Grinstead-Crawley-Horsham (The Carfax). An associated 34A started at Westerham and joined the main route at Crockham Hill. The 34 and 34A worked right along

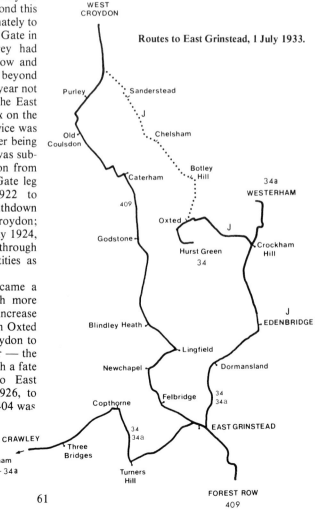

Routes to East Grinstead, 1 July 1933.

the boundary between East Surrey and Southdown which, by the agreement signed on 2 June 1915, was notionally a line drawn from Haslemere through Horsham and Handcross to Crowborough. The Forest Row to Uckfield road was by the same agreement open to both companies.

In London General Country Services days ST buses were running hourly from West Croydon station to Uckfield on a through journey time of 2hr 58min, building up to a half-hourly frequency at weekends that required an allocation of 13 or 14 vehicles. The 34/34A offered an hourly facility from Crockham Hill, with two-hourly departures from Hurst Green and Westerham; this was always a single-deck route. The advent of the LPTB caused an amputation of the Forest Row to Uckfield section of the 409 which gave it the form it retained for the next 46 years; East Grinstead was really the boundary of the Board's operating area but the road to Forest Row was an 'unrestricted outward working'. The 34/34A road was, for much of its length, the designated LPTB boundary line; contact was made at various points with Maidstone & District (at Edenbridge and East Grinstead) and with Southdown (at East Grinstead, Crawley and Horsham — its service from Haywards Heath connected at Turners Hill, a link still existing in the 1983 timetables). On 4 October 1934 the 34 became, logically, 434, and the 34A became 464; later Route 434 was altered to start from Edenbridge and the 464 became a more local rural route from Holland via Hurst Green, Oxted, and Limpsfield to Westerham. By this time, of course, there was a Green Line coach service from Edenbridge over the old 404 route to Croydon and on to London, Route F.

The 409 and the 434 thus assumed their individual identities. They are, of course, quite different in character: the 409 is a trunk route with a frequent headway between West Croydon and Godstone (the main operating garage), less frequent though regular beyond that point; Route 434 links a string of small settlements in Kent and through Sussex, only East Grinstead and Horsham in the 1930s and 1940s being of any size — the postwar development of Crawley as a new town has altered the population balance in the area out of all recognition. It is evident that Edenbridge has never produced a high level of traffic; the Green Line route terminating there was withdrawn on 31 August 1939 and never reinstated and even the replacement service from Chelsham (465) was later localised to start at Holland. However, the main services through East Grinstead were sustained by the high level of passenger use during the 1950s and into the 1960s; RTs — and later RMLs — were allocated to Route 409 and 434 became an RF preserve.

The recent changes and withdrawals have followed very heavy falls in passenger numbers. While a vigorous service has been maintained

Right:
Passengers have cause to wonder! This Leyland PD3 was one of three purchased from Southdown Motor Services in 1975 when London Country was seriously short of working rolling stock. Put into an LS class, it was allocated to Godstone and worked mainly on Route 409 alongside RMLs. Atlanteans were introduced on 9 July 1977 and the Leylands were immediately put on the sale list, having had an interesting extension to their lives. The imaginative quality of LCBS advertising is exemplified by the Green & Golden Rover poster. *London Country*

Above:
MB380 threads its way through the centre of old Crawley. This bus, in red livery, was sent to Crawley garage to cover the extension of Route 434/473 to Horsham in place of the 405. A green vehicle of the same type was found to take up the duty early in 1969 and MB380 returned to the Central area. *Edward Shirras*

Right:
Atlantean AN118, seen here in East Grinstead, was one of the first order supplied to London Country in 1972. Most suffixes to route numbers have now been discarded and 438 is now basically an hourly service from East Grinstead to Horsham; it offers a faster journey than the rather circuitous 434. *Edward Shirras*

between West Croydon and Godstone (with much of the road now highly urbanised), the rural stretch of 409 south of Godstone has seen progressive thinning of the timetable. The collapse of the Green Line service to East Grinstead (708, later 719) on 26 October 1979 in a sense promoted a revival of the 409 which, though shorn of its East Grinstead to Forest Row section, became an hourly express working over its old road via Lingfield and

Above:

STL1469 approaches the stop near the Chequers Inn on the Brighton Road at Horley, a spot much changed in appearance over the years. Curiously the stop sign is for coaches and is of the type adopted in the early days of the LPTB. The driver is giving a hand signal to indicate that he is slowing down, though there is no other traffic about — the road is astonishingly empty by today's standards. This front-entrance Weymann-built bus would have been almost new. *London Transport*

Newchapel, with a few journeys only running to the former bus times. From the same date 434, with its associates 473 via Rowfant and 474 via Colgate, the first replacing Southdown journeys in 1972, the second a Tillingbourne Horsham route in 1977, were cut back to start from the bleakly-named Stone Quarry Estate in East Grinstead, the road to Edenbridge and Westerham being passed to Route 485.

A further upheaval was occasioned by the closure of East Grinstead garage after 54 years activity — the Southdown garage in the town had succumbed much earlier in 1971. From 31 December 1981 alternate journeys on the 409 express were sent via Dormansland as the 419 express, each working every 2hr. Bus journeys on 409 operated only as far south as Lingfield. The 434 group were cut back to Crawley, the 474 having gained a further diversion through Sharpthorne and West Hoathly on 30 Nov-

ember 1980, replacing withdrawn Southdown facilities; anyone choosing to travel from East Grinstead to Crawley by the 474 will travel in a gigantic S — it is just as well that an hourly service (on Route 438) is offered via Felbridge and the main road! Finally, to complete the list of economies the 485 was withdrawn altogether, thus ending service on another section of the old 404. The present bus provision in the East Grinstead area probably represents a final stage before total withdrawal in the face of high car ownership levels. The major traffic flow remaining appears to be to Crawley with its extensive industry and shopping facilities; passenger numbers to local settlements like Dormansland appear sufficient only to sustain a minimum bus service, while the road beyond to Edenbridge is more than adequately catered for by a twice-weekly Maidstone & District connection. The Southdown routes to Haywards Heath and Uckfield, at one time hourly operations, are much reduced to five or six journeys a day and must be at the limits of viability. Clearly, buses in this area have only a small share of passenger movement and the days when 409 offered a half-hourly service to East Grinstead, paralleled by a Green Line coach every 30min over the same road, have now gone. Those who do not travel by car may well be tempted by the fast, regular-interval trains from East Croydon to Oxted, thence to Lingfield, Dormans and East Grinstead or to Edenbridge Town. What survives of the demand for public transport in this area appears orientated towards the railway rather than the road.

Croydon to the South and West

Dorking was early in the lists of LGOC 'Summer Sunday' services, the 107 reaching the town from Epsom in 1914; LGOC buses arrived at Guildford after the war, the 85 from Putney Bridge and Kingston via Leatherhead on 11 May 1921 and 115 from Kingston via Esher on 20 July in the same year. The last service throughout its existence (and subsequent renumbering as Route 215) was always a Central bus preserve, but the other routes were either shared with or taken over by Country buses or its predecessors. Thus, as part of the programme of development in association with the LGOC, East Surrey began S6B between the Marquis of Granby in Epsom and Guildford via Ashtead, Leatherhead and East Horsley on 16 November 1921 taking over that section of the 85 road; the route was extended back to Sutton (Cricketers) on 14 April 1922, renumbered S8 on 5 June in the same year, and operated from West Croydon from 7 March 1923. On 1 December 1924 S8 became 408, the number still extant. (The 85 continued in the summer of 1922 as a through service to Guildford, though in the following year it was diverted at Leatherhead to run to Dorking.) The 107, working daily to Dorking in 1920, became 70 in December 1924 and as 70D ran between Morden

renumbered 470, was diverted at Ewell to run to West Croydon over the existing 408 road. For many years 408 and 470 were interworked, sharing a common road from West Croydon to Leatherhead before striking out independently for Guildford and Dorking. On 2 September 1936 both routes were

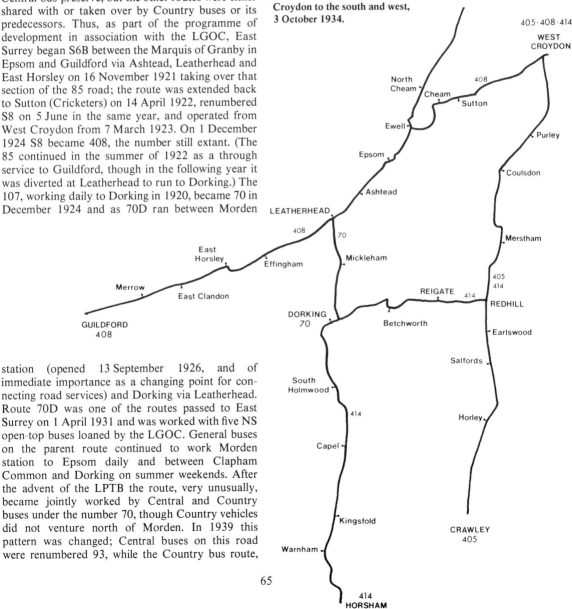

Croydon to the south and west,
3 October 1934.

station (opened 13 September 1926, and of immediate importance as a changing point for connecting road services) and Dorking via Leatherhead. Route 70D was one of the routes passed to East Surrey on 1 April 1931 and was worked with five NS open-top buses loaned by the LGOC. General buses on the parent route continued to work Morden station to Epsom daily and between Clapham Common and Dorking on summer weekends. After the advent of the LPTB the route, very unusually, became jointly worked by Central and Country buses under the number 70, though Country vehicles did not venture north of Morden. In 1939 this pattern was changed; Central buses on this road were renumbered 93, while the Country bus route,

extended eastwards to Warlingham and Chelsham, partly for operational reasons but also to provide part of the service between Wallington and Chelsham which, with the 403 routes, built up to a 5min headway. In the 1953 timetables 408 and 470 worked every 10min between Warlingham (with some journeys from Chelsham) and Leatherhead, with two buses each hour going on to Guildford (Onslow Street) and two to Dorking. In 1961 these services, together with the offshoot 408A to Merrow, Bushey Hill initiated in January 1954, were allocated 23 buses — five from Guildford, 17 from Leatherhead and one from Chelsham. They were all RTs, of course.

Apart from changes of vehicle type and some thinning of the timetables, Routes 408 and 470 had a long period without major alteration, though both routes were cut back to West Croydon in the 1970s. However, there was a full-scale upheaval on and from 31 August 1980 when, in connection with the Weyfarer scheme, 408 was made into an express operation and lost its ANs in favour of Leyland Nationals; the intention was to make the trunk route more attractive to long-distance travellers, a through journey being scheduled for 1hr 40min, a reduction of 16min on the previous time. The 408A however retained its ANs and style of working. The changes involving 470 virtually ended the route altogether apart from a vestigial remain of two schooldays only journeys, a somewhat pathetic remnant of the former full-scale timetable. The section between Leatherhead and Dorking is now covered throughout the day by Green Line 714. There has thus been significant reduction of frequency between West Croydon and Leatherhead (now two buses hourly) and between Leatherhead and Dorking (now a coach each hour). Clearly this level of service is adequate

for the level of traffic on these formerly very busy roads.

If the routes via Leatherhead owed their origins primarily to the LGOC, the 405 to Crawley and the 414 to Horsham via Redhill were developed very early East Surrey activities. Having opened the Reigate to Redhill service on 23 May 1911, East Surrey reached Merstham on 12 December 1911 and Horley on 15 March in the following year. A detached service between Brockham Green and Holmwood, started 19 February 1914, was subsumed in a through Redhill to Dorking service on 7 April, extended to the Duke's Head at Beare Green on 31 May. Crawley and Handcross (Red Lion) were reached on 21 February 1916, though services were later withdrawn as a wartime measure. However, on 21 August 1920 East Surrey opened an ambitious circular route starting at Reigate and running through Redhill, Horley, Crawley, Horsham and Dorking, thence back to Reigate; a week later Handcross was served by some buses diverted from the main line of route. In the following year, in conjunction with the LGOC, East Surrey began operation of a new route, S5, from West Croydon to Redhill Market Place over part of the General 59 road. (This LGOC route, latterly 59B, had started as a summer service via Wray Common to Reigate in 1914, interestingly by agreement with East Surrey after an abortive attempt to start the

Above:
Leyland National SNB309 was one of its type that displaced Routemasters from the 414 in the autumn of 1977. It is seen here in Reigate on its way to Horsham, a terminus the route ceased to serve after 31 August 1980 when it was cut back to Capel; Green Line 714 took over most of the bus work south of Dorking. *John Marsh*

service in the previous year.) All these sections were subsequently absorbed in other services; thus S5 was extended to Crawley (The George) on 14 April 1922, from which point alternate buses worked to Handcross or Horsham (The Carfax): from 1 December 1924 West Croydon to Handcross became 405, West Croydon to Horsham via Crawley became 412. Also from 14 April 1922 a new route, partly over old ground, was opened between Merstham (The Feathers) and Horsham via Reigate and Dorking as S25; with extension to West Croydon on 17 April 1924 this was the basis of the 414 which it became later in the year. With the withdrawal of 412 on 15 April 1930, the following day 405 assumed the form it was to retain for many years, working between West Croydon and Crawley; the Crawley to Horsham section passed to the 34 from East Grinstead and Handcross was served by a local route from Horley.

From that date there were very few changes in route or schedule on either Routes 405 or 414,

though one generation of vehicles replaced another, of course. The service provided was basically every 30min on each route, thus affording a 15min frequency between Croydon and Redhill; at one time 24 buses were needed. The expansion of Crawley New Town brought about the extension of 405 via Northgate to Southgate, giving these areas the advantage of through journeys; peak hour buses routed via the industrial area were numbered 455. These Crawley services proved remarkably healthy and retained a half-hourly service on weekdays and a Sunday operation as well. A recent development, from 21 August 1982, has turned the former 455 journeys over to Route 422 which runs with 405 as far as Redhill and then takes its own line of route to Banstead and Sutton; all journeys on these routes serve Gatwick Airport, now an important interchange. Route 414, however, has suffered from thin traffic south of Dorking on the somewhat bare road through Warnham and from 31 August 1980 the service was withdrawn between Dorking and Horsham except for a few peak-hour journeys as far as Capel. Green Line 714 thus became responsible for this section and 414 is now basically an hourly service from Dorking to West Croydon with a supplementary hourly working from Reigate; between them 405 and 414 offer a 20min service from Redhill to Croydon. The amount of tourist traffic on these routes is now minimal and they have settled to a more work-a-day activity; thus on Sundays each route offers a bus every 2hr, and, as elsewhere, they are rarely fully occupied.

Change at Reigate

Two very long-established routes meet at Reigate, making it possible to travel all the way from Kingston to East Grinstead by changing at the Railway station in Reigate, at Red Cross or at Bancroft Road. These are the 406 from Kingston station to Redhill and the 424 which currently runs from Reigate station to East Grinstead. Of the two, Route 406 has had a remarkably uneventful history. East Surrey opened a route from Redhill Market Place to the Marquis of Granby in Epsom on 5 June 1920; this became S6 on 16 November 1921 as part of the General scheme, was extended to Kingston on 14 April 1922 and assumed the number 406 on 1 December 1924. And that is the whole story, or very nearly; there have been variations of frequency, or course, and changes of vehicle allocation, but for 60 years the 406 has worked through suburbs like Tolworth and Ewell which vastly increased their size

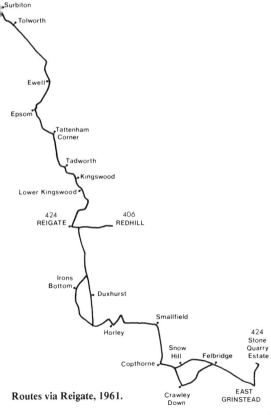

Routes via Reigate, 1961.

in the 1920s and 1930s, on to Tadworth and Kingswood, and down Reigate Hill. There have been very few changes of road, though in the 1950s and 1960s there was a diversion between Tattenham Corner and Tadworth station via Merland Rise numbered 406A; this has now become the main line of route. (Green Line 727 which also links Reigate and Kingston travels by the main road.) Mention should also be made of the works service 406C which ran for many years from Redhill to the Windmill Press at Kingswood, and of 406F which was once a most intensive service ferrying race-goers from Epsom station to the race course; in its heyday this service made demands on almost every garage south of the Thames. Now both printers and punters go by car. At its peak the 406 required 16 RTs from Leatherhead and another six from Reigate; current allocations are more modest though 406 is still a major service. ANs work hourly over the whole route, every 20min between Tadworth and Kingston; additional buses are provided in the peak hours.

The 424 is a very different kind of service and has had a rather more complicated history. In contrast with the suburban role of 406, Route 424 is essentially a rural service, though at one time it offered facilities over considerable distances. Started on 28 June 1920, East Surrey Route 22 provided buses from Reigate to Redhill, by the direct road to Horley and then on to Copthorne (Duke's Head) which was the terminus. In the following year, from 1 July, buses worked via Copthorne village and ran through to Felbridge, East Grinstead and Forest Row. Curtailed at East Grinstead in 1922, from 5 May 1924 buses again ran to Forest Row and were further extended to Hartfield. The next changes (from 20 May 1925) cut out the Reigate to Horley section altogether and Route 22 was therefore reduced to a Horley to Hartfield service until its withdrawal on 25 January 1927. The following day, under number 24, a joint service was worked with Autocar from Horley Post Office to Tunbridge Wells (Opera House) on an hourly frequency; alternate journeys ran via Smallfield and Shipley Bridge. Later in the year the Smallfield buses were sent via Snow Hill and those running through Shipley Bridge were numbered 24A. Horley was rather an unsatisfactory terminus, especially as some buses for the service had to be sent down from Reigate, so from 31 October 1928 the route was formally extended to Reigate via Duxhurst; alternate journeys were diverted through Irons Bottom from 30 January

1929, Routes 24 and 24A subsequently became plain 424 and there has never been differentiation on this route since — passengers have always had to know if they were destined for Duxhurst or Irons Bottom, or for Snow Hill or Crawley Down in the later section of their journey. The deep purple buses of Autocar did not penetrate the Surrey countryside after the advent of the LPTB on 1 July 1933 and 424 settled down to work from Reigate to East Grinstead in very much the form it is in today; initially buses turned at Forest Row, but by the following year they were starting from the Crown in East Grinstead. The section beyond that point to Tunbridge Wells eventually became Maidstone & District property, which of course it still is, a two-hourly service being provided on Route 291.

A single-decker service for many years (four Q types were allocated from East Grinstead garage at one time), double-deck vehicles were eventually required and seven RTs worked the service in the 1960s by which time the 424 had acquired a limited local function in East Grinstead by extension to the Stone Quarry Estate. The route is now much reduced in status, running every 2hr between Reigate and East Grinstead — still to Stone Quarry after stopping at the Crown. A few journeys run via Duxhurst, the majority via Irons Bottom, and all serve Crawley Down; the service ceases in the early evening and does not run on Sundays. However, Atlanteans now carry this number and work along the boundary between Surrey and East Sussex. There must be few who now remember when the 24 went all the way to Tunbridge Wells, but in fact the new Maidstone & District Invictaway Service 900 covers much of this road, offering a through facility from Tunbridge Wells via East Grinstead and Horley to Gatwick Airport. This is not a destination that existed in the 1920s, of course, and passengers at that time had more modest intentions in mind than to fly to New York or on a package holiday to Majorca.

Above:
MBS4 started life as a Central area bus and was noteworthy as the only Strachans-built vehicle thought worth overhaul. It was accepted by LGCS on an exchange basis in 1973 and repainted; it went the rounds of the garages, which suggests it was not very popular. Here it is operating from Leatherhead and is at Epsom on a crewed working on the 406 on 28 October 1977. The vehicle was withdrawn in December of the following year.
Brian J. Garrard

Right:
XA46 was one of three Atlanteans transferred from the Central area to the Country department in 1969 in exchange for three of the Daimler Fleetlines for performance comparison tests. It is seen here in East Grinstead; the 'Green Rover' advertisements were necessary on a red bus! The entire XA class was sold in 1973 — later Atlanteans were much superior vehicles.
Edward Shirras

Right:
XF8 was the last of eight Daimler Fleetlines purchased by London Transport in 1965, most of which spent their lives at East Grinstead. The Park Royal bodywork provided seats for 72 passengers. These buses were intended for experimental service (hence the X) in which the upper deck was shut off during off-peak hours and the bus operated only by the driver. These vehicles were the first rear-engined double-deckers taken into the London Transport fleet. XF8, seen here near Sidlow Church, was withdrawn in December 1978. *Edward Shirras*

Guildford to Windsor

A through bus service from Guildford to Uxbridge via Woking, Chertsey, Staines and Windsor may now seem an unlikely facility, but for some time in the 1930s it existed. Bus services in the lower Thames Valley were early enterprises of the LGOC, the 141 from Hounslow Central station reaching Virginia Water at Easter 1914; after a gap caused by wartime difficulties the service to Egham and Virginia Water was resumed in 1919, becoming a daily service on 30 June 1920. The number allocated was 117, still in use as far as Staines. Route 61, started 4 January 1922, worked from Kingston Garage to Chertsey and was extended to Windsor via Chertsey Lane, Egham, Englefield Green and Old Windsor on 1 April in the same year; also on 1 April 1922 Route 79 from Kingston to Woking was initiated. Further south in the Guildford area the Aldershot & District Traction Co was well-established by 1914 with a network of routes including one from Guildford to Woking and Walton-on-Thames begun at the end of that year. Despite recent route changes, including considerable withdrawals

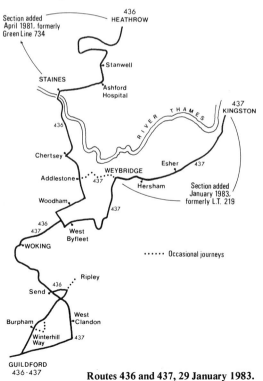

Section added April 1981, formerly Green Line 734

436
HEATHROW

Stanwell

STAINES

Ashford Hospital

RIVER THAMES

436

Chertsey

437
KINGSTON

Esher 437

WEYBRIDGE

Addlestone 437

Hersham

Section added January 1983, formerly L.T. 219

Woodham

437

436
437

West Byfleet

WOKING

Occasional journeys

Ripley

Send

West Clandon

Burpham

Winterhill Way 437

GUILDFORD
436·437

Routes 436 and 437, 29 January 1983.

from the area by London Transport, a glance at the map will still show LT and Alder Valley (successor to Aldershot & District) in charge of considerable territory, with London Country holding a corridor between them.

East Surrey ambitions included running its buses into the lower Thames Valley and Windsor was a particular target because of the lucrative tripper traffic which seemed to get bigger every year. The key to achievement of these aims came with the purchase of J. R. Fox & Sons' Woking & District company by Aldershot & District on 14 January 1931, a purchase made with the active (and financial) support of the LGOC which immediately arranged for part of the route network to be operated by East Surrey. Mr Fox had begun with a local route in Woking on 1 April 1921 and subsequently extended southwards to Send in 1923, Ripley in 1924 and to Guildford in 1929. With increasing prosperity, Woking & District put on two new hourly services on 1 September 1928: Woking to Ottershaw and Chertsey, and West Byfleet to Woodham, Chertsey, Staines and Egham. This second route was subsequently extended to Windsor Castle, though an ambitious scheme to project to Maidenhead was disallowed. When the Fox concern reached Windsor it was over a road from Staines via Egham and Englefield Green already well-served by buses, including those of the LGOC which was running the well-established 117 from Hounslow and a local route, 117D, between Slough station and Staines. There was also the Thames Valley route which had begun as a Windsor Castle to Staines service in 1922; by 1929 this was running as Route 21 and started at Maidenhead. The following year, from 1 April, the Woking & District services were remodelled to provide a 30min frequency between Chertsey and Windsor. At the point of take-over by East Surrey on 14 January 1931 there were eight buses hourly over the Staines to Windsor road — two East Surrey (formerly Fox), four LGOC and two Thames Valley. The LGOC of course worked additional journeys from Hounslow on summer weekends.

Another operator in the Woking area was B. H. Martin who owned the Red Bus or Bus-de-ville and whose main route was Woking to Chersey via Maybury Inn, Pyrford, West Byfleet, Byfleet and Addlestone. This firm was acquired by East Surrey on 11 March 1931. For a short time East Surrey ran the former Fox and Martin services to the existing schedules, but there were substantial revisions from 20 May 1931 when the routes were numbered. The through Woking to Windsor service became 38, the complementary route from West Byfleet, 39. Other services were as follows:

36: Woking-Send-West Clandon-Guildford
37: Woking-Send-Ripley
40: Woking-Byfleet-Addlestone-Chertsey
40A: as 40 except via Pyrford

The purchase of the Woking & District operation included the Fox premises in St John's Road, though these were used only until 31 May 1931 when East Surrey moved to the former Aldershot & District garage in Walton Road, that firm having found a new site. Further changes included the working of some LGOC routes by LGCS from 1 March 1933

— the 117D became 417 — and the acquisition of 'full rights of road' between Staines and Windsor on 10 June 1933, from which date LGCS took over the Thames Valley timings and two buses. A further reorganisation by LGCS provided through running from Guildford and Ripley to Windsor by extending Routes 36 and 37 over the former 38 and 39 roads from Woking, and these numbers were abandoned. Routes 36 and 37 became 436 and 437 on 3 October 1934, and 507 (not extended to work Staines-Windsor-George Green-Uxbridge) became the once-familiar 457 shortly after on 1 December. An interesting development came on 3 July 1935 when 436 and 437 were extended to Uxbridge via Iver Village and George Green respectively, thus creating very long hauls from Guildford or Ripley; the numbers 457 and 458 were withdrawn. However, this arrangement lasted less than a year and on

Above:
This is a Dennis bus seating 26 passengers, new in 1928 to C. Aston of Watford. It was acquired by LGCS on 9 May 1933 and shifted from its Watford haunts to work the hourly Guildford to Windsor service that East Surrey had taken over from Woking & District on 14 January 1931. The vehicle has been repainted and carries the number 37 that became 437 in the scheme of 4 October 1934. It was sold in 1936. *J. F. Higham*

Left:
This is an example of the RLH class, RLH33, which served on lowbridge routes for 20 years. It is an AEC Regent with Weymann body; there are seats for 53 passengers, the upper deck seats being in rows of four. Buses of this type were active in the Weybridge and Woking areas for most of their life. RLH33 has just arrived at Ripley from Guildford as a 415 and is about to take up a 436A working to Staines. These buses were replaced by AEC Swifts of the SM class in July 1970. *Edward Shirras*

which, after Burnt Common, ran via Burpham along the main road. Initially single-decker operations — Qs worked for some years — these routes were subsequently allocated lowbridge double-deck types, first STLs and then the RLH models. In fact the history of these services is largely dictated by low railway bridges during a time when passenger traffic was sufficient to warrant double-deck operation. The 1962 lists show Routes 436 to 436A working through to Staines once again, though via Burpham rather than West Clandon, paralleled for much of the way by 463: Guildford to Walton-on-Thames, which took over the Clandon road. With minor variations, including the renumbering of 436A to 420, this pattern of routes persisted well into the London Country period, though the RLH buses were replaced by AEC Merlins which did little for the reliability of the services they worked on, nor it would seem for the morale of the drivers; Addlestone garage has been persistently short of staff. However, recent changes have seen an interesting projection of the 436 into London Airport, from 25 April 1981, replacing failed Green Line 734. Route 436 has thus become basically an hourly service throughout the day between Guildford and Heathrow; a supplementary local service is offered to Winterhill Way in Burpham, and the occasional journey to Ripley. The sight of time-worn RPs at the central bus station at the airport was not a particularly inspiring one, but they were probably as comfortable as the Boeing 747s the passengers had just left — Leyland

Above:

The railway bridge in Chertsey Lane, near Staines is one that has caused operating problems for many years and the limited clearance available even to a lowbridge bus is seen in this shot of RLH 32 during its last days of service in July 1970. It was one of 13 buses of its type allocated to Addlestone; five more were kept at Guildford. They were all replaced by vehicles of the SM class which were brought into service on 1 August 1970, and they brought problems of another kind. *London Country*

18 March 1936 Routes 457 and 458 were reinstated between Uxbridge and Windsor and 436 and 437 were correspondingly cut back. For operational reasons the buses and crews still worked right through and there was a 5min layover at Windsor Castle to allow the conductor to change the destination blinds. This rather curious procedure was abandoned by June 1938 when Route 436 from Guildford was curtailed to run only as far as Staines, with the companion 436A from Ripley; 437 assumed a new identity as a local service between Woking and Addlestone via Woodham. Subsequently, in the interests of running sections with double-deck vehicles, the routes were split again and by 1949 were running as 436: Staines to Woking via Chertsey, Addlestone, New Haw and Woodham, 436A: Woking to Ripley, and 436B: Woking to Guildford via West Clandon; a more direct service between Woking and Guildford was offered by 438

Below:

Route 437 has changed its form many times over the years. By the time this splendidly turned out RF was at work on the route it had shrunk to Woking to Weybridge via West Byfleet, New Haw and Addlestone. With the changes implemented on 29 January 1983, however, the route now runs from Guildford to Kingston. RF666 was new in 1953 and is seen here converted for one-man-operation. *Edward Shirras*

74

Nationals took over. Various modifications evolved Route 437 which for some time worked from Guildford to Weybridge every hour, via West Clandon; however from 29 January 1983 this route was projected to Hersham, Esher and Kingston over the former London Transport Route 219 which was withdrawn. Although serving major objectives, 436 and 437 suffer from somewhat circuitous route paths, especially between Guildford and Woking where the parallel Alder Valley 286 takes 30min to Woking and 72min to Staines against the 40min and 88min respectively of Route 436. Anyone wishing to travel from Guildford or Woking to Kingston would, of course take Green Line 715 or 716 which afford faster trips.

Since the cutting of Routes 436 and 437 at Staines the road from that town to Egham and Windsor has had a separate history. For some time the routes concerned were 417 to Langley Village and 458 to Uxbridge, the first a double-decker working, initially by STs, the second a single-decker operation. Journeys were alternately via Old Windsor (Village Road) and the Bells of Ouzeley on the so-called Straight Road. Subsequently this section was subsumed in the 441 which has now been a trunk route through to High Wycombe for many years, with up to four buses an hour provided as far as Hedgerley Corner. Since the Thamesline changes of 31 May 1980, Route 441 has been basically an hourly service from Staines bus station to High Wycombe, supported by an hourly 443 from Staines to Windsor (via the Village Road in Old Windsor) projected to

Above:
SNB543 heads out of Guildford shortly after the 437 was revised to work through to Kingston on 29 January 1983, following withdrawal of London Transport operations to Weybridge on Route 219. The bus is the most recently delivered Leyland National to be taken into stock by LCBS, being registered in 1980. The weakness of the one-line destination display is highlighted here; 437 takes a circuitous route to Kingston, while Green Line 715 is a much more direct route. The scene of urban desolation has, alas, been characteristic of towns in London country for nearly 20 years as old buildings have been replaced by faceless constructions; traffic lights, yellow lines, no-right-turn signs and other cluttered street furniture complete the picture. *Michael Dryhurst*

Uxbridge over the former 457 road across Iver Heath, thus re-establishing a link severed many years before. There is also an hourly short working from Staines to Cherrywood Avenue in Englefield Green.

It is thus now possible to travel from Guildford to Windsor and Uxbridge by London Country with only one change of vehicle, at Staines. However, Alder Valley still provides a through service between Guildford and Slough via Brookwood, Bracknell and Windsor; it is neither a very direct nor frequent service, but it is part of the Weyfarer and the romantically-named Forestride schemes which have their own adherents. It is always pleasing to have a choice.

Thames to Chilterns

Bus services in the Slough area started by the Great Western Railway on 1 March 1904 were the first motorbus operations in London country and among the earliest anywhere. The network became considerable, with buses from Slough station — always the principal standpoint — travelling by way of Farnham Road or Stoke Green to Hedgerley Village, Burnham Beeches or Beaconsfield station; there was also a Windsor to Ascot route that began on 5 April 1905. Development was interrupted by World War 1, but through the 1920s the GWR was very active indeed and new services were initiated to the Trading Estate — seemingly a Mecca for all bus operators in Slough and Windsor — and to Taplow. Amersham & District reached Slough in 1922, buses working from Chesham via Amersham, the Chalfonts, Gerrards Cross and Stoke Common; this route was later designated Route 3, the forerunner of the 353. The company extended to Windsor in the following year and later opened a service from High Wycombe, numbered 14, via Beaconsfield, Hedgerley Corner, Farnham and Slough; this and some of the GWR services became the basis for 441. The third major service from Windsor and Slough to the northwest, the 335, was pioneered by Frederick Lewis (later the Lewis Omnibus Co Ltd), who worked from Watford via Rickmansworth, Chalfont St Peter, Gerrards Cross and then Fulmer; for a period in the 1920s Thames Valley also ran on this road from Chalfont St Peter but withdrew on 31 December 1928 when it had to move out of the Uxbridge base from which the service was worked. In addition to these operators there was a plethora of small firms active in the Windsor and Slough area, including F. C. Owen who ran a Windsor Castle to Farnham Royal service and E. A. Shand whose Cream Service ran to Farnham Road. An interesting late development was the initiation by Premier Line of a route from Aylesbury (Kingsbury Square) to the Lord Raglan at Windsor in the early summer of 1931; though worked by coaches, this was a bus route and a 30min frequency was maintained; it was designated Route F.

The first sign of rationalisation in the Slough area came with the acquisition of the GWR services and vehicles by the LGOC in December 1931. Operations were taken over by LGCS on 10 April 1932 and the routes were numbered 41 (those via Farnham Road) and 42 (if via Stoke Green); the 14 buses were transferred to the garage in Alpha Street, Slough and later to Windsor, when it opened. The

Traffic Commissioners were also at work by this time and initially refused a licence altogether for the Premier Route F; however, on appeal, Premier was allowed to run to Slough (Uxbridge Road) from Aylesbury every 2hr in a co-ordinated service with Amersham & District Route 19, also every 2hr, between Great Missenden and Windsor. The advent of the LPTB caused few immediate changes in the services but total changes of identity; Amersham & District was acquired on 1 October 1933 (though vehicles retained their Amersham & District title until 23 November), Lewis also on 1 October and Premier Line on 20 December. The takeover of F. C. Owen's service on 1 February 1934 was especially significant in that his route to Farnham Royal was numbered 441 — the first mention of this number. Otherwise most of the existing numbers were retained until the scheme of 3 October 1934 when

Routes through Slough, 1983.

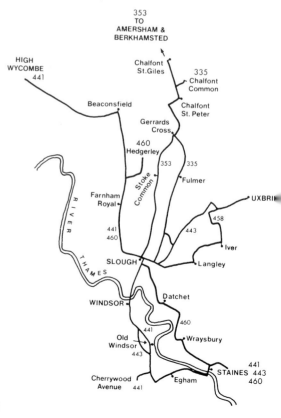

Above:
The light reflected off the destination display hides the fact that Routemaster RML2348, working the 441 from High Wycombe, is on its way to Staines. It is seen here, one day in March 1978, alongside the Thames at Old Windsor. New in December 1965, this bus spent most of its life at Windsor before being sold to London Transport in 1980. Route 441 is currently worked by Leyland Nationals.
Michael Dryhurst

there was a reallocation which produced route numbers familiar today; these included:

335: Windsor-Fulmer-Gerrards Cross-Rickmansworth-Watford (formerly Lewis)
353: Windsor (Hospital)-Stoke Common-Gerrards Cross-Amersham-Chesham-Ley Hill (formerly Amersham & District Route 3)
369: Windsor (Lord Raglan)-Stoke Common-Gerrards Cross-Amersham-Aylesbury (worked in two sections: Windsor to Great Missenden — formerly Amersham & District Route 19, and Slough to Aylesbury, formerly the Premier service)
441 (why not 341?): Windsor-Slough-Hedgerley Corner (with some journeys to the village)-Beaconsfield-High Wycombe

The 441 timetable incorporated the former Amersham & District Route 14, the former GWR times and some local independents' services as well. The 369 was the only subsequent casualty, being withdrawn on 13 May 1936 when an increased service

was provided on 353 which, on the same day, was extended to Berkhamsted. From that date the route structure has proved remarkably static, though the Windsor turning point has been variously given as St Leonards Road and the Coach Station, the same place of course. Double-deck vehicles of the ST type were allocated to Route 441, lowbridge STs to 353 and Qs to 335; RTs were allocated to all these services in the heyday of that type. Thus single-decker working was eliminated on the Windsor to Staines section when that was turned over to Route 441 — this was always an intensive service; for many years a 15min frequency was scheduled over much of its road.

After leaving the tourist scenes of Windsor and enduring the urban delights of Slough, all these routes — 335, 353 and 441 — traverse some pleasant wooded country with attractive settlements large and small; the Beaconsfield to High Wycombe section is perhaps less pleasing than others, but at least it is now mercifully traffic-free after the opening of the M40 and buses have a more or less free approach to Wycombe itself. Travellers who venture on to Amersham are rewarded by Chiltern hills and trees and a remarkable atmosphere redolent of the 1930s — Hovis teas are still available and one can even see people armed with guide-books and maps actually walking, a regrettably rare sight in London country in these times. Through the years there have been adjustments to timetables and changes of vehicle type, of course, but these routes have survived largely unchanged except for the 335 which, from 31 August 1980, ceased to run through to Watford. Of interest was the shuttle service between Slough and Eton included in the 441 schedule, put on

when the town bridge was declared unsafe; this ceased on 23 March 1974 when replaced by an Alder Valley service — Eton is thus surrounded by London Country but no longer served by it.

The current position shows Route 441 to be basically a through hourly working from Staines to High Wycombe, supported between Slough and Hedgerley Corner by an extension of 460 to Hedgerley Village; Route 460 also works from Staines, but via Wraysbury — the old LGOC Route 162B. The 353 is still a substantial service, working hourly all the way to Berkhamsted with a local wriggle in that town, alternate buses travelling through Ashlyns Estate. The 335 is really the only casualty of diminished patronage, being reduced to a handful of journeys (five on Mondays to Fridays, six on Saturdays) mainly between Slough and Chalfont Common. Windsor is, of course, very much a Leyland National preserve and these buses currently rattle along the pleasant roads there. It is nostalgic to think of the more discreet AEC types that once ran these services, but pointless — at least the services are in being and, hopefully, are sufficiently well-patronised to ensure their future.

Top:
Merlin MBS438 waits near Slough station to depart on the short shuttle to Eton, put on when the Thames Bridge at the top of Eton High Street was pronounced unsafe for vehicles. This bus was delivered in 1968 and at first operated on an Autofare basis; the arrival of decimal currency on 21 February 1971 however caused its conversion to conventional OMO with the driver collecting the fares. These buses did not have good reputations for reliability and this vehicle was among those disposed of in 1978. Alder Valley now operates into Eton.
Edward Shirras

Above:
SM510 waits at the Windsor garage terminus in St Leonard's Road to take a 353 journey to Berkhamsted. Buses of this type were allocated to the route in 1971, replacing the double-deck working by RTs which had consistently run on the route since October 1950. This bus, a Metro-Cammell build, seated 41 passengers and was licensed for another 19 standing; it was not altogether unsuitable for the lengthy 353. Following withdrawal of this class the route was made a Leyland National activity in 1979. The 353 is now, of course, part of the Chilternlink scheme and an hourly through service is maintained on weekdays; there is also a substantial Sunday service.
Michael Dryhurst

Routes from Uxbridge

The little market town of Uxbridge, terminus of the tram route from Shepherds Bush and of the Metropolitan Railway, was an obvious bridgehead for bus services to Windsor and the Chilterns. However, the LGOC was unable to put its interest into material form until after World War 1 when a single B type bus was sent from Acton to start Service 95 from Uxbridge to High Wycombe on 16 March 1921; some three months later the allocation was increased to four buses which worked Uxbridge-West Wycombe-Beaconsfield-West Wycombe-Uxbridge. These vehicles were based at Turnham Green, which meant lengthy garage journeys and complicated crewing arrangements. The agreement between the LGOC and Thames Valley passed further development of services in the area to that company which assumed responsibility for Route 95 on and from 7 June 1922, worked as W21 from the recently completed LGOC garage in Uxbridge (which Thames Valley managed also). New routes were pioneered to Gerrards Cross, The Chalfonts, Amersham and Great Missenden (W23), to Windsor via Cowley, Iver, Langley and Slough (W22), and — joint with National — to Denham, West Hyde, Rickmansworth and Watford (W24). All these services were in operation by September 1922 and though operated daily were not on regular headways; Thames Valley provided small single-deck buses, either Daimler or Tilling Stevens vehicles, though later double-deck Thornycrofts were employed.

Traffic was less than anticipated and by January 1923 Route W23 was cut short at Amersham station and W24 abandoned altogether, though after a few months National resumed service between Watford and West Hyde. The Bassom numbering scheme removed the W prefix and the services, all starting from the Eight Bells in Uxbridge, became 502 to West Wycombe, 503 to Windsor Castle and 504 to Amersham. Though the numbers appeared in the timetable books, Thames Valley was not very punctilious about placing them on the vehicles.

The agreement between the LGOC and Thames Valley expired on 31 December 1928 and the following day General repossessed the Uxbridge garage and took over the routes operating from it with its own buses. Amersham & District took over operation of Route 502 to West Wycombe in June 1930, and in effect 504 to Amersham when that service was subsumed in the express Service 17 (Amersham to Oxford Circus) started on 26 January 1931 — this,

of course, became part of the Green Line system. The LGOC itself worked 503 to Windsor until 1 March 1933 when the route — and the operating base at Langley Road, Slough — passed to London General Country Services; by this date there was also a 507: Uxbridge to Windsor via Iver Heath and George Green. All these routes were now very clearly in the London country category.

The 500 series numbers survived until 1 December 1934 when the Uxbridge services, now starting from the RAF station, became 455 (formerly 502A, formerly 502 to High Wycombe), 458 (formerly 503 to Windsor via Iver Village) and 457 (formerly 507 to Windsor via Iver Heath, now extended via Pooley Green to Staines). Two rural services owned by Filkins & Ainsworth Ltd of Harefield, acquired on 31 October 1933, were worked from the Eight Bells to Harefield (309A), with an extension as Route 357 to Northwood on Sundays. Mention should also be made of the frequent Green Line Services Q and R to High Wycombe and Chesham respectively; on the Buckinghamshire roads the fast coaches had an advantage over the bus and catered more successfully for the kind of traffic offering.

Apart from the projection of the Windsor services to Guildford and Ripley as 436 and 437 respectively for a period in 1935 until 18 March 1936, and the subsequent exchange of the Windsor to Staines section from 457 to 458, the pattern of services from Uxbridge remained in being for some years. In 1938 they were all single-decker operations, Reliances, elderly Leyland Tigers and the newer T types being used, though Cubs were still adequate for the Harefield journeys. Traffic to Windsor was, of course, heavy and seasonal, that to the Chilterns never reached more than satisfactory figures. It is now hard to imagine actors and film crew travelling in anything but their own large cars, but a service to Pinewood Studios was introduced on 15 February 1937. In addition to journeys on 457, Route 309 from Rickmansworth was projected to run hourly to the Studios. Special tickets over-printed 'PS' were issued on all Pinewood journeys, presumably to ensure accurate accounting on what were subsidised services supported by the film company. Route 309 was withdrawn from this section on 4 August 1937 and all journeys from Uxbridge worked under the number 457C; this route lasted until the late 1950s. During the war an important development was the restoration of the old W24 in the form of 321 which worked from Luton via St Albans and Watford; this

Above:

RTs always looked well to the very end of their time. Garston-based RT4495 started at Grays in July 1954 and is seen here working a 321 from Uxbridge. Buses of the same type were used on the express Route 803 which covered the same road, only rather faster.
London Country

Below:

RF55 was delivered in 1951 and spent its best years on Green Line work. Here it is seen near the Crown at Slough on 8 July 1973, the first day of Route 452 which was actually no more than a renumbering of former 457A: Uxbridge-George Green-Upton Lea-Slough-Windsor. Withdrawn in 1977, the bus was in service for 26 years.
Edward Shirras

began on 6 October 1943 and added a significant trunk route to the Uxbridge network.

Subsequently all departures from Uxbridge LT station were taken by RTs, the only single-decker workings being the 458 to Slough (with a few journeys to Windsor) and its associated 459 to Richings Park Estate; these were allocated to RFs. A major development in the 1950s raised the status of the Harefield services to a trunk route through to Northwood, Watford and Hemel Hempstead, the 347, and an express service was run over the 321 road to St Albans and on to Hatfield and Welwyn Garden City, on 803, which began on 21 March 1956. The High Wycombe road, however, was less busy and the 455 was reduced to a few journeys on the main A40, being interworked with the 305 which described a great arc through Chalfont St Peter after leaving Gerrards Cross; these routes were early casualties of affluence in that they ran through country where car ownership was high. They also suffered some unreliability as the approaches to High Wycombe were subject to daily congestion before the opening of the M40.

In the early days of London Country these services remained in being except for 803, now superseded by half-hourly departures from Uxbridge on Green Line Routes 724 and 727; the 321 lasted until 31 March 1979. Frequencies of operation were perhaps optimistic in relation both to the number of passengers offering themselves and to the availability of staff and vehicles. Thus in May 1975 Routes 452 (formerly 457A) and 457 were advertising three buses per hour to Windsor during the peak, with another two on 458; the 305 worked hourly on its circuitous journey. The RTs had by now disappeared from these routes which were operated by Merlins, when working, and elderly RFs when they were not.

Two reorganisations in the area, Chilternlink (13 April 1980) and Thamesline (31 May) considerably altered the provision on the routes out of Uxbridge. Route 305 maintains an hourly departure on its Chiltern tour to High Wycombe, with just two journeys on the direct road under the number 325 (changed from 455 on the closure of High Wycombe garage and the transfer to Amersham — High Wycombe was always regarded as a '4' garage). The 457 and its associates disappeared after 36 years, being replaced by 443 from Uxbridge to Staines via Slough and Windsor, basically hourly, journeys sent through Upton Lea carrying the number 442. The 458 is still a half-hourly service, being usefully extended across Slough to the Trading Estate and Cippenham; on Sundays, buses working under the number 482 take a different route in Slough and terminate at Britwell. All these services are scheduled for Leyland Nationals. While bus operations in the area have declined over the years, it is pleasing to note that Green Line activity is intense, being especially suited to the current needs of travellers.

Trunk Routes in Watford

The major bus routes in the Watford area have very early origins indeed, most of them dating back to the horse and motorbus interests of the London & North Western Railway. From a base in the goods yard of Watford Junction the railway inaugurated a motorbus service between Croxley Green and the Junction on 23 April 1906, extending to what was then called Callowland in North Watford in 1909 and reaching the Three Horseshoes in Garston on 12 May 1913. The horse-drawn service from Boxmoor station to Hemel Hempstead, dating from 1884, was turned over to a Milnes Daimler bus on 9 August 1909 and subsequently extended to Piccotts End; this was supplemented by a through service from Watford Junction to Hemel Hempstead which began running

interest waned, so that by agreement bus work in the town was passed to General. The first mention of new routes in Watford was in the traffic circular dated 17 January 1920 under the heading 'Advance Information of Services in the Watford Area'. Four

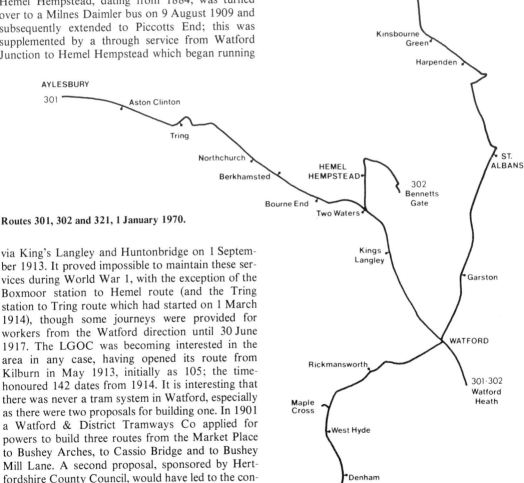

Routes 301, 302 and 321, 1 January 1970.

via King's Langley and Huntonbridge on 1 September 1913. It proved impossible to maintain these services during World War 1, with the exception of the Boxmoor station to Hemel route (and the Tring station to Tring route which had started on 1 March 1914), though some journeys were provided for workers from the Watford direction until 30 June 1917. The LGOC was becoming interested in the area in any case, having opened its route from Kilburn in May 1913, initially as 105; the time-honoured 142 dates from 1914. It is interesting that there was never a tram system in Watford, especially as there were two proposals for building one. In 1901 a Watford & District Tramways Co applied for powers to build three routes from the Market Place to Bushey Arches, to Cassio Bridge and to Bushey Mill Lane. A second proposal, sponsored by Hertfordshire County Council, would have led to the construction of a line from Bushy Arches to North Watford. However, nothing came of either.

The interregnum occasioned by the war strengthened the LGOC hand in Watford and the railway services were listed, all to begin operation on Wednesday, 4 February 1920:

143: Watford Junction-Rickmansworth High Street (every 30min)
144: Watford Junction-Berkhamsted Town Hall (hourly)
145: Watford Junction-Hemel Hempstead Posting House (hourly)
146: Bushey Arches (Wheatsheaf)-St Albans (every 30min)

143 was intended as a single-decker route, the others were allocated double-deck vehicles. However, considerable delay was caused by the fact that the Leavesden Road garage was not ready for occupation and did not open until 25 August 1920. Very shortly after, three B type buses began working Route 143 between Croxley Green (The Sportsman) and Garston (Three Horseshoes) and two others were allocated to Route 145 between Bushey station (Railway Arms) and Boxmoor station. Route 147 was introduced as a daily service between Bushey station and Hemel Hempstead on 20 October 1920, and a month later, on 24 November, Route 143 was extended from Garston to St Albans and 145 from Boxmoor station to Berkhamsted. The original plans were thus implemented in rather different form. There was also a 'Summer Sunday' Route 146 which ran from Golders Green to Boxmoor (Station Hotel) — this appeared in April 1920. The LNWR retained its interest in its services from Boxmoor and Tring and passed them to the London, Midland & Scottish Railway, the buses in crimson lake livery being a familiar sight in the area for another 10 years.

The LGOC tactics of offering two rates of pay to its Watford crews, one for Routes 143, 145 and 147, and a higher rate for services southwards through Harrow, proved explosive, and after a prolonged strike National was brought in as agent and took over management of the Leavesden Road garage on and from 25 May 1921. Watford was always henceforth in the London country area, the LGOC (and later red Central) buses reaching the town from the south being provided from other garages. From 6 August 1921 National-operated routes were numbered:

N1: Croxley Green-Garston-St Albans (formerly 143)
N2: Bushey-Boxmoor-Berkhamsted (formerly 145)
N3: Bushey-Hemel Hempstead (formerly 147)

Of related interest was the mounting of two additional services via Rickmansworth on 13 August 1921 — the N6 from Watford to Amersham and Chesham (extended to Berkhamsted in May 1922), and N24, a joint service with Thames Valley, to West Hyde and Uxbridge. This last service was too

ambitious for the traffic offering, however, and was withdrawn in December 1922. It was subsequently revived in May 1923, but only as far as West Hyde. N2 was extended to Northchurch in 1923 and the Bassom numbering scheme in the following year established the long-familiar 301: Bushey station-Northchurch, and 302: Bushey station-Hemel Hempstead. As it was outside the Metropolitan Police District, N1 retained its National designation; it was extended to Fleetville in St Albans and in 1927 took over the former N24 journeys to West Hyde. Leavesden Road was vacated in 1925 when Watford High Street garage opened, but this did not affect the route structure then in being.

The 301/2 roads became subject to intense competition and in 1929 a co-ordination scheme was evolved which established a shared timetable, journeys being marked by the name of the operator so that the intending passengers knew what colour and type of bus to expect. Thus National shared the operation with C. Aston of Watford, E. and F. Prentice's Chiltern Bus Service of Tring, the West Herts Motor Services Ltd and the Aylesbury Motorbus Co. The inclusion of this last company in the scheme allowed the extension of Route 301 to Aylesbury and 301/2 settled down to run Watford Heath (every 30min)-Watford High Street (four buses hourly)-Pond Cross Roads (every 10min)-Apsley Mills, and every 20min on from that point to Hemel Hempstead (302) or Aylesbury (Kingsbury Square), though some Aylesbury journeys required a

Above:
ST111 was one of nine vehicles of its class sent to Watford High Street garage in April and May 1930 for the N1 (St Albans-Watford-Rickmansworth-West Hyde). These were standard LGOC buses, recognisable by the rounded cab. This bus passed to LGCS and then to the LPTB; it spent all its life in the Country area and was withdrawn in August 1948. The vehicle behind is also an AEC Regent, new in 1930, but with a Short Brothers body seating 48 passengers. It belonged at this point to the Lewis Omnibus Co Ltd of Watford; when acquired by the LPTB on 1 October 1933 the bus became ST1133. It lasted a little longer than its companion here, being scrapped in 1949.
D. W. K. Jones

change of vehicle at Berkhamsted. With the advent of the LPTB the independent operators were taken over and all buses on the routes became London Transport vehicles; the 1934 lists indicate Route 301 working between Watford Junction and Aylesbury and Route 302 starting at Watford Heath. These routes were fairly level and undemanding roads and were worked for many years by the so-called Bluebird STs based at Hemel Hempstead, Tring and Watford High Street.

The road from Watford to St Albans was also subject to competition, notably from the Lewis Omnibus Co Ltd which worked between Rickmansworth and St Albans Market Place. Another link in the chain that was to form the 321 came with the LGOC's acquisition of Road Motors of Luton on 8 April 1925 — its most lucrative service was that between Luton and St Albans. National worked this as N51 on behalf of General from 1 January 1927, keeping its own extensive services in the Luton area entirely separate. A co-ordination exercise similar to that on the Watford to Boxmoor road was finalised in February 1929 and National ran with Comfy Cars of Harpenden and Express Motor Services of St Albans to provide a 15min service and inter-available tickets. These companies were acquired by the LPTB, Express on 1 January and Comfy Cars on 5 February 1934, though the St Albans to Luton service retained a separate identity (latterly as 321A) until incorporated into the 321 to run between Luton

(Park Square) and West Hyde (Chalfont Lane) on 5 December 1934. The route was further extended to Uxbridge, over the earlier National/Thames Valley road, on 6 October 1943.

Changes to these routes during the rest of the London Transport era were relatively minor, though the length of Route 321 has caused rostering problems that have divided it into two sections; thus in 1947 Route 321 ran from Luton to Maple Cross supported by a new 351 between St Albans and Uxbridge. The number 351 was subsequently abandoned as a route number on this road and by 1962 two overlapping sections — Luton to Maple

Above:
**A view of Watford High Street garage in the mid-1930s.
The heavy equipment about would be in diminishing use as
overhauls and repairs of newer vehicles were transferred to
Chiswick. Green Line coaches were never operated by this
garage; the T type coach with rear door and seats for 27
passengers had probably been brought over from
Leavesden Road where space was always at a premium.
ST1070 was a Bluebird ST delivered new to LGCS in
August 1932 to take over routes in the Banstead area;
when the interchange with LGOC fell through buses of this
class were allocated to Hemel Hempstead and Watford
and spent most of their lives on the 301 and 302 routes;
this vehicle must recently have undertaken a works journey
to Aspley Mills. Third to the right is STL 1019, a front-
entrance STL with Chiswick-built body seating 48
passengers. All three buses look well cared for.**
London Transport

coaches, and lost some of its importance as a trunk
route.

At the beginning of the London Country era, 301
worked from Watford Heath or Little Bushey on to
Aylesbury, while 302 from the same termini was
projected beyond Hemel Hempstead centre to Bennetts End, thus adding a local function to its duties.
RTs which had worked the routes for nearly 25
years were displaced by AEC Merlins and Leyland
Nationals in 1975, a somewhat deadly combination
of vehicles. A major innovation in 1976, starting
15 May, was the diversion of 301 into Hemel itself;
this marked the end of the individuality of 302 which
lost its Bennetts End leg on 8 January 1977. With the
closure of Tring garage there was some reorganisation of the timetable and 302 was extended to work
through to Northchurch, its only differentiation from
301 being its diversion via Durrants Road in Berkhamsted. With the setting up of the Watfordwide
system on 21 March 1979 both services were cut
back to start at Watford town centre and assumed
their current form. There is now an hourly service on
both routes, though on weekdays only, and it ceases
in the evening. What traffic there is outside these
hours is carried by Green Line 708.

The 321 (when London Country became
responsible for it) was running through from Luton
to Uxbridge. It was extended into the new bus station
in Luton on 4 September 1976 and was rescheduled
when Luton garage closed in 1977. The express 803,
latterly timed to work between Maple Cross and
Welwyn Garden City, was withdrawn on 2 Septem-

Cross and Kinsbourne Green to Uxbridge were
worked under the single number 321. By this time it
was over-laid by express Route 803, Uxbridge to
Welwyn Garden City, started 21 March 1956, a
remnant of an abortive Green Line scheme. A more
successful Green Line initiative, the launching of 727
between Luton and Crawley in 1967 meant that 321
was covered over its entire length of route (with the
exception of the historic digression via Bowling Alley
in Harpenden) by the faster, more prestigious

Right:
STL2684 was one of the postwar buses based on the AEC Regent II Provincial chassis with a Weymann body; they were non-standard vehicles and included in the STL class for administrative convenience. They were not very popular with crews, perhaps because of the crash gearboxes, but similar buses served other companies well for many years. They were withdrawn and sold as soon at the RT programme got well under way. *F. G. Reynolds*

ber 1978 after years of unreliability — it is astonishing that it appeared in the timetables for so long; the Green Line service flourished, however, having been supplemented by Route 724 between St Albans and Uxbridge. From 31 March 1979 the 321 was withdrawn from the Uxbridge to Watford section and became a Watford (Vicarage Road) to Luton service; it was supported by a new 327 from Rickmansworth station which worked daily to St Albans with some extensions to Harpenden and Luton. However, from 4 June 1983 Vicarage Road was served by a Watford local route, W10, and with the abandonment of the number 327, 321 became a daily Rickmansworth station to Luton service. The basic weekday interval is half-hourly, with additional journeys at peak times; the Rickmansworth to Garston section is also covered by the Watfordwide service from Maple Cross, W4. These roads are clearly still very busy ones providing a great deal of traffic.

Below:
RT3458 stands in the shower in the recently opened Garston garage in July 1952. This impressive bus was delivered to Watford High Street garage in March of the same year and in the fullness of time passed to London Country Bus Services in 1970. The full destination display is exactly set and an illuminated route number appears under the canopy. Route 351 at this time ran from Uxbridge to St Albans and was the other half of the 321: Rickmansworth to Luton. *London Transport*

Hemel Hempstead to Bishops Stortford

The road from St Albans to the Stone House, Hatfield has been provided with an intensive bus service for many years since National first appeared on a route to Welwyn in 1921. Until the scheme of 6 August in that year identified the route as N5, it was worked under the number 201 in the timetable book. The LGOC had considerable ambitions in Hertfordshire and, with an interest in the National base at Bishops Stortford, planned a route right across the county through Hertford, hitherto undeveloped territory. These plans, inhibited initially by lack of vehicles, were entirely frustrated by the Harvey & Burrows enterprise which began working a joint service with Road Motors of Luton between St Albans and Hertford on 14 July 1921; a fortnight later Harvey & Burrows began a Hertford to Bishops Stortford service on its own account. General then initiated diplomatic pressure sufficient to persuade Harvey & Burrows to withdraw from the St Albans to Hertford road and National took over joint operation with Road Motors on 8 September 1921; on 14 December in the same year, following an agreement that gave Harvey & Burrows free rein on the Waltham Cross road, National began operating the Hertford to Bishops Stortford route. The subsequent withdrawal of Road Motors from the St Albans to Hertford section (doubtless under pressure or persuasion) at the end of September 1922 left National in charge of considerable activity; the route pattern established from 1 October 1922 comprised:

N5: St Albans-Welwyn-Hitchin
N10: St Albans-Hatfield-Cole Green-Hertford
N10A: St Albans-Hatfield-Essendon Mill-Hertford
(this was the former Road Motors route)
N11: Hertford-Ware-The Hadhams-Bishops Stortford

Subsequently N5 lost its Welwyn to Hitchin section to the 303 from New Barnet and in April 1928 assumed a new identity as N5A, terminating at Pear Tree Village in Welwyn Garden City; in August in the same year frequency was shared with the City

service of Flowers & Etches. N10 and N10A were extended beyond Hertford to Rye House in the summers of 1927 and 1928, while some buses on N11 were put through to Wareside as N11A. The most significant projection came in August 1929 when the N10 and N11 routes were joined to provide through running all the way from St Albans to Bishops Stortford. The initial aim of the LGOC was thus achieved.

These services passed to LGCS and then to the LPTB, running under new numbers from 3 October 1934. Route 5A became 350, but only a few weeks later part of the service became 330, the number familiar today. All journeys between St Albans and Bishops Stortford were worked under number 340, whether via Cole Green or Bayford Turn, or via Stanstead Abbots or Wareside later in the journey; 341 comprised the short working between St Albans and Hertford via Bayford Turn. The long through working was apparently found unsatisfactory and from 27 November 1935 Routes 340 and 341 were rationalised to run between St Albans and Hertford only via Cole Green and Bayford Turn respectively; the Hertford to Bishops Stortford services were worked under numbers 350 (via Wareside) and 350A (via Stanstead Abbots and Hunsdon). Apart from the 330 and sundry short workings between St Albans and Hatfield which were double-decked, all these services were single-decker operations; Qs appeared on the 340 and 341, though rather elderly Ts sufficed for the Bishops Stortford service. In 1939 the 341 was allocated double-deck vehicles (STLs)

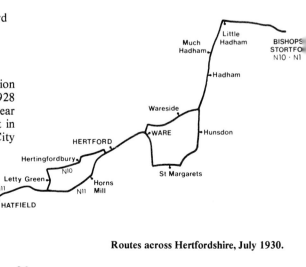

Routes across Hertfordshire, July 1930.

An NS (left) stands in the entrance of the garage in South Street, Bishops Stortford, having arrived from St Albans Market Place, a journey scheduled for 2hr 25min. The bus carries the London General Country Services Ltd title and though equipped with pneumatic tyres is otherwise unmodified from its original form. The Eastern National vehicle alongside is an ADC416A with a 32-seat body constructed by Strachan & Brown, delivered to National in 1927. There was joint use of this depot for some time; LGCS operated services from Stortford to Saffron Walden and to Henham on behalf of Eastern National until 30 June 1933, when the advent of the LPTB put an end to such cooperation. *D. W. K. Jones*

Right:
This B type bus turned out for the N11 appears to be in rather poor condition, its appearance not improved by the removal of the slats from the lower bodywork. The side route boards were a feature of this class, not perpetuated in its successors, and probably derived from tramcar practice. The two drivers are in the uniform white coats, while the second sports the bow tie that many of them adopted. *George Robbins collection*

Right:
The NS waiting at Hemel Hempstead has been considerably altered since it first took the road; now fitted with pneumatic tyres, it also has a roof and a windscreen for the driver. It is, of course, in LGCS livery. N14 was a National venture on behalf of the LGOC; it became 314 and later was subsumed in the 340 as part of a through route to Welwyn Garden City. The vehicle behind is a first series T type Green Line coach. *J. F. Higham*

Route 320, with its companions 330 and 340, was the modern successor to N14 and N5 and ran from Hemel Hempstead to Welwyn Garden City via St Albans and Hatfield. LR7, obviously and splendidly new, is seen in St Peter's Street, St Albans; it is an Olympian with Roe bodywork and entered service in May 1982. *G. B. Wise*

and 340 was abandoned as a through service — a low railway bridge at Cole Green limited the road to single-deck buses.

Subsequent modifications of these services were associated with the development of the new towns at Hatfield and Welwyn Garden City, the increase in population sustaining a high level of service through the 1950s and 1960s. An interesting innovation was the projection of the 330 back to Hemel Hempstead, also a new town of course, on and from 17 October 1956 when the route incorporated 314: Hemel Hempstead to St Albans. Route 314 dated back to May 1922 and began as N14. Another development was the extension of 350/350A beyond Hertford to Potters Bar and New Barnet via Cole Green and Essendon; these journeys were worked by RF vehicles, all other services being allocated RTs.

With the advent of London Country there was eventually considerable modification of these services though the main route structure remains largely unchanged. Routes 330 (now 340) (Hemel Hemp-

stead to Welwyn Garden City), 341 (St Albans to Hertford) and 350/351 (Hertford to Bishops Stortford) are still important services. The 330 sprang variants 320 and 340 depending on line of route taken in Hatfield, and offered a 20min service, all of which works under No 340. The 341 works from Marshalswick and also schedules departures every 20min, one terminating at Hatfield Garage, one at South Hatfield and one running through to Hertford. Some of these through journeys double-run into Essendon, a change introduced on 28 April 1981 following the withdrawal of 350/351 west of Hertford. These latter services, basically every two hours, are operated by Leyland Nationals; the other routes sport Atlanteans or Olympians which run through almost continuous conurbation from Hemel Hempstead to Hatfield and Welwyn Garden City; the Hatfield to Hertford section of 341 is through rather bleak country along dual-carriageway, though there are compensations if the bus is timed to run to Essendon. However, between Ware and Bishops Stortford rural Hertfordshire is still readily identifiable, and Little and Much Hadham, despite recent estate building, retain their village character. A journey from Hemel Hempstead to Stortford offers the traveller interesting contrasts of town development; St Albans, Hertford and Stortford retain in large measure the appearance and quality of the 1920s and 1930s, while in other places there are brash shopping centres that are not easy to distinguish one from another.

Buses from New Barnet

New Barnet station on the main line from King's Cross has been the terminus of London country routes for many years, occupying a role similar to that of Croydon in the south, though its network of routes was never as flourishing or extensive. However, the LGOC was anxious to establish services starting at the station and National began operating N7 'for and on account of General' on 8 September 1921; this route, after entering Barnet High Street, worked along the Great North Road through Potters Bar to Hatfield; after Little Heath buses were timed at Mymms Drive to serve Brookmans Park station, a considerable walk away. A second route, N13, was introduced in 1922; buses worked through Borehamwood, then a very small settlement, to Elstree and Watford. The following year N13 was extended eastwards to Enfield Town on 19 March, reaching Waltham Cross in November 1923. The Bassom numbering scheme designated the Hatfield route (formerly N7) 303 and the N13 became 306, both numbers still carried today. The 306 was eventually worked to Epping Forest, the Volunteer, and for a short time to Epping Town, making a through journey of some 28 miles from Watford; however it subsequently settled down to run between Enfield and Watford. In April 1928 the 303 was extended north from Hatfield to Hitchin over the former N5 road — N5 had started as a St Albans to Hatfield and Welwyn service in 1921, being extended to Hitchin the following year, taking over from a route that National had started themselves between Hitchin and Welwyn in the autumn of 1920. National operations in the area had been greatly facilitated by the opening of the garage in Hatfield in 1922.

Services on these routes were not very frequent, reflecting the somewhat sparse country through which they ran; after the diversion of some journeys on 303 to Potters Bar station in 1929, there were buses every 30min from New Barnet station as far as Potters Bar, then every 2hr (Mondays to Fridays), hourly (Saturdays and Sundays), beyond to Hatfield station and the small towns of Welwyn, Knebworth and Stevenage, the buses turning at Hitchin Market. A through journey in 1930 took exactly 2hr and a feature of the timetable is the lack of any 'layover' time, buses having to take up return journeys immediately. Certainly the 'wheels turning' principle was applied to this road with a vengeance.

By 1934 the 306 was working from Enfield to Watford (Gammons Lane) alongside an exactly similar 312 which ran via Little Bushey rather than Bushey Heath; the next change saw the disappearance of the 312, and the cutting back, on 24 March 1937, of 306 to start from New Barnet station. On 2 February 1937 alternate journeys on 303 were worked via Brookmans Park station and Welham Green as 303A, the main route continuing via Bell Bar. Routes 303, 303A and 306 were worked by Q type buses and were joined at New Barnet station by another Q type operation, the 342 which ran via the 303 to Brookmans Park, then taking its own rather rural way to Essendon, Cole Green and Hertford; this route was subsequently

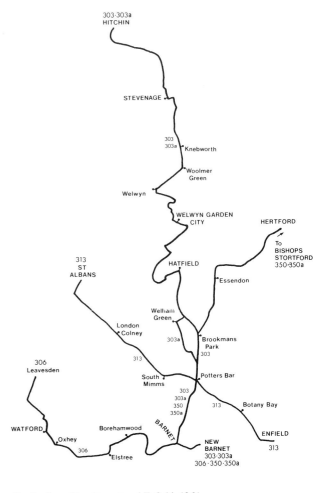

Routes from New Barnet and Enfield, 1961.

89

Above:
This single-deck S type vehicle, S859, was one of a batch allocated to National for work on Route N13 (later 306) from Watford to Enfield, where this bus is standing. Buses of this class had long careers in the Watford and North London services; first in use in 1922, 13 were handed over to LGCS in 1932, though by that time they had pneumatic tyres. The passengers apparently sitting on the roof are, of course, on the top deck of the bus alongside, also an S type. *George Robbins collection*

Below:
The shelter would appear to be new and the official photographer is recording its arrival in Stevenage High Street in August 1934. The crew of NS285, their passengers and the two girls about to board have clearly been alerted and are carefully posed. NS285 looks well in the mid-green livery adopted for Country buses of the LPTB; 'General' is still carried as the fleetname — 'London Transport' came later. Interestingly, the bus still carries the legal address of LGCS — Bell Street, Reigate; it does not however carry garage code or running number plates, though it would have been based at Hatfield. The successors to the NS type on this route were the Qs. *London Transport*

extended to Hertford Heath and Broxbourne. There was a great deal of Green line activity in parallel with the 303/303A, services from London building up to three per hour as far as Lemsford. The withdrawal of these services on 29 September 1942 led to the introduction of another bus service from New Barnet; this was the 340 to Potters Bar (over the 303 road) then via North Mymms, New Hatfield and Longcroft Green to Welwyn Garden City — the buses ran on the Barnet by-pass, a rather faster road than the Great North Road. Another wartime development was the introduction of double-deck vehicles to 303/303A and the 306.

The 303/303A timetable in April 1952 shows hourly departures on each route for Hitchin, St Mary's Square, a half-hourly service on 306 to Watford and an hourly departure for Hertford and Broxbourne on 342; there were also some rather irregular workings on the 340 to Welwyn Garden City. RTs appeared on 306 in November 1948 and on 303/303A in January 1949; the 1962 lists show 10 vehicles allocated to the 303 routes which had become even more important with the development of no fewer than three new towns on line of route — Hatfield, Welwyn Garden City and Stevenage. Higher capacity vehicles, the RMCs were drafted to work the route in 1969. Thus at the end of the London Transport era New Barnet station was busy with two departures hourly to Hitchin (303/303A), two to Watford (306) and an hourly bus for Bishops Stortford on 350/350A which had taken over the Essendon and Hertford road from the 342. However, the advent of London Country and the tightening of London Transport boundaries radically affected the Barnet and Potters Bar area which became a London Transport preserve — unusually, Potters Bar garage is one of only three such LT establishments outside the GLC area. London Country services to New Barnet were first reduced to peak hour workings,

then withdrawn altogether. The 306 was withdrawn between Barnet and Borehamwood (Rippon Way) on 15 May 1976, and on the same day 350 and 351 (successor to 350A) ceased to run south of Essendon, thus cutting a long-standing connection. A few departures survived on 303 and 300 (formerly 303A), but these disappeared on 20 May 1978. New Barnet station thus ceased to have any London Country buses standing on the forecourt after 57 years.

However, some four years later London Country returned to New Barnet having taken over the northern section (or tentacle) of London Transport's Route 84 to St Albans, a route dating from 24 September 1912 when it started from Golders Green; in recent years it has worked from Arnos Grove. Thus green buses, double-deck Leylands, began a half-hourly service on 24 April 1982, in deference to history carrying the old 84 route number; for the rump of the route to Arnos Grove LT had to be content with 84A. With characteristic enterprise London Country is sending some buses through to Whipsnade Zoo during the summer months. So far as the earlier routes are concerned,

300 and 303 continued to work every 30min Mondays to Fridays and hourly on Saturdays, from Potters Bar station — as good an interchange point as any — to Hitchin; there is no Sunday service. However from 2 July 1983 all journeys were routed via Welham Green as service 300 and only a few special 303 journeys via Queen Elizabeth II Hospital in Welwyn remain. The 306 has really severed its connection with the Barnet area; it now starts from Borehamwood, Stirling Corner, working hourly to Watford and Garston. The vast amount of new town and LCC building in this part of Hertfordshire has entirely changed the role of the bus services, though places like Knebworth and Welwyn still offer glimpses of the 1920s which allow the imagination to recall journeys along the Great North Road in open-top Ks and NS buses.

ROUTE 310

The Lea Valley

Much of the bus activity in the county town of Hertford was initiated by the enterprising local firm of Harvey & Burrows whose first service began on 1 January 1921; this linked Hertford and Wormley and the first bus, joined by a second vehicle a fortnight later, was sent via Ware, Hoddesdon and Broxbourne. The motorbus came somewhat late to this part of London country; north of Waltham Cross where the MET trams terminated facilities on the road were minimal until Harvey & Burrows set to work. The LGOC quickly mounted a rival service from Waltham Cross to Ware on 11 May 1921, reaching Hertford itself on 1 August; however this Route 132 was withdrawn on 13 December in the same year. By agreement Harvey & Burrows was left to the Lea Valley road in exchange for the Hertford to Bishops Stortford service which General passed to National to operate. However, in May

1924 all the Harvey & Burrow's licences, vehicles and staff were transferred to National after purchase by the LGOC; included in the deal was the garage behind the Town Hall in Ware, an important asset in developing services in the area.

National numbered the Lea Valley service N25 and buses ran every 20 or 30min throughout the day between Hertford (Fore Street) and Waltham Cross (Queen Eleanor Cross); the journey time was exactly 1hr. In the Bassom renumbering N25 became the familiar 310. Buses turned at Waltham Abbey in 1925 but were put through to Enfield, The George in 1926; the route thus became very similar to its present form. Enfield was an important town in the 1920s and 1930s, being far away enough from London to have an independent existence of its own; even so, the roads northwards were very built up as far as Waltham Cross — the influence of the trams was important here — and only at Cheshunt did urban building give way to acres of glasshouses in the Lea Valley. Further north again, Wormley, Broxbourne and Hoddesdon were all quite separate settlements on the road to Ware. There was a great deal of competition involving the LGOC itself whose buses ran on Sundays as far as Rye House, and Biss Brothers which worked a 69, also on Sundays, from Camberwell Green all the way to Ware and Hertford. Development of the 310 service in 1929 extended Sunday working beyond Hertford to Stapleford, Watton and Stevenage over the road pioneered by Harvey & Burrows in 1921. The following year part of the Sunday service was worked to Puckeridge, Buntingford, Chipping and Royston. The 1930 timetable shows Route 310 as basically a half-hourly service between Enfield and Hertford North station; on Sundays part of the service ran every 2hr through to Stevenage, Trinity Church on a running time of exactly 2hr. The Sunday Royston buses, also every 2hr were numbered 316 and left the line of route at Ware where a connecting bus to Hertford was provided. Pleasant small towns though Stevenage and Royston undoubtedly were at the time, there is some cause to wonder what the Sunday excursionists did when they

Sunday routes from Enfield, July 1930.

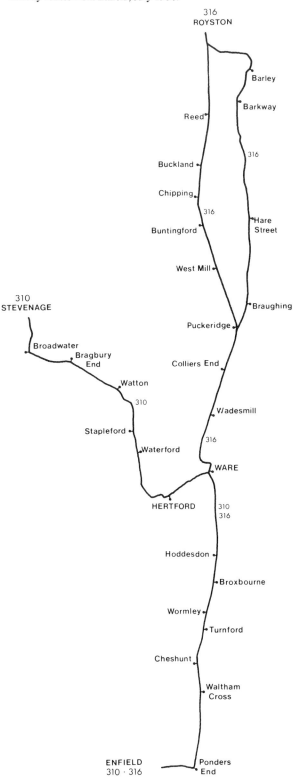

Left:
Hertford High Street in the early 1920s is enlivened by a Harvey & Burrows bus which is plying on the Hertford-Ware-Wormley-Waltham Cross route later taken over by the LGOC and handed over to National for operation in July 1924. The other buses belonged to Road Motors and J. R. Street & Son. There is considerable activity in the street; neither the motorcyclist nor the lady cyclist behind him appear very intent on the road, while a man and woman are being driven in style in a taxi. Route 310 now passes through rather different scenery.
George Robbins collection

Right:

Right:

This bus was an unusual vehicle in National service as it was a Leyland 36hp acquired by the LGOC from the Alberta Omnibus Co Ltd, one of the so-called pirates, in 1926. This was one of seven vehicles taken over and doubtless the LGOC could find no better use for it than in Hertford. N31 at this point ran from Hertford to Buntingford and Royston on weekdays; on Sundays the service was worked through from Enfield as 316. *W. Noel Jackson*

Below:

This vehicle, an ADC416, originally had a coach body, but this was replaced in 1930 and the bus passed to National. Here it is working a Sunday 310 journey from Enfield to Stevenage, a through run taking just 2hr. The open windows suggest a warm day and the bus appears to be full. *W. Noel Jackson*

go there. The weekday services on these roads were N26 (Broxbourne-Hertford Heath-Stevenage) and N31 (Hertford-Buntingford and Royston).

These services passed to LGCS and then to the LPTB whose 1934 renumbering scheme identified Route 310 as the Sundays only service between Enfield (George) and Stevenage (Trinity Church), with 310A as the weekday service from Enfield to Hertford North via Ware, though some early journeys were sent via Hertford Heath. The 310B was the weekday offering on Tuesdays, Thursdays, Fridays and Saturdays from Hertford as far as Aston. The through running to Royston had disappeared by this point and the 331 from Hertford to Buntingford, initially with some journeys to Royston, began its own history. By 1938 the 310 had assumed the identity it still retains and became the trunk service from Enfield to Hertford. It was worked mainly by ST vehicles, though the route had the doubtful distinction of having double-deck Q vehicles among its allocation. A wartime change, from 30 September 1942, sent alternate buses via Bullsmoor Lane and Turkey Street — hitherto the 310 and its predecessors had always worked through Ponders End; by 1949 all buses worked by this route along the Great Cambridge Road. RTs arrived in September and October 1948 to smarten up the service, 18 of them being allocated to 310 and its offshoot 310A: Enfield-Hoddesdon-Rye House. After a lengthy stint these buses were replaced by the first Atlanteans introduced by London Country on 29 April 1972, though the RTs remained in evidence for some time. On and from 29 January 1977 the 310A, renumbered 316, was extended beyond Rye

House to run to Hertford via St Margarets and Great Amwell to reach a common terminal with 310 at Sele Farm Estate; workings to this estate however were much reduced later in the same year. From 11 October 1980 all Sunday journeys were sent through St Margarets as Route 316 on the rather circuitous route adopted and 310 thus became a weekdays only service.

A batch of associated changes introduced on 25 April 1981 produced the current pattern of operation. The 310 is basically a half-hourly service on weekdays between Enfield, (Little Park Gardens) and Hertford bus station, supported as far as Cheshunt (Rose & Crown) by buses on Route 360 which terminate in the Rosedale Estate; these are AN-worked services. Route 316 supplements the 310 between Waltham Cross and Hoddesdon Clock Tower before assuming its own line of route through St Margarets to Hertford; on Sundays, as already indicated, it provides the only bus link and starts at Enfield. Of interest are the routes which terminate at Waltham Cross bus station and run via Hertford Heath to Hertford; these comprise 324/334 through to Welwyn Garden City and the 390 which reaches Stevenage, Lister Hospital. There is thus a multi-destination provision on the 310 road; it is pleasing to note the use of the number 316 — which lapsed in the early 1930s — and the fact that it is again possible to travel all the way to Stevenage without change of vehicle. Another historic connection, that between the Enfield area and Royston, has been restored by Green Line 798, also from 25 April 1981; doubtless the coaches offer a more comfortable, if less exciting, ride than the NS open-toppers that were at work in 1930.

Above:
ST1082, a Bluebird ST, is here allocated to a 310A duty. This bus was new in August 1932 and worked from Hertford for some years. It ended its career at Watford in October 1947 and was scrapped very shortly after; the bodywork of these vehicles tended to sag rather obviously in middle life. The A suffix on the route number denoted a short working from Enfield to Hertford; 310 was kept for the Sunday runs to Stevenage. *D. W. K. Jones*

Below:
The current scene at Hertford bus station is set by Atlantean AN101 and Leyland National SNB211 waiting to begin journeys. The SNB was one of the last of the 'Phase One' Nationals delivered to London Country in 1976, while AN101 has a Metro-Cammell body and was new in 1972. The 316 takes an extraordinarily circuitous route round the estates between St Margarets and Hoddesdon; otherwise it parallels the 310. *J. Rickard*

The Long Haul in Essex

Throughout its existence, and in its various forms, the 339 has marked the eastern boundary of the London country area in Essex. At its most extended, buses on this service worked from Bishops Stortford, into and out of Epping, along to Ongar, then south to Brentwood and on to Great Warley — a total distance of 31 miles through some very rural territory. The line of route, every inch of the way, represented the limits of the interests of the LGOC and its successors; beyond was a rural county properly catered for by Eastern National.

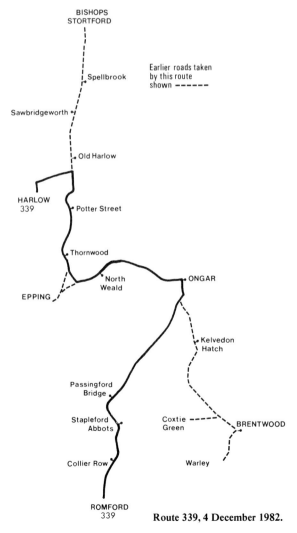

Route 339, 4 December 1982.

National activity in Brentwood began with the opening of a small depot in the yard of the Yorkshire Grey on 8 February 1920 and the mounting of two services: one to the Thatchers' Arms at Great Warley and the second, which became Route 11, to Ongar (The King's Head) via Kelvedon Hatch. LGOC intentions in the Brentwood area were then — and remained — ambivalent; National was persuaded to move out in March 1921 and set up elsewhere, which it did at Dane Street in Bishops Stortford. From here buses worked to Harlow and Epping Town on Route 14; following the formal agreement with the LGOC these were extended to Ongar and then sent on over the former Route 11 to Brentwood, the through service opening on 12 August 1921. This lengthy route, with all the operational problems derived from working from a garage at the extreme northern end, became N9; it was included in the Watford and North London timetable, being worked 'for and on account of General'. The depot at Bishops Stortford, later moved to South Street, was funded jointly by the LGOC and National. In July 1926 Route N9 was extended beyond Brentwood to Great Warley, and the service in this form passed to London General Country Services in 1932; there were four through journeys (taking 2hr 10min) with extra buses at the Great Warley end of the route.

The LPTB numbering scheme designated the N9 as 339 on 5 September 1934 when considerable changes were made in the Epping area following the opening of a garage there and the closure of the base at Bishops Stortford. The route was somewhat diminished in importance by reduction to work mainly between Great Warley and Ongar, only garage journeys running through to Epping with the odd extension northwards to Potter Street. The Epping to Bishops Stortford traffic was provided for by Green Line coaches on route V; similarly coaches on Route W had a bus fare facility between Epping and Ongar. The kind of service that the 339 became can be judged by the allocation to it of three small Bedford buses which worked the main service and its off-shoot, 339A: Great Warley-Brentwood-Coxtie Green, which had come to the LPTB from the City Coach Co Ltd on 21 August 1936. These Bedfords were of course replaced by Leyland Cubs.

The withdrawal of Green Line just before the war had no immediate effect on the 339 operation, as two replacement bus routes ran from Epping over its existing and former roads, the 392 to Ongar and the

396 to Bishops Stortford. However, the 392 time-table was eventually absorbed in the 339 schedule, and with the increase in traffic associated with the RAF station at North Weald double-deck vehicles were allocated to it. At the end of the war Green Line coaches were restored between Epping and Bishops Stortford, though they never reappeared on the Ongar road; the 339 and the 396 met at Epping and the overlapping section between that town and Potter Street was deleted from the 339 route. By 1962 Route 339 required an allocation of five RT buses and Route 396 (and its associated 396A which worked via the new town) a total of 19 — this vast increase due, of course, to the great expansion of urban development in the area, especially around Harlow itself. With the opening of a garage there, and the consequent closure of Epping, from 22 June 1963 the 339 recovered some lost ground and ran from Harlow to Great Warley. This again raised the question of 339A, which had always remained a small bus operation, and the Great Warley to Coxtie Green run had for a time to be worked by a bus sent up from Grays; however, this expedient came to an end when the route was handed over to Eastern National in 1964.

With the reorganisation of Green Line routes on the Epping to Harlow and Bishops Stortford road on 2 April 1977, the bulk of the passengers between these points were accommodated by the coaches. Route 396 disappeared after nearly 38 years, a lengthy stretch for a temporary route, and all the buses from Harlow to Epping came into the 339 timetable. Some rationalisation in the Brentwood area resulted in the section of route between Great Warley, Eagle Way, and the Four Wantz roundabout at Ongar passing to Eastern National which could operate on this road much more conveniently than London Country; it adopted the number 239, a logical choice.

Route 339 thus became a fairly modest service, buses running hourly from Harlow bus station to Epping Underground, then after reversal on to North Weald, Tylers Green and Ongar, terminating at the Two Brewers. However, the long-threatened reduction of services on the Central Line to Ongar was the occasion for a considerable upheaval of bus services in the area. First, London Transport took over the road from Epping to Ongar, working from Loughton station on weekdays, Buckhurst Hill on Sundays, as Route 201 on an hourly frequency. The 339 assumed a new form; this route was diverted away from Epping — after 61 years! — and buses ran direct between Thornwood and North Weald. The route was also extended beyond Ongar to Romford station via Passingford Bridge and Stapleford Abbots over the former London Transport Route 247B which was withdrawn. All these changes dated from 4 December 1982 and 339 operated as an express service, basically every hour from Harlow to Romford. Further revision on 12 May 1984 gave a new route number 501 operating in conjunction with the 500 (ex-Green Line 712). This route, which once had great importance as a boundary marker, has been adapted more than most to changing needs and circumstances.

Left:
A lineal descendant of the 339 was the 397A: Bishops Stortford to Harlow via Templefields Industrial area, though when Bedfords worked the route in the 1930s Templefields were fields in reality as well as in name. RT609 was a comparatively early member of its class, being sent new to Hemel Hempstead in July 1948. It is standing on the parking lot of Harlow garage and the tower in the background is part of the fire station.
Edward Shirras

Below:
Traffic on the 339 at one time demanded the use of the 72-seat RMLs of which Harlow received nine in 1966, though this vehicle was not one of them. It is photographed at Epping station on 1 May 1971. This bus had a somewhat unfortunate record, being incapacitated for three and a half years before being sold to London Transport; it was scrapped for spare parts.
Ian Allan Library

Riverside into Essex

For many years the principal services from Grays have been those to Romford and to Rainham, worked for much of the period under the numbers 370 and 371. Route 370 may be traced back to a National initiative — Service 40 from Grays through South and North Ockendon to Upminster begun on 1 October 1924, through very rural territory. The LGOC took an interest in the service in December 1928 when the route was extended to the New Mill Inn, Romford and worked it jointly with National — the only example of shared operation north of the Thames. LGOC buses carried the number G40, National 40, and an hourly service was provided. It should be noted that Grays was a National, later Eastern National depot, never part of the Watford and North London scheme; even after the formation of Eastern National early in 1929, the National Omnibus & Transport Co remained legally responsible for services in the area until 30 September 1930. The LPTB acquired the route on 1 September 1933 with operation shared between Central and Country buses from Romford (RD) and Grays (GY) garages respectively; the number 370 replaced G40 in the Grays reorganisation — the first of several — on 18 July 1934, and from 12 December in the same year the route was worked entirely by Country buses. Interestingly, Eastern National 40A which exactly paralleled the parent route from Grays (War Memorial) through the Ockendons before branching off to Great Warley and Brentwood was not acquired by the LPTB.

There was also an alternative route from Grays to Romford via Aveley and Rainham, numbered 371 in the 1934 lists, which National had started in 1923; it had a somewhat varied career, being routed away from Purfleet in 1926 when it became part of the Watford and North London scheme and was numbered N36. With the closure of National's small Romford base, the service was run from Grays and therefore ceased to be run for and on account of General on 23 May 1928. On acquisition by the LPTB this Route 36 became 371 (on 18 July 1934). A year later there was a substantial reorganisation in Grays; from 5 June Route 371 and its supporting 375 to Rainham (White Post Corner) were withdrawn altogether between Grays and Rainham and replaced by Green Line Z1 and Z2 with bus fares offered between Dagenham and Purfleet, Stonehouse Corner. The 375 was left as a small-scale local service in Rainham, while the road from that town to Romford passed to Central buses, initially as Route

253. However, a through service over much of this road was maintained as a return journey on Sundays; this was Route 351 and was primarily for visitors to Oldchurch Hospital.

The history of 370 to Romford was uneventful for the next 18 years or so, though the frequency of operation increased and passenger loadings improved with the development of the vast LCC estate at Belhus. The Grays to Rainham service, however, was subject to considerable change when, on 31 August 1939, Green Line services were suspended and were replaced by bus services which ran as far as East Ham; Route 371 ran via Aveley, the 371A along the Purfleet by-pass. Routes Z1 and Z2 were, however, quickly restored, resuming on 1 November, but the withdrawal of 29 September 1942 brought about a resumption of 371 and 371A, this time reversed — ie 371 via Chandler's Corner and 371A via Aveley. A feature of wartime travelling that few will forget is the use of 'producer gas' for the ST buses allocated to this very level route; speeds were by no means distinguished and operation was decidedly unspectacular. The growth of postwar traffic allowed both Green Line coaches and Country buses to run over the same road, and 371 became Grays-West Thurrock-Aveley-Wennington-Rainham.

The reorganisation of services in Grays consequent on the takeover of some Eastern National services there on 30 September 1951 restored through-running in the town after years of division at the War Memorial. From 2 January 1952 Route 370 was extended eastwards via Chadwell St Mary to Tilbury Ferry and 371 worked to Feenan Highway via Little Thurrock — ie by the more direct road. With minor variations of route and times 370 and 371 were busy throughout the RT era and the larger RMCs were drafted to 370 which, with its off-shoot 370A to Purfleet, required an allocation of 12 buses with an extra four on Saturdays. A new facility was the 369 running between Aveley and Ockendon station via Belhus, though the strategic importance of the route only came to be realised later. A significant recasting of services in the Grays area (again!) on 1 September 1979 withdrew 371 in its old form, the replacement route 375 running from Rainham via Aveley and Grays to Stifford Clays, with some peak-hour journeys on 373 from Rainham to Chadwell St Mary. This change probably reflects the diminished traffic deriving from the dock area. Route 370 was, on the other hand, confirmed in

Above left:
Grays garage, March 1935. There is a somewhat mixed collection of vehicles here. From left to right they appear to be a first series T type Green Line coach (though its door appears to have been moved to the front); an AEC Reliance; an elderly NS, judging by its registration number one originally allocated by the LGOC to East Surrey; a Gilford 168OT; another Reliance; (rear view) an ST, probably the newest bus in sight; (rear view) a Leyland Titan; another Green Line T type; an NS; and a Gilford 26-seater. The 10 buses in the photograph appear to be of seven different types. Route 372 (on the NS) was a local route from Grays to Purfleet (Post Office).
London Transport

Left:
ST171 was a Central area bus equipped with the 'producer gas' trailer in August 1942 in an effort to save petrol. Grays was a garage afflicted with these devices which allowed buses to operate with reasonable efficiency on level ground. They were therefore allegedly suitable for the 370 and 371 routes. Other features of wartime include the netted windows, with small apertures, and the white circle on the bottom panel of the rear. Curiously the trailer appears to be without any form of rear light.
Ian Allan Library

Above:
BT2, seen here in Romford, was one of 15 buses in its class based on the Bristol VRT chassis with Eastern Coach Works body seating 74 passengers. After delivery in 1977, these buses were allocated to the 370 and from 9 July in that year worked OMO. These were among the most distinguished double-deckers ever operated by London Country but the small size of the group put the company at the end of the line for spares and the decision was made to sell them. BT2 became, appropriately, part of the Bristol Omnibus Co fleet in 1980. *Michael Dryhurst*

being, running in the late 1970s up to frequencies of every 15min throughout and operated with Bristol VR buses, among the most distinguished double-deck vehicles ever employed by London Country. A significant exchange of services on 1 September 1979 brought the long-standing Eastern National Route 40, latterly 269, into London Country hands; it was given the number 369 and offers five journeys on weekdays between Grays and Brentwood (Robin Hood & Little John), the short workings to Ockendon station being incorporated into the timetable as additional facilities. In a change instituted on 10 July 1982 one journey hourly on 370 was diverted at Feenan Highway to run in a great loop back to Little Thurrock and Grays; these journeys were numbered 371. The timetable thus appears to have a considerable local emphasis, though the Romford to Grays section remains intact. Thus the bus network in the Grays area has, so far as the major services are concerned, retained a large measure of continuity despite numerous cosmetic changes, though this is by no means true of the local routes. This was known as a high-riding area, with well above average passenger loads; even in a decade of diminishing traffic this ridership has been sustained and the level is reflected in the extensive facilities still provided. Throughout the history of bus work in Grays and Tilbury, however, this has always been something of an outpost of London Country operations; even now the local timetable is published by Essex County Council — in very pleasing format, incidentally — and there is no LCBS publication corresponding with all the others in that company's series.

Route Miscellany

Many services running today have had long and continuous histories. The 423, currently West Kingsdown to New Ash Green via Swanley, Leyton Cross, Dartford and Longfield, started on 30 January 1929 as 23, an East Surrey service from Dartford to Stanhill Farm on the Birchwood Road; subsequent extensions were made to Birchwood (The Alma) on 16 April 1930 and to Swanley (Lullingstone Castle) on 8 October in the same year. With the takeover of the Maidstone & District Service 42 on the Longfield road, a route operated with splendid open-top Leylands, a through service from Swanley to Hook Green was mounted, appropriately numbered 423. The Longfield to Hook Green section, never a money-spinner, was passed over to the 489A from Gravesend in the 1950s and later abandoned; at the other end of the route buses on 423 were extended beyond Swanley to Farningham, West Kingsdown and Wrotham, partly to cover for the withdrawn 478 and to supplement Green Line coaches. For a time LCBS divided the service so that most Longfield journeys were sent to and from Belvedere on Route 400, but the route has settled down to its original form with a useful extension into the new housing at New Ash Green. It is a very substantial and busy service linking rural communities and hospitals with Dartford. Another route between Swanley and Dartford, but via Hextable, has been identified by the number 477 since the advent of the LPTB. It was originally part of S7, later 407, from Sidcup station via Old Bexley, Crayford, Dartford, Hextable and Swanley to Crockenhill (Chequers) started by East Surrey for the LGOC on 14 April 1922. For a while the route, extended to St Mary Cray, was taken back to Sidcup station, thus assuming a very curious shape; however, after a period of running to Bromley North the route was cut back to Orpington on 23 May 1928. On 1 July 1933 the two legs from Dartford assumed separate identities and, extended to Gravesend (Denton), worked as 407

from Sidcup and 477 from Orpington. Each route has had its own history ever since. Route 407 became 467 on 6 February 1946 when it became Horton Kirby (Westminster Mills) to Sidcup; the service now offered between the same termini has been 492 since 30 August 1975, though there have been variations of route between Dartford and Bexley. The 477 ceased to run to Gravesend after 3 June 1947 and has worked from various points in Dartford, including the Temple Hill Estate, to Chelsfield via Orpington. It is currently worked by five AN vehicles.

Another survivor with a long history is the 425. This began as an Aldershot & District service from Guildford to Dorking via Chilworth on 2 February 1914, with an extension to Leatherhead the following day. Withdrawn during the war, service was resumed on 11 September 1919, but only as far as the White Horse in Dorking; later the London, Brighton & South Coast Railway station in Dorking, now Dorking North, became the terminus. Some buses on Route 25, as it became, were started from Aldershot. East Surrey and Aldershot & District began joint working on the service as far as Guildford on 29 February 1928, the LGOC providing four K type single-deck buses for the purpose. From 1 August 1933 the Aldershot company ceased to work on this road and the LPTB numbered the route 425. A half-hourly service was offered for many years, reflecting the good day-to-day business, shopping and tourist potential. Two six-wheeled Renown buses worked the route in the 1930s and 1940s alongside Q types; at the height of demand in the 1950s nine RFs were required to work the schedule. LCBS extended the route eastwards to Redhill via a great loop through Brockham Green and Leigh, but the old order was restored on 31 August 1980 when the 425 became basically an hourly service throughout the day from Dorking North to Guildford.

Two very long-established rural routes from Dorking are those to Sutton and to Ranmore Common. The first started as a Dorking to Holmbury St Mary via Westcott, Abinger Hammer and Sutton service, numbered 22, on 4 June 1927, though the line of route was altered to run via Parkhurst and Holmbury St Mary to Sutton (Volunteer) in 1931. The number became 422 in October 1934 and a full-size saloon, which was out-stationed at Holmbury, was allocated. Later an RF spent each night on the forecourt of the Royal Oak in what was a very exceptional arrangement. Extended to Ranmore Common for some years the Sutton route became a 412 activity; currently there are four buses each weekday, with an additional journey on Saturday; in the existing timetable they work east of Dorking to Pebblecombe and Box Hill. The 433 appears in the October 1934 lists as a route between Ranmore (Dog Kennel Green) and Coldharbour. Its origin was

Above:
BN44 is taking the 412 journey across Ranmore Common in April 1976; the bus stop sign has been prostrated in a recent accident. The 'narrow' Bristols are identifiable by the position of the side lights above the headlights; they were not very intensively used in LCBS service. This bus, new in 1974, was withdrawn quite soon in its career and in 1982 was in store in Swanley garage. *John M. Chapman*

an East Surrey service from Dorking North to Coldharbour started as Route 33 on 18 April 1930. Two Cubs, one from Dorking and one from Leatherhead, were later required to work the service, though in due course one Guy Special sufficed. Daily traffic was somewhat thin, but at weekends and holiday times the buses were packed with walkers and trippers. With the years this traffic fell away and the Coldharbour leg had gone by 1969; Ranmore Common was then served by the extension of 412 noted above. Since 1 September 1979 Ranmore has been served by two return journeys on Tuesdays and Fridays only; operation is by the 'spare bus' on 425 and that number is used.

The current 462 service from Leatherhead station to Chertsey is the remnant of a much more substantial operation to Staines and Slough initiated by the LGOC as 162B in 1926. East Surrey for some reason declined to run this route, though eventually it passed to LGCS and was numbered 462 in LPTB days. It remained a through service for some years, requiring five Cubs from Windsor, but increased traffic on the section north of Staines brought double-deck vehicles into use and the designation 460. The 462, reduced to Leatherhead to Staines, was allocated RF vehicles and an hourly service was maintained, though by 1975 this had been somewhat

Above:
RF175 turns away from the Duke's Head in Addlestone when 462 still ran through to Staines. The route has contracted considerably in recent years and currently there are four journeys on Mondays to Fridays between Leatherhead and Chertsey station. This bus, initially a Green Line coach was among those modernised in 1966/7 but was put on to bus work early in its LCBS career; the pale green waist band was changed to an attractive yellow. *Michael Dryhurst*

Above right:
On the very last day of the 336A, 30 March 1972, the second of two Guy Specials kept at Garston for the route was turned out as a duplicate. This was also the last day of scheduled work for the buses (GS33 and GS42) and they were sold in the following June. RT4031 looks on with some complacency, though it did not have very much longer to go either. *Richard L. Dafré*

reduced to a two-hourly working with additional journeys at each end between Leatherhead and Fetcham and between Addlestone and Staines. The MAP surveys highlighted the poor earnings of the 462 which, from 31 August 1980, shrank to four return journeys between Leatherhead and Chertsey on Mondays to Fridays. The 460 on the other hand, running through much more populous country, has continued to flourish and now runs beyond Slough to Hedgerley via Salt Hill; this extension dates from 31 May 1980.

A service which has maintained its form and identity over the whole period of London country operations has been the 362. The number dates from 3 October 1934 and combined two former Amersham & District services; these were 1: High Wycombe to Amersham, Chesham and Ley Hill and 2: Amersham (Crescent) to Chesham (Sportsman), with some journeys to Ley Hill. At first there was a supporting service, 362A, from High Wycombe to Holmer Green, but by 1949 all buses on 362 were sent through Holmer Green; the Q types allocated gave way to RTs which worked the route for 20 years. In 1975 alternate journeys were started from Pond Farm Estate in Chesham before joining the main line of route at the Broadway, from which point a half-hourly service was maintained. Following the introduction of Chilternlink in 1980, the 362 has been sent deep into Alder Valley territory, peak hour

buses working through to Marlow. Another very long-standing service is the 307 from Hemel Hempstead station to Harpenden. This was a railway bus service, initially between Boxmoor station (the old name) and Hemel Hempstead Broadway going back to 9 August 1909; extension to Harpenden via Redbourn came on 18 February 1929 when buses replaced some trains on the branch line (which lost

its passenger service altogether in 1947). The railway buses passed to LGCS on 11 April 1933 and the route took the 307 designation shortly after, offering — in addition to the through service — some works journeys to Apsley Mills. The timetable has remained much the same over 50 years, even to the inclusion of the journeys to Apsley, though the terminus in Harpenden is now Masefield Road. H7 now provides additional facilities from Hemel to Cupid Green before branching off to Woodhall Farm Estate.

In rural Hertfordshire two routes pioneered by Mr Thurgood's People's Motor Services Ltd in the late 1920s are still in being. The first is the route from Hertford to Sacombe, Dane End, Benington, Walkern, Stevenage, Willian, Letchworth and Baldock which was given the number 384 after acquisition by the LPTB in 1933. A full service, apart latterly from Sunday working, has been maintained under the same number for 50 years. Letchworth became the northern terminus, though the route was cut at Stevenage on 25 April 1981, buses between these points running under number 382. The second is the 386 which for many years ran right across the northern part of the county from Hitchin to Bishops Stortford via Stevenage, Buntingford, Braughing, Puckeridge and Standon. The service has never been a daily one, being restricted for many years to Tuesdays, Thursdays, Saturdays and Sundays, though the Sunday journeys have long since disappeared. Two Cubs were earmarked for the service, replaced in due time by the Guy Specials. The through Hitchin to Bishops Stortford journeys were withdrawn when the service was revised to work in two sections on 31 May 1975; buses now work from Hertford to Hitchin on Tuesdays and Saturdays and to Stortford on Thursdays and Saturdays, with a Friday run to Stevenage. Thin though the timetable is, it is pleasing to see it in being, clearly appropriate for the deeply rural country through which the buses run. Leyland Nationals are, of course, the order of the day.

In the 1930s the LPTB was responsible for a number of works services, some of which offered midday return journeys from factories to homes. There was a whole batch of these in Gravesend; four worked from Rosherville to King's Farm Estate (479), Park Avenue, Perry Street (480, later 496A), Echo Square (482) and Huggins College in Northfleet (483); there was also Route 484: Dover Road Schools to the Imperial Paper Mills. There were special journeys to Apsley Mills, including those from Friars Ash (Route 377), Hemel Hempstead (378) and Harpenden (379); Route 324A: Hemel Hempstead to Abbots Langley also worked via the mills. There were two short routes from Rainham Clock Tower, 393A (later 375) to Rainham Ferry and 393B to Manor Way. A theatregoers' bus was

This Albion bus equipped with a sturdy railway workshop body was engaged on the Boxmoor to Harpenden service shortly after formal acquisition by LGCS on 28 April 1933 — note the sticker on the front saloon window. The destination box arrangements are interesting, as are the unused roof boards; clearly the indicator boards at waist level were easier to manage. *J. F. Higham*

offered to patrons of the Playhouse, Welwyn Garden City on Wednesday evenings in the 1930s; this was numbered 323 and had been initiated by E. G. Hewitt's Premier Omnibus Co Ltd. This firm had also run an express service from Watford to Ware Park Sanatorium, as the hospital was then known; London Transport ran this as Route 349, curtailing at Hertford in 1938 and withdrawing altogether on 18 December 1949. Another hospital service was that to Oldchurch Hospital, served by Route 351 (Grays to Romford) on Sundays only; this lasted until 1946. Until 1983 LCBS Route 472 ran every Wednesday and Sunday from Leatherhead to Nethern Hospital in Coulsdon; it appeared to do good business, especially on the shuttle worked from the hospital itself to the main gate and on to Hooley.

London Transport was always reluctant to run services jointly with other operators. Exceptions were Route 448 from Guildford to Ewhurst where the timetable was shared with Tillingbourne Valley until that company took over entirely in 1964, painting a Guy Special in the company's own distinctive colours. The cross-town Routes 326 and 326A in High Wycombe inherited from Amersham & District were interworked with Thames Valley, an arrangement surviving into the Alder Valley and LCBS era. The withdrawal of Green Line from the Amersham to Aylesbury via Wendover Road during the war brought joint working with Eastern National on Route 359; latterly with United Counties, this co-operation ceased in 1964 although through buses were worked from Amersham to Aylesbury until 1972. Despite the penetration of each others territory by Alder Valley and LCBS following implementation of the MAP schemes, most routes are kept discrete. Perhaps mention should be made of the LCBS operation of an evening journey from Crawley to Handcross on Southdown Route 161, and of the operation shared with United Counties of Route 44 from Stevenage to Luton via Codicote.

The record for the shortest route in London country probably goes to 481 from Epsom station to The Wells; a through journey over marginally more than a mile of road took 9min. After a long period of independence, Route 481 disappeared and from 28 October 1978 The Wells has been served by a double-run on 479 which works from Kingston to Bookham. The most personal service was perhaps that offered on Route 336A between Loudwater Village and Rickmansworth, a route taken over from the estate developers in 1950. For many years the bus, initially a Cub, then a Guy Special, was garaged in the old coach house in the grounds of Loudwater House. The driver, who lived nearby, took his bus to Garston once a week for servicing. This highly individual route was withdrawn on 30 March 1972, and with it went the last Guy Special in regular use. The most infrequent service was provided on Route 854 from Guildford to Chichester through some splendid Sussex countryside; inherited from Tillingbourne on 3 September 1980, the timetable offered one return journey on the first Wednesday of every month. Regrettably, it was withdrawn on 1 September 1982 after just 25 journeys, so it will be seen no more even by the sharpest-eyed enthusiast.

3
Components of the Scene

The four components of the bus scene are the passengers for whom the buses are provided, the staff who run the services, the vehicles, and the garages from which they work. All repay study; passengers and staff from a sociological angle and the vehicles from a technical standpoint; the garages have their interest too, though perhaps less to the students of architecture than to the bus historian. The increased availability of private transport in recent years has tended to limit bus passengers to certain identifiable social groups, and to limit their numbers absolutely. There have been changes too in work practices and customs that make the busman who devotes his whole working life to the industry a comparative rarity. The most dramatic changes, however, have been in the technical development of the motorbus; the sturdy open-toppers of the 1920s may be contrasted with the sophisticated machines of today; physical size has increased very considerably, though reliability is probably no greater. After a period when passenger comfort was a major consideration, bus interiors have tended to become more stark. Some early depots were in fact inn yards, by analogy with the stage coaches; however, effective maintenance of motor vehicles quickly demanded more elaborate premises in which to provide it. Few garages are more impressive, as garages, than the LPTB-designed ones of the 1930s; after 50 years they still have a touch of modernity.

The Passengers

Who travelled on the buses? For many years almost everybody, irrespective of sex, class, occupation or age. The motorbus in the 1920s, especially in areas like London country, initiated and sustained a social revolution of great significance. People who lived in rural communities suddenly found they could travel into the towns to work, for shopping and for entertainment. The old isolation of the village ceased the day the bus arrived. Jobs in towns were usually better paid than jobs in the country and incomes through the 1920s and 1930s tended to rise. It must be remembered that despite the economic crises and mass unemployment that were features nationally, London and its hinterland tended to miss the worst effects; the vast areas of Middlesex and Metroland that became urbanised — or suburbanised — in a decade are evidence of continued and sustained wealth. Shopping centres developed in places like Croydon, Kingston and Watford, and all towns of any size included in their amenities the cinema — the Odeons and Gaumonts of the 1930s reflecting the Hollywood dream.

Left:
The passengers entering the upper saloon of the so-called 'Godstone' STLs were in an entirely characteristic Weymann Motor Bodies Ltd decor. These buses, delivered in 1933, were lowbridge vehicles, hence the gangway on the offside and the arrangement of seats in alternate rows of three and four, with five at the back. The design of the seating fabric and the style of the light bulb covers are typical of those in vogue in the 1930s in provincial companies. *Ian Allan Library*

Below left:
A nostalgic view for all prewar lovers of Cadbury's chocolate, Heinz spaghetti and other delights: this is the café leased to a contractor at Sevenoaks bus station in September 1937. There were chairs for eight diners, a modest provision mostly under-used considering the number of passengers then handled by the station. It was London Transport policy to work from bus stations where these were operationally convenient and where appropriate passenger amenities could be provided.
London Transport

The traffic was not all one way, of course. Townspeople took to the buses and headed for the country resorts. The Chilterns and the Surrey Hills, Rye House and Knole Park became venues for large numbers of people who came by bus on Sundays, especially in summer. People travelled in their best clothes for these occasions; leisure wear was almost unknown and photographs of the period show men in suits (and often hats), women in formal dresses on the tops of open buses or queuing for the journey home. Such expeditions, and others to the next town for shopping and 'the pictures' or to Windsor or Virginia Water are part of many memories of family jaunts in the 1930s. Cars were then relatively few, owned by a fortunate minority; even the Austin Seven and the £100 Ford were remote from most people's expectations. This period also began the move from town to country in another way as more affluent townspeople moved out to live in the villages, welcomed for the most part by the villagers except those who disliked change or newcomers. The process began the social revolution in the country which has made many formerly sleepy and moribund villages into more lively, if less rurally-orientated, communities. Some villages had the first new housing for a century during this period, both council and speculative.

Thus the bus became a trusted and valued facility; services during the 1920s and 1930s were frequent and reliable. If the passengers were segregated at all they were sorted out by time of travel. Thus artisans and workmen travelled before 08.00 either on the service buses or on specials — there were several networks of these in the London country area, including Gravesend and Northfleet for the paper

mills and cement works; the largest single demand, noted by the LPTB in 1939, was at Apsley Mills where up to 20 extra vehicles were provided on Routes 301 and 302 in addition to a number of 'works journeys' on other routes. Shop workers, office workers and business people travelled between 08.00 and 09.00, the more leisured — usually women — on shopping forays mid-morning. Schoolchildren, surrendering their scholars' tickets, made up some of the morning clientele, and were the first of the returners from about four o'clock onwards. In the evenings the buses were kept busy with cinema-goers, football fans, those intent on pubs or clubs, and the habitues of greyhound racing, now almost extinct. Saturdays were exceptionally busy days, requiring every available bus on the road — in the 1920s and 1930s before the era of the five-day week, many people worked at least on Saturday mornings; many schools were in session until 12.30. Sundays were also very busy, especially in high summer, and much of the traffic was unpredictable; on sunny days queues tended to form and lengthen while efforts were made to round up vehicles and crews.

The war confirmed the supremacy of the bus. There were other forms of public transport available, of course, though in London country only Dartford was served by the trolleybus. The former tramway system here had succumbed in 1935; those in Gravesend and Luton — the only other examples in the Country area — had been replaced by buses much earlier. In the south, in the 1920s and 1930s, the Southern Railway had mounted a progressive series of service developments that provided towns and villages with fast, regular-interval electric trains; the railway was — and remains — an important competitor for short and median distance travel in Kent and Surrey. In the north the routes from King's Cross, Euston and St Pancras tended to be main line services to such places as Newcastle, Manchester or Sheffield, and suburban provision was relatively limited; this feature preserved the entity of towns like St Albans and Hertford, while Epsom and Redhill became sprawling and vastly expanded. The dependence on the bus between 1939 and 1945 was almost absolute, and in return the bus industry provided an almost exemplary service. Petrol for cars was tightly rationed and the buses had the roads almost to themselves. The same happy situation continued into the postwar period when the numbers of passengers carried in London country — and elsewhere — rose steeply; with a considerable amount of money about and only limited opportunities to spend it, the tendency was to spend it on what is now termed 'optional travel'. However, the travel boom did not last; increasing prosperity through the 1950s and into the 1960s combined with changed social attitudes and habits to put greater and greater emphasis on personal rather than public transport.

While a car was at one time a much-enjoyed luxury, perhaps associated with Rowntree's Motoring chocolate and fast runs to Maidenhead in the 1930s, it became a convenience for those who had to make regular journeys and then almost a necessity; at least in terms of convention those who could obviously afford a car in the 1960s and who did not run one were looked upon as somewhat eccentric. The age of the car was apparent everywhere, in the car parks, in the streets, in the garish filling stations, and in the traffic queues. Towns and cities had to come to terms with the motor vehicle — multi-storey car parks disfigured the skyline, parking meters rose like forests.

Traditional bus traffics fell away; first to go were the Sunday excursionists — people now took their cars into the country or further afield. The coming of TV, especially after 1955, diminished evening traffic progressively; cinema attendances withered, greyhounds ran before fewer spectators. Social changes have occurred, too, which have reduced the pleasure of evening walks or watching football matches. In this dispiriting situation of declining numbers of passengers, the bus industry seemingly assumed that the problems were only temporary and would go away; routes and services continued in being, largely unaltered from more prosperous times, though patently under-patronised and unremunerative. The car was seen as an enemy; transport unions would have liked to restore the viability of the bus by legislation or other pressures reducing the use of private transport; the attitude of management was less clear — public statements reflected a bafflement that people were not using the splendid services provided. Yet fares increased as passengers became fewer and unit costs went up; staff shortages made timetables unreliable as journeys were cancelled without notice; elderly vehicles and some of their newer replacements were mechanically unreliable and breakdowns caused further devastation of the timetable. It is accepted that any under-used system tends to have low staff morale and a vortex of related problems. In many cases people who had every intention of relying on public transport found that their livelihoods depended on their acquiring their own cars.

And who does that leave to travel on the buses in the 1980s? Basically, those who are too young, too old or too poor to run their own means of transport, those who are members of a car-owning family temporarily deprived of the vehicle, and, of course, the transport enthusiasts who exist in considerable numbers and are not always instantly recognisable. Recent surveys, especially those forming parts of the Market Analysis Projects, have clearly identified the present bus-travelling public; in Maidenhead and Slough, on Mondays to Fridays 68%, and on Saturdays 63%, are female — this is true of every age group, even among the five to 13-year-olds, where boys, it would seem, either walk or cycle! Of passengers on Mondays to Fridays 37% are between 14 and 24 — the youthful proportion increases to 43% if the five to 13's are included. About 20% are over 60, only 37% are between 25 and 59. Some 41% of these passengers did not own a car; 54% were in car-owning families but without immediate access to the vehicle; an honourable 5% had a car available but nevertheless travelled by bus. The figures are only marginally different on Saturdays, but on Sundays the passengers are almost equally divided between the two sexes; on Sundays, too, the participation of the under 24 group amounts to 48% of those travelling.

On Mondays to Fridays, in the Maidenhead and Slough area, 34% of journeys made are to and from

Above left:
Some characteristic middle-of-the-day passengers wait at Hitchin for the driver to appear. At the end of the London Transport era Route 304 ran from Hitchin to Whitwell, Wheathampstead and St Albans; this bus is working a local leg to Park Street. RF661 disappeared in the early years of London Country, probably displaced by the Merlins or Swifts. *Edward Shirras*

Above:
These, of course, are not passengers at all. The apparent somnambulists are officials at Aldenham posing with RW1, the first bus designed for rapid-transit in the Country area with front entrance and central exit. It is a Reliance with Willowbrook body, and it entered service from Garston on 26 September 1960 on Routes 322/322A from Watford to Hemel Hempstead. There were two others and the trio did not prove universally popular with drivers or passengers as it was difficult to stop the bus where there was pavement at both entrance and exit, especially on country roads. They tended therefore to get moved from garage to garage and were sold early in their careers. The comparative lack of success of this experiment did not deter those responsible for the Merlins that came later in the decade. *Ian Allan Library*

work; shopping journeys form 18% of the total, education 19%, medical 2%, social 6% and 'other' 21%. On Saturdays shopping journeys predominate at 47%; on Sundays 'social and other' total 87% — large numbers of transport buffs must travel on that day. Figures for Guildford are slightly different; on Mondays to Fridays 26% of all journeys are shopping trips, on Saturdays 55%, perhaps reflecting the quality of shopping facilities available. Bus operation in London country is generally against a background

of relative prosperity which results in there being 0.33 cars per head of population in Surrey and in Buckinghamshire, 0.29 in Berkshire, with a national average of 0.26. The MAP reports spell out the significance for bus traffic of the tendency for families to have a second car. With some slight rounding off of the figures, it is possible to construct a notional passenger load of a bus in London country on, say, a Wednesday morning; if we assume a total of 26 passengers on board — not an unrealistic figure — then there will be two men over 60, three between 25 and 59, three young men between 14 and 24 and one boy of 13 or under; there will also be three women over 60, six between 25 and 59, six young women between 14 and 24 and two girls under 14. Of these 26 passengers, 10 are going shopping, five are on the way to work, three are on trips with a social purpose, one is going to school, one is on the way to the doctor and six are on unspecified missions. Some 14 of the passengers are in car-owning families; one has a car available but has chosen to go by bus.

The figures given in the MAP reports spell out very clearly the strengths and the weaknesses of the current bus marketing position. Clearly, there is a defined group of people — those under 24 and women of all ages — who are currently served by the bus, a group that is likely to retain its size, perhaps grow a little in times of economic gloom. (This is the point to note, perhaps, how inconvenient present bus design and operating methods are for women with shopping bags and pushchairs and small children; the very act of boarding the vehicle and paying the fare to the driver is a complex operation in itself, not without stress.) There is thus a base for the bus operator to build on, though the traveller making a daily journey to and from work is a rare bird and the 'optional' or pleasure passengers are

few; these were the categories that were the foundation of the bus industry's prosperity in the early years. It has been suggested on many occasions that improved facilities, reliable services and acceptable fares will positively generate traffic, winning back to the bus the car-owner who will be pleased to leave his vehicle in the garage. Undoubtedly there are journeys where conditions are so unpleasant, or parking potentially so difficult, that car-owners do take to the bus. However, it is doubtful if the numbers are very significant, except where StevenageBus or C Line have held on to good shares of the market. Public transport is almost by definition bound to be less convenient than personalised transport in terms of availability, flexibility, speed

and comfort. There is also something of a myth that people travel for fun and that they can be won away from their TV sets by cheap fares; most passengers take a very utilitarian view of transport, regarding it as solely a means to get them from home to destination and back again. The enthusiast is different, of course; he travels for the intrinsic delights of the journey; he revels in matching timetables with performance. It may be possible to increase the number of enthusiasts, but they can hardly add up to numbers that would make much difference to company balance sheets.

Above:

This bus has the distinction of being the very first Leyland National in London Country service and is, appropriately, LN1. It was delivered in June 1972 and is of the type with front entrance and central exit doors. It is seen here in yellow and blue livery for Stevenage Superbus work. The mid-morning passengers are typical — except for one man all are women laden with shopping which hinders the search for the 'exact fare' requested. *London Country*

Left:

About the only regular daily travellers on the buses who turn up in large numbers are now those going to school or college, a trend becoming evident when this photograph was taken in 1969. RF638 is seen here at Bookham on a 432 schools journey to Horsley (despite the blinds); similar schools journeys are now very much a feature of the timetables. RF638, new in 1953, did not make the old bones of some of its contemporaries, being out of service after the comparatively short period of 20 years.
Edward Shirras

112

The Staff

The backgrounds of the first drivers and conductors of motorbuses run by East Surrey or the railway companies at Watford and Slough are not known; many LGOC crew members started with horsebuses and graduated to the mechanical variety, as retirement lists in the 1930s will confirm. It is possible that the railway bus drivers had some experience with steam locomotives and found their expertise transferable, but that is only a possibility. Certainly the drivers who started with East Surrey before 1914 needed some technical knowledge — their machines were reasonably reliable, but minor faults put right on the spot kept the vehicles running. They also needed considerable physical strength — swinging the starting handles of early engines on cold mornings was a very heavy duty — and stamina: their hours were long, the driving positions open to the weather. Conductors needed other skills, of course, more social than mechanical.

World War 1 vastly increased the numbers of men available who had experience of motorised vehicles, and in the rapid expansion of services in London country that began in the early 1920s their knowledge and driving skills were invaluable. Those crews recruited by East Surrey and National were of a generation who, having survived the war, settled to a steady existence and remained loyal to their job and to their employers until they retired. They were a very disciplined body of men, the sense of order experienced in the forces being appropriate to a service that depended on time. The smaller operators in the 1920s and 1930s often started with a one driver, one bus system, and were usually more enterprising and adventurous than the employees of the large companies, prepared to risk capital and to seek out new traffic. With the success of their businesses they enlarged their fleets to five, six or seven vehicles — sometimes more — and learned the management skills on the job. On purchase of their firms many proprietors set up business elsewhere — G. Readings of Surrey Hills Motor Services set up Black & White Motorways at Cheltenham, for example; W. P. Allen of Farningham & District expanded his interests at Clacton-on-Sea and in East Kent and Lincolnshire. Others, however, settled for supervisory grades in larger organisations or were promoted even higher in London Transport days.

Those who had jobs in the 1930s tended to stick to them and to be proud of them. A chief inspector who started as an East Surrey conductor recalled 'the real esprit de corps and pride in the job'; an aspect of his early years that remained firmly in his memory was 'the feeling of belonging and real comradeship; and we always helped the less fortunate'. Inspector Jones who retired in 1961 regarded himself as fortunate to get a job with East Surrey as a conductor in 1931; he started at Leatherhead, was sent to Brixton to work Green Line in 1933, to Southall in 1934, to Amersham in 1935, came back to Leatherhead briefly in 1936, then was transferred to Chelsham; on becoming a road inspector in 1937 he moved to London, then in 1939 to Hertford, back to London in 1941 and in 1942 came to Dorking where he spent the rest of his career. Conductor T. W. Hedges who retired in 1962 at the age of 70 saw 41 years' service, all of it at Dunton Green where he worked with three generations of the Webb family — grandfather, father and son — all Jim Webbs and all drivers at Dunton Green. Les Giles who ended 41 years of service as an enquiry office attendant at Slough in 1971 expounded somewhat old-fashioned views: 'Discipline was severe, but fair; it made you feel good because it kept every one up to a good standard. My advice is — hard work, and loyalty to the guv'nor, you won't go wrong'. Driver Frank Chalk who retired at 70 from Garston in 1977 started with Biggerstaffs in 1928; he swore by the older buses — 'they rarely broke down' and regarded the new vehicles as 'rubbish'. Fred Gwalter of Northfleet who left the industry in 1978 after 43 years had family connections going back to the Gravesend trams.

As in World War 1, World War 2 brought women to the bus platforms, but not to the driver's cab. Those who joined the LPTB early in the war were volunteers who chose bus work in preference to a factory, office or shop job. Later, women were

directed by the Ministry of Labour and some of them found the work not to their liking. However, some of these wartime recruits remained in service for many years, usually on the platforms, sometimes in canteens or in offices. When they retired from Northfleet in 1980 when the 480 went OMO, Deanna Durban and Sadie Painter were the longest-serving conductors there, having started in 1940. When Amersham became a totally OMO garage in 1971, the displaced conductors included four women with 30, 28, 27 and 26 years service; there were four men with 25 each. The very last bus operated by London Country with a conductor was a 477 which arrived at Swanley with Gert Sloper on the platform, as she said 'near to tears' after many years of bus work.

During the 1950s problems of staffing became acute in some areas, especially near London Airport and in the northwest; driving skills were easily transferable to what were often better-paid jobs and conductors found semi-skilled work of various kinds, usually on a 'day' basis and no longer on shifts. Some former Central busmen, and some former tram staff, moved out to the new towns, to Hatfield in particular, where they served out their time. Recruiting drives were mounted in Ireland and though some recruits were alleged to have got no further than Liverpool, many stayed and are still in service. A hostel was opened at the Grove in Watford to help solve the problems of accommodation. The buses came to be staffed by a solid nucleus of men and women with 15 or more years service and an ever-changing body of men and women who stayed but briefly. Some garages were described as transit camps for road staff, and dissatisfaction was rife.

'Under the present procedure,' wrote one conductor 'having passed safely through his schooling, served his probationary period, he is then interviewed by the District Superintendent, given a blessing and promptly forgotten. From then on an interview with the guv'nor means trouble. He becomes just another cog in the vast machinery of London Transport. A few months and frustration sets in. He looks for employment where things are not so impersonal.'

The crew of this Dennis 32-seater appear very much in the guise of army personnel, the driver having removed the wire support from inside his cap in World War 1 army fashion. The bus is a Road Motors Ltd vehicle engaged on the Luton to Wheathampstead service which became Route 61 when National took it over on 8 April 1925. From 1927 the service was worked 'for and on account of General' and in 1928 was projected to St Albans as N8B, the forerunner of long-standing London Transport Route 365. *D. W. K. Jones*

Below:
A driver stands in front of his K type single-decker (K1053), new in 1923 and allocated to National for the Watford and North London area. The bus is engaged on Route 313 from St Albans, though it appears to be on a short working from Potters Bar. The 'General' title is in evidence on the radiator head but the driver's uniform is clearly National. One of the hardest aspects of the job was 'swinging' the engine to start, a task he might be about to try. *George Robbins collection*

Above right:
Many conductors spent some 25 years of their working lives looking forward into the lower saloon of the RT. The pleasing proportions are matched by the clean design of the seats and the neatness of the window fittings. Most RTs had a bell-cord running the length of the ceiling on the nearside — this vehicle, exceptionally, has bell-pushes. *Ian Allan Library*

This 'alienation', as organisational analysts would describe it, is in marked contrast to the reference in the same copy of the London Country Magazine to the Swanley Veterans' Club; with a minimum qualifying service of 25 years, there were (in 1957) 13 members at the garage whose time on buses totalled 399 years! Drivers Atkin and Parfitt had reached 36 years, garage staff C. Fitch and W. Baker, 34.

An acute crew shortage in 1959 followed a staff turnover of 13.2%, yet 99% of the scheduled bus and coach mileage actually operated. When the longer-serving busmen — those who had started in the 1920s and 1930s — began coming up for retirement in the 1960s, the position deteriorated. Their place as an identifiable group was taken by the women recruited during the war and the men who joined London Transport immediately after it — both rather smaller sections of the work-force. They and the more transient employees had many problems to face including the decline of the service, their loss of status and the growing confusion of purpose in which they worked. In the traffic conditions of the 1960s it became almost impossible to do a good job; time-keeping and reliability suffered and public reaction to a late-running journey or cancellation was often hostile. Driving was in any case no longer a special skill — it was a widely accomplished technique. Another factor in the 1960s was the increased application of one-man-operation which added to the uncertainties of employment of platform staff.

London Country in 1970 thus inherited staff problems among its legacies from London Transport. The company's drive for OMO has now made the conductor extinct; the displaced men and women, especially the long-serving, have apparently been sympathetically treated, many being redeployed as general hands. While work remained for them at some garages they were ferried daily from their home bases — many conductors on Route 480 were in fact staff from Dunton Green. Some of the older drivers who were temperamentally unsuited to one-man-operation were similarly found other jobs. Recruitment has continued and London Country now has a number of women driver-operators who have quickly — and enthusiastically — found their metier behind the wheel. The mechanics of driving a bus are, of course, much easier now with self-starters and power-assisted braking and steering; for the most part the vehicles, including the Leyland Nationals, are pleasantly light to drive. However, the technical demands of driving are perhaps greater in the traffic conditions that are met day by day, especially in peak hours and the nearer one gets to central London. Certainly the element of frustration must be considerable. The driver-operator has a very demanding job, of which actually taking his or her vehicle from one point to another is only part; he (or she) is money-taker, ticket-issuer, guide, adviser, occasionally disciplinarian and general public relations officer as well. While the busman's job is now more demanding, it is probably more rewarding at least in its exploitation of social skills. The passenger may well admire the speed with which the driver takes 20 or 30 passengers on to his Atlantean, but the pressure is considerable. This is the point, perhaps, to note the incidence of long-term illness recorded in staff magazines over the years and to bear in mind that the busman's job has changed from being physically demanding to being stressful in other ways. London Transport and its successors appear to have been sympathic in drafting those unfit for platform work as general hands, loading reporters or even — as at Harlow — as canteen assistants.

This account has made no mention so far of the engineering staff who tend to work behind the scenes and only occasionally receive notice. In May 1921 Mr Frank Newton appeared to be responsible, single-handed, for the welfare of 12 AEC Y type buses based in the yard of the Railway Hotel at Sevenoaks. He is photographed at work in the open air, cigarette in mouth, apparently mending a radiator. In comparison Northfleet had an engineering staff of 43 in 1978. The establishment at Windsor, following the Market Analysis report, shows the current balance of administrative, engineering, garage and platform staff:

- Traffic Superintendent — 1
- Depot Engineer — 1
- Engineering Foreman — 1
- Deputy Traffic Superintendent — 1
- Inspectors — 7
- One-man operators (Drivers!) — 77
- Clerks/Typists — 8
- Driving Instructors — 2
- Canteen Staff — 7
- Loading Reporter — 1
- Fitters/Mechanics — 16
- Craftsmen — 10
- Advertisement Fixer — 1
- Cleaners/General Hands — 14

Total — 147

This gives a ratio of operating staff to 'indoor' staff of 52:48, ie for every driver on the road there is a member of the support team. In May 1981 Windsor had a 'run-out' of 26 buses and 13 Green Line coaches; the buses comprised 23 Leyland Nationals (SNBs), two double-deck Atlanteans and one RP acting as a ferry bus mainly employed in taking drivers to pick up their duties at Slough. There are, or should be, some vehicles classified as 'engineering spares'. Photographs of garage staff give the impression of splendidly resourceful cheerfulness, even in the face of the Leyland National, and it would be difficult to find higher praise.

House magazines over the years have tended to take on a bland quality that conceals differences in performance between garages. It has been a recognised feature of organisational analysis that some

Left:
The controls and instruments of the Guy Special (GS class) were nothing if not simple; the most complex piece of machinery in sight is the ticket machine. The relatively few drivers who worked on their own in London Transport times graduated from the Leyland Cub to the Guy; they usually chose to do so, perhaps finding the job more satisfying in giving them contact with passengers, something they lacked in the isolation of a normal bus cab. These small buses had well-known clienteles on the rural routes they worked on. *W. H. R. Godwin*

Below left:
A driver's mirror view of a fully-seated Merlin introduced in 1968 and allocated to such routes as the 305 from Uxbridge to High Wycombe. The Metro-Cammell-Weymann body has characteristic London Transport design features and looks a pleasing environment in which to travel. However the vehicles were cold and unreliable and there was a tendency to bounce and rattle unless fully loaded, which of course these large vehicles seldom were. These buses were licensed for 60 passengers, including 15 standing. *London Transport*

Right:
Drivers tend in recent times to be less punctilious about uniform, though the driver of this Leyland National probably has more excuse than most to appear in casual gear as he is taking a Sunday duty on the 318. This 'Leisure bus' was introduced on 25 May 1980 with the financial support of the Lee Valley Leisure Park authority and runs on Sundays and bank holidays in the summer months; the route is from Broxbourne station to Waltham Cross via Claytonhill and Waltham Abbey, with some journeys to Dobbs Weir. The confusion of 'Lee' and 'Lea' is interesting; both forms appear on Ordnance Survey maps. *S. J. Butler*

units function very well, while others — with apparently exactly the same human and material resources — are rather less effective. Statistics are not available to support the fact that some garages have a higher vehicle break-down rate than others; most evidence is impressionistic — why is it, for example, that buses running out of Hemel Hempstead have often looked unwashed and uncared for, while those kept at Reigate are very presentable? From the operating standpoint, why did East Grinstead sustain a very good record of reliability over the years while Harlow achieved a very low reputation in the 1960s with press reports of late-running, non-running or abandoned buses? Supervisory staff undoubtedly characterised certain garages as maintaining high profiles of dependable service; among these the old East Surrey garages were staffed by men and women who went about their jobs with steadiness and cheerfulness. In contrast, Hatfield at one stage achieved a poor record for late-running and slack operation, put down by some inspectors to the fact that many staff there were former Central busmen 'who could never keep time'. Some of the larger garages tended to have less happy staff/management relations than smaller ones; this was especially true of Watford High Street where card-schools in the canteen at one time took precedence over taking out the buses. And why did Amersham bus crews take such a consistently cheerful view of their work while those at Leatherhead were said to be 'most awkward'?

London Country were, in 1982, fully staffed and hopefully this situation will continue. The work available to busmen and women is now much more varied than it was. In addition to operating the bus routes, drivers many be responsible for Green Line coach journeys, either regularly or occasionally — the former more rigid segregation of Green Line crews no longer applies; they may be members of the private hire or excursion panel, and they may undertake National Express work either on service journeys or taking duplicate coaches. The characteristics of bus work in London country have thus changed very considerably over 60 years; distances travelled and hours worked have altered and there is no current equivalent to the demands of Route S9, a lengthy stint just 2min short of 3hr on the road from West Croydon to Uckfield station. In an open vehicle, on a bleak February day with wind and sleet, that must have been a test for passengers and crew alike.

The Vehicles

The first vehicles sent by the LGOC to work in London country were B type buses, some of which had been built before 1914. However, they retained their sturdy and reliable qualities and demonstrated their capabilities while working for East Surrey and National. Some of those allocated to East Surrey were AEC YC type chassis (ex-War Department), with the 40hp Tylor engine, a more powerful unit than was usually fitted; this explains why East Surrey was able to operate up Westerham Hill while the LGOC buses from the Bromley direction turned at the top. In addition to double-deck B type buses, National also ran a few single-deck versions. The postwar development of the bus was rapid, the K type seating 46 passengers appearing in 1919, the S (for 52 passengers) in 1920 and the incomparable NS (or Nulli Secundus) in 1923; each was a technical improvement on its predecessor. East Surrey worked 30 K types, in addition to the 12 it owned, while National ran four single-deckers; the 28 S types allocated to National in 1923 were also single-deck buses. A modification of the S type, known as the PS — or 'Provincial S' — was a more heavily designed vehicle with a Ransome body; East Surrey received 32 of these from the LGOC and operated them alongside 12 the company owned itself; National received 15. When they became available, the LGOC allocated 21 NS buses to East Surrey (which purchased 10 on its own account) and 31 to National. At first the buses provided for East Surrey were painted in that company's dark blue livery, those for National appearing in a light silver grey with darker lower panels; by 1923, however, the red livery akin to that of the LGOC was in use, though buses carried their operators' titles and head office addresses on their sides.

While the double-decker fleets tended to remain static in numbers, there was considerable expansion in single-decker numbers; in 1926 some (single-deck) ADC419s were sent to the two companies for coach work, and these were followed two years later by a much larger number of type 416 single-deck buses. East Surrey operated 11 of these; in addition to 19 the company owned itself there was also a solitary double-deck vehicle on this chassis. National received no fewer than 53 plus two small coaches on virtually the same chassis identified as the 427 type. National also worked 14 AEC Reliances received in 1928, though the LGOC took back nine of these after a short time; East Surrey received five buses of the new T type — the AEC Regals — when they

became available. It will be noted that the LGOC was reasonably generous in providing new or relatively new buses to its London country operators. The decade between 1919 and 1929 was in fact a period of rapid technical development of the motor-bus. Progress might have been even more dramatic if the Public Carriage Office of the Metropolitan Police, which controlled the design and use of buses in London, had not been staffed by such ultra-conservative officials as it was. Even so, larger vehicles followed the allowing of increased weight limits; pneumatic tyres were fitted to single-deck buses from 1925, and in the same year four-wheel brakes became standard; covered tops were fitted to

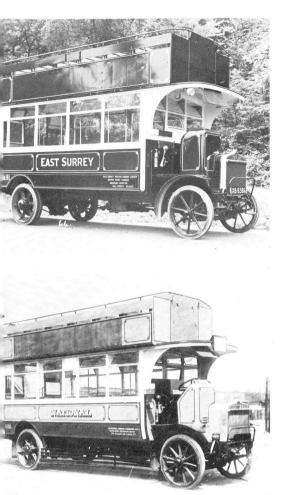

double-deck vehicles in 1926 — the NS was the first; vehicles equipped with the new tyres were allowed to run at speeds up to 20mph in 1928 — the previous limit, 12mph, still applied to most buses, of course. In 1929 the standard width of the bus was increased to 7ft 6in, and in the same year windscreens were permitted in drivers' cabs — an innovation, indeed, that at last brought the driver out of the stagecoach age and into the era of the motor car. All these improvements combined to make the bus crews' job less arduous and the passengers' journeys more comfortable. The culmination of these developments was marked by the appearance of the AEC Regent chassis or ST type double-deck bus — its single-deck running mate was the Regal, or T type. The LGOC sent 19 Regents to National, including six lowbridge buses with dual gangways on the top deck, and rather more — 70 — to East Surrey which also owned 14 on its own account. Each generation of new vehicles, of course, displaced a predecessor, though the new services planned and mounted during this period demanded a progressively larger fleet.

Some indication of the scale of the exercise is given by the number of LGOC-owned vehicles operated by East Surrey in June 1929; these totalled 103 and included:

K type	30 d/d and 4 s/d
PS	32
NS	21
ADC416	1 d/d and 11 s/d
R	1

At this date East Surrey also operated 66 vehicles of its own, most of them of similar types. At the end of the National era in London country in 1932 the company was using the following vehicles on the Watford and North London services:

● S type	13 s/d
● NS	31
● ADC416	55 (all s/d, including 2 427s)
● R	5
● ST	19

Some additional Regents were built for LGCS in 1932; these 23 buses were always known as the Bluebird type from the colour of the seating; an additional feature was the projection of the upper deck right over the driver's cab.

By this date the fleet lists had become very complicated, and were to be made even more complex by the addition of vehicles of companies acquired, by the moving of buses between the Central and Country fleets — more exactly, until the advent of the LPTB, between the LGOC and LGCS garages, and by the acquisition or purchase of large numbers of coaches for express or Green Line work which 'cascaded' down to bus duties as newer types arrived. The vehicle count of the Country Depart-

ment of the LPTB on its first day, 1 July 1933, shows an extremely mixed fleet in operation:

NS	57 (including 36 open-top, 13 unlicensed)
PS	11
S	6 d/d and 13 s/d
T	26
ST	120
LT	2 (this was a six-wheeled chassis, the Renown)
ADC416	86
ADC426	4 (1 unlicensed)
R	6

These were all AEC buses. Other makes were as follows:

Leyland Lion	9
Leyland Titan	41 (including 3 lowbridge and 9 open-top)
Guy	12 (4 unlicensed)
Tilling Stevens	4 (3 s/d and 1 d/d)
Morris	8 (1 unlicensed)
Commer	6
General Motors Co	1
Thornycroft	8 (1 unlicensed)
Daimler	2 (both unlicensed)
AJS	1
Bean	2 (both unlicensed)
Maudslay	3
Dennis	6 (2 unlicensed)
Chevrolet	1 (unlicensed)
W&G	1 (unlicensed)
Albion	4 (1 unlicensed)
Gilford	7

The total is 447, including 29 unlicensed buses. There was also the coach fleet comprising 446 units, of which 266 were Regals or T types; the others were largely acquired vehicles of various makes including Gilfords which were to haunt the engineering department for some years to come. This is the point to note, perhaps, that bus and coach fleets became interworked to some extent — a coach might be turned out for a bus duty and buses were used extensively for Green Line duplication. Some classes of vehicle — notably the T type — included buses and coaches, though the coaches were furnished to a higher standard. Additionally, when they were supplanted by new vehicles coaches drifted downward into the bus fleet. It becomes increasingly difficult to give an account of the vehicles worked in London country without referring to both buses and coaches.

After 1 July 1933 the acquisition of independent companies proceeded apace and the London Transport collection of vehicles became even more numerous and varied. Some of the stock was never operated by the LPTB, though it must have passed the new tests prescribed in the 1930 Road Traffic Act. It was newer than might have been expected, though doubtless the real 'bangers' had been scrapped when vehicle testing began. Much was only two, three or four years old when acquired; some buses, ordered by a company, were delivered new to the LPTB. For example, two Dennis Aces ordered by Gravesend & District Bus Services Ltd went straight into the London Transport lists; new rolling stock was also owned by Enterprize Motor Services of Gravesend and the Grey Motor Coach Service was running a new Morris from Dartford to Ash. There were really three classes of vehicle: small buses seating 12 to 20 passengers, legally entitled to be operated without a conductor; larger vehicles seating up to 30, run as buses (with a conductor) or as coaches and private hire vehicles (without one). The third category, double-deck buses, was relatively small; Lewis operated six Regents, new in 1930, and C. Aston of Watford ran two Leyland Titan TD1 buses with Dodson bodies. Most independents did not really need such large capacity buses; they were expensive compared with the commercial chassis and in any case there was usually nowhere to keep them — double-deck buses required garages with high-pitched roofs. The oldest bus acquired by the LPTB appears to have been a Reo owned, appropriately, by the Reo Omnibus Co (L. W. Didcock) of Chertsey; this was a small bus seating 10 passengers, new in 1924. It would be pleasing to think that the LPTB ran it, if only for a short while, but Mr Didcock had given the vehicle up and it was unlicensed on acquisition. The four Crossleys belonging to Filkins & Ainsworth of Harefield would have even greater claim to fame if, as some authorities believe, they were built as wartime ambulances. The People's Motor Services fleet was outstanding, with one Chevrolet 14-seater dating from 1927, two Laffly 26-seaters (1928), four Gilfords (1929) and 12 Thornycrofts delivered between 1930 and 1932. The owner of the firm, Mr W. Thurgood, had built the coachwork of all of them except one of the Gilfords which was a Duple-bodied coach. In contrast to this, the St Albans & District fleet of 14 buses was of nine different makes: Lancia, Reo, W&G, Guy, Commer, Bean, BAT, Leyland and AEC. Elsewhere Bedford, Chevrolet and Ford were popular — these were archetypal cheap chassis; Dennis and Leyland were also found in good numbers and were generally considered 'up-market'.

Among the buses taken over from the larger operators, the 34 Leyland Titans taken from the Maidstone & District fleet were outstanding; these buses, some originally Short Brothers open-toppers, had seats for 48 or 50 passengers and were new between 1928 and 1931. All were in use by the LPTB until 1936, though all had gone by 1939. These were numbered between TD133 and TD166 and were joined in 1935 by another four from the Redcar fleet (TD192-TD195). Thames Valley con-

Above:

The bus is a Gilford 166SD, formerly 26-seater coach with Duple body owned by the Skylark Motor Coach Co Ltd, new in 1928 and acquired by Green Line Coaches on 6 February 1932. In Skylark service it ran between Hertford and Guildford or from High Wycombe to Oxford Circus and for a period, Dorking. It became GF2, worked mainly in the Slough and Windsor areas, and was withdrawn in 1937. This stop is the George at Farnham Royal. The bus appears to be working only with the driver, in which case six seats would have been removed to allow legal operation without a conductor. *London Transport*

Left:

ST157, an AEC Regent with lowbridge body built by Short Brothers, pulls up by the newly erected shelter in Rickmansworth Road, Little Chalfont, in September 1934. This vehicle was one of a batch supplied by the LGOC to National in May 1930, starting its life on N6: Watford to Berkhamsted, which later became 336 — the spelling on the destination blind is wrong. It was one of the last of its class to be withdrawn, surviving until October 1952. It is to be hoped that the young ladies safely reached their destination after such earnest enquiry. *London Transport*

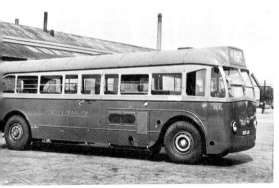

Left:

The handsome lines of the Q are seen in this photograph; the Birmingham Railway Carriage & Wagon Co's bodywork is recognisable by the distinct rearward slope of the roof. The fitting of direct injection oil engines to these buses cured early tendencies for them to overheat, but the single rear wheels were sometimes responsible for a slide on slippery roads, a fault never eradicated. Arthur Henry Hawkins was much taken by this type of bus; this particular vehicle, delivered in July 1935, started at Watford High Street (WA) and was at work until August 1953. *Ian Allan Library*

Left:

A Leyland Cub, C54, moves smartly away from The Ship at Weybridge on its journey from Walton-on-Thames to the Waterman's Arms at Hersham in 1937. The Short Brothers body is both elegant and functional. This bus was one of several sold at the end of the war to the Belgian Economic Mission in September 1945. Others soldiered on until 1953 when they were replaced by the GS class. *London Transport*

Above:
Windsor in August 1949 shows the garage dominated by STL buses with front entrance bodies specially designed for the Country Bus Department. There is also a 10T10 and an earlier T model, both initially on Green Line work but now working as buses. The restricted blind displays, a relic of wartime economy, are evident. Such a scene would have been familiar since the late 1930s; however, hidden away in the line are two RT buses, seventh from the left and in the far corner. They were delivered to the garage in the previous year and were the forerunners of those that would replace the entire STL class. *London Transport*

Left:
STL2461, among the last of its class built just before the war, was originally a Central (red) bus but found its way into the Country fleet; its appearance is quite different to that of the front-entrance vehicles that were the standard STLs working in the Country area. It is seen here towards the end of its life, set up for a Green Line duplicate on 725. All buses of this type were withdrawn from passenger service in the Country area by 31 August 1954, though some were kept on the road for training purposes. They were replaced, of course, by the RTs which rapidly became ubiquitous. *Lens of Sutton*

Left:
RT1027 waits in the parking lot at Priory Road, Dartford; new in November 1948 it looks well after 15 years. Alongside, the bulky vehicle is a Ford Thames Trader bus specially built for service through Dartford Tunnel; as the carriageway was single, cyclists were regarded as a potential hazard (except at night) and were compulsorily transported in the upper deck of the bus; the bicycles were put into racks on the lower deck space. Within two years these buses — there were five of them — were withdrawn, having seen very little service as cyclists bound for Purfleet and beyond were very few and far between.
Michael Dryhurst

tributed two more (TD168 and TD169) and some others were transferred to the Country Bus Department from the Central fleet; these included two Dodson-bodied vehicles from the United Omnibus Co with seats for 56 passengers, and another from the Enterprise Transport Co Ltd. The Amersham & District stock totalling 43 buses handed over to the LPTB on 24 November 1933 was wholly single-decked with the exception of two lowbridge Regents with Short bodies. Most were of Dennis manufacture but Chevrolet and Gilford were also represented.

There was some shuffling about of the vehicles operated by the Country Bus Department which also inherited some Dennis double-deck buses, quite hideous in appearance, formerly owned by the Paterson Omnibus Co Ltd of Ilford; drafted to Windsor, which always seemed to be afflicted with venerable buses, these vehicles though new in 1929 and 1930 looked extraordinarily antiquated and were notoriously unreliable. Another double-deck bus that did not endear itself to operating staff was the Maudslay. There was some interchange, too, among vehicles acquired from express operations; the 220 Gilfords, for example, were sorted at least twice and allocated to duty — or the scrapyard — according to their capabilities. The policy of the new Board was to sort the acquired vehicles according to makes, discard those regarded as unsuitable, and move towards a standardised fleet. Initially, at least, there was a considerable surplus of rolling stock as rationalisation schemes took effect and the sight of numerous vehicles of various hues milling around town centres became a memory. The withdrawal lists of 1933 and 1934 confirm this, though many of the buses disposed of by the Board ran for many years in the service of other operators who were said to have secured bargains. At this point the most prestigious vehicle in the Country fleet was the LGOC-inspired Regent, the ST; its counterpart, the Regal, operated most of the Green Line schedules. The first bus of characteristic LPTB design, though also of LGOC origins, was the STL, a front-entrance version exclusive to the Country Department appearing in 1935. These buses were STL959-STL1043 and STL1056-STL1059 with Chiswick-built bodies; another 50, STL1464-STL1513 were given Weymann metal-

framed bodies, making the total 139. These buses, as delivered, were given large luggage spaces over the rear wheel arches; these were seldom used and eventually were replaced in some vehicles by additional seats. The gap in the numbering was filled by the 'Godstone' STLs, a distinctive lowbridge design by Weymann — these buses worked the 410 route for most of their lives. At weekends many Central area red STs and STLs with rear entrances — really a superior design to the draughty front-entrance vehicles — appeared on Country area routes during the 1930s and during the war some STLs were permanently allocated to the Country garages; 49 were thus in green livery in 1947.

Single-deck working was standardised on the AEC Q type vehicle, an ingenious design with the engine positioned on the offside of the bus behind the driver. As designed there were seats for 37 passengers who entered and left by a central door; the bodywork was by the Birmingham Railway Carriage & Wagon Co. The Country Department had 102 of these buses allocated to it and on occasion some front-entrance versions of the same type were loaned from the Central fleet. There were also five double-deck versions, but they spent much of their lives languishing in store. Services that could be operated successfully by small one-man-operated buses were allocated the Leyland Cub, a pleasing design for 20 passengers; the gear lever and handbrake were positioned to the right of the driver so that he could handle ticket issue without impediment. These numbered C1-C76, of which C1 had a Chiswick-built body, C2-C75 were given Short Brothers bodies and C76 was acquired from St Albans & District. There were also new designs of coachwork for the Regal chassis: the 9T9 (T403-T452) and the most distinguished 10T10 (T453-T718); these were designated Green Line coaches though, along with the 6Q6 and the striking TF types, they cascaded down to bus use over the years. By June 1938, after five

Above:

West Croydon has for many years been a busy focal point for bus routes from the Central area and from the country. RML2348 is one of the 100 Routemasters allocated to the Country area in 1965/6; these were designed to seat 72 passengers and were normally employed on the most demanding services. After three years at Godstone, this bus moved to Windsor where it remained until sold to London Transport in 1980. It has since reappeared in red livery. *Edward Shirras*

Right:

RF200 prepares for departure at Rickmansworth. Though somewhat battered and unkempt, it had seen its best days in Green Line service, being among those modernised in 1966/7. The waistband is now yellow (under the mud) and the other identifying feature of the rejuvenated vehicles was the pair of double headlights. This bus lasted until 1977 and was scrapped after a life of 26 years. The 309 goes back to Filkins & Ainsworth which handed the route over to the LPTB on 31 October 1933. *Edward Shirras*

Below:

SMW4 is an example of the AEC Swift with Marshall body seating 53 passengers; this bus was delivered to South Wales Transport in 1969 but transferred to LCBS in 1971. WIth its 11 companions it spent most of its life at St Albans, having replaced the MBS class. It did not lead a full life and was sold in 1978. *Edward Shirras*

years strenuous — and costly — activity, the Country area fleet showed considerable advance in technical terms and with regard to passenger amenity and comfort. Almost all the vehicles acquired by the LPTB and its predecessors had been sold; only a few remained to delight the enthusiast. Thus there was only a handful of double-deck Leylands still in operation — eight at Windsor, eight at Grays and five at Northfleet. There were only three single-deck Leyland Tigers or Titans left on the road, also at Windsor which always operated with the antiquities of the fleet. Eight Bedford 20-seat buses were still active, Dunton Green and Epping running out four each. There was also one Dennis Mace, formerly with the Penn Bus Co, which was working at Hertford. The veteran ST1139 — the first Regent delivered and the last numbered — was allocated to East Grinstead. Conversely, Northfleet was operating 24 front-entrance STLs, four Qs and seven Cubs; Chelsham was similarly equipped with new type vehicles. The London Transport Country Department fleet in 1939 thus presented a very modern appearance, with the possible exception of the ST type buses which began to look progressively aged both in external line and in internal decor.

During the war the Country Bus Department fleet

was enhanced by the addition of numbers of Central area STLs. The STs, being petrol-engined, tended to be out of favour, though many were converted to run on 'producer gas' derived from a coke-burning plant towed behind the vehicle. Hemel Hempstead, Addlestone and Grays suffered from these operations. In 1945 the Country vehicles were in reasonable shape, though some replacements were necessary; three non-standard types of vehicle were introduced — a version of the STL (numbers 2682-2701) which, with crash gearbox, was never very popular with staff, and a batch of 30 single-deck buses (T769-T798) with a Mann Egerton body that might have been designed in 1930. The lowbridge buses were in urgent need of replacement and 20 vehicles based on the AEC Regent Mark III chassis with Weymann bodies were delivered in 1950; these pleasing vehicles were known as the RLH class and another 32 were supplied in 1952. During the war the Country garages were never allocated (except temporarily) any of the Bristol, Guy or Daimler utility buses that were operated in Central London and elsewhere. In the immediate postwar period, however, some new Bristol buses worked on some routes — mainly 336 and 410 — before being drafted to their rightful owners.

The postwar plans of the LPTB and its successor, the London Transport Executive, were centred on three standard types of bus. The first was the RT — a prewar design, appropriately modernised. The first of these in the Country area were delivered to Tring and Hemel Hempstead in July 1948 to replace the now creaking Bluebird STs; by April 1949 227 had arrived in the Country garages, allowing all the STs to be discarded. Between February and October 1950 another 197 were licensed, thus facilitating the withdrawal of the front-entrance STLs (among others). Further deliveries were made, though in smaller numbers, until the last new vehicle arrived at Hertford in March 1958; many had been held in store for several years. These splendid buses were to grace London country for the next two decades, some of them in unhappily unkempt state surviving well into the 1970s. The second standard type was the RF which in the fullness of time became another distinguished veteran. This underfloor-engined Regal Mk IV chassis was designed for bus and coach work, with slightly different interior designs; 187 were allocated to Country bus work initially in 1953, though the number was subsequently increased when some Green Line routes were double-decked. The third new vehicle was required to replace the Leyland Cubs, now nearing 20 years old; this was the Guy Special, an interesting and well-designed bus for 26 passengers, with bodywork by Eastern Coach Works. Eighty-four of these were delivered and proved very well-liked, though policy changes in the 1960s by which small buses were replaced by RFs or the routes withdrawn limited their lives. Thus from

1953 until the arrival of the lengthened Routemasters (the RMLs) in 1965, the observer in London country would be most unlikely to see any buses other than the three types described — the RT, the RF and the neat GS, all in shades of green.

The Routemaster arrived in London country as the RMC class for Green Line work in 1962, followed three years later by a batch of longer vehicles, the RCLs — also for coach work. In time,

of course, these vehicles were allocated to bus duty and proved a sturdy resource; of more immediate benefit to the bus side was the delivery of 100 long Routemasters, RML2306-RML2355 and RML2411-RML2460, in 1965. The arrival of these buses marked the end of a very long period when the AEC had supplied sturdy machines for LT road services; though the company remained in being, it was never again to repeat the successful designs of former years. In particular the Merlins of various classes proved mechanically unreliable, difficult to drive and unattractive to passengers. The first of these, known as the MB class, were delivered to Country garages in 1967 and fitted with full seating and designed for normal OMO; their great disadvantage lay in their length — 36ft of bus caused problems of manoeuvre in congested town streets and narrow country roads alike. The next group, also 36ft in length, appeared in November 1968 and was fitted with front entrances, central exits, autofare ticket machines and 32 seats; 34 standing passengers were provided for. These buses, coded MBS, achieved instant unpopularity with staff and passengers alike — they were really a by-product of the London Bus Reshaping Plan and designed for Central area work, where in fact they were no more successful. However, the programme had by now gained momentum and was difficult to stop; the shorter version, 33ft long, the Swift, was known as the SM and, with 38 seats, moved a little nearer to the requirements of a country bus and a little further away from the mass-transit concept.

Thus LCBS inherited a fleet that was basically

Above:
RP69 stands alongside AN4 immediately prior to entering service. RP indicates an AEC Reliance with Park Royal bodywork; this class was delivered between November 1971 and April 1972 for Green Line work and had a broad light-green band along the sides. The most unfortunate feature of these coaches was the seating which was visually restrictive and physically uncomfortable. The Atlantean, among the earliest in London Country service, was also a Park Royal vehicle — note the close similarity in frontal style. The blinds of the Atlantean are, of course, wrongly set, in fact this vehicle was first put to work on the 310 from Hertford garage. *Ian Allan Library*

Top right:
The most recently arrived double-deck buses in London Country service are the Leyland Olympians with Roe bodywork — very distinguished vehicles indeed. LR15 started work on the recently acquired 84 in May 1982; it brings yet another frontal design to the double-deck fleet. *G. B. Wise*

Above right:
BL7, an example of the 8ft wide Bristol LHS class, came into service in 1973. The LHSs were intended to replace the RF class which, in turn, had replaced the GS class on routes that were rural in character or hazardous for large vehicles. By tight fitting of seats (and extreme thinness of cushions) 35 passengers could be stuffed into these buses. They were not very attractive nor capacious enough for peak journeys and many have recently been withdrawn from service; by November 1982 only seven of these buses were allocated for duty (five at Amersham and two at St Albans), and BL7 was not one of them. *Edward Shirras*

renowned for being intensely cold and became known to drivers as Siberian Morgues. London Country, intent on moving towards OMO throughout the fleet, needed new vehicles in any case and this need was intensified by the poor public image of the AEC Merlins. The only readily available single-deck bus was the much heralded Leyland National, and successive deliveries of these have been made, starting with some standard two-door buses classified LN in June 1972. Subsequently there have been another 47 of the LNB version (ie with only one door) and large batches of the SNB, shorter, more manoeuvrable versions for bus work. Fortunately 87 SNC type vehicles, with better, more comfortable seating and improved decor (originally for Green Line) have now been drafted to bus work; certainly the standard Nationals are somewhat unlovely vehicles with a very primitive concept of passenger comfort. They are also very noisy, emitting an unmistakable clatter when on the road. There have, of course, been modifications over the years and some technical improvements have been made, though the interiors remain stark and unattractive. The single-decker fleet is completed by some vehicles less distinguished than the Nationals in appearance and amenity although widely used by NBC companies. These were the ECW-bodied Bristol LHs, the BL class (8ft wide) and the BN class (7ft 6in); though 67 of these were supplied to the company they have been progressively disposed of to other operators after relatively short working lives. Additionally, of course, there are the down-graded coaches of the RP and other types.

The double-deck buses present a rather better appearance and are mainly Leyland Atlanteans with coachwork by Park Royal, Metro-Cammell-Weymann and Roe. There were (in 1983) 291 of these vehicles in use and they are being supplemented by the distinguished Leyland Olympians (LR class) first deployed on the former London Transport Route 84 to St Albans. London Country bus services in May 1983 required the following run-out of vehicles:

	Mondays to Fridays	Saturdays	Sundays
Double-deck	279	233	37
Single-deck	387	334	106

The 279 double-deckers comprised Leyland Atlanteans (AN class) and Olympians; the single-deck numbers included 26 LNB ('long Nationals'), 337 SNB/SNC buses and just six BNs. There are, of course, additional vehicles available, usually 'engineering spares'. It is pleasing that London Country maintains, and occasionally runs, two buses from the historic past; these are RF202 and RMC4. They are cared for at Northfleet and Dorking respectively, and are much prized.

unsatisfactory at both ends of the scale. On 1 January 1970, the company had available 488 RTs (dating from 1948), 363 RFs (dating from 1951) and 17 RLH buses (dating from 1950/2) together with the more recent, but by no means new, Routemasters of bus and coach classifications. The recently-delivered buses were perhaps even more unsatisfactory because they were unsuitable for country bus work in the first place and tended to have low levels of passenger and driver comfort. These included 33 MBs (new in 1967/8) and 76 MBSs (new 1968), with 138 vehicles of the similar (but shorter) SM class ordered in the last days of the LTB for delivery to LCBS in 1970; these buses were

Garages

East Surrey began operations in Reigate from the premises of Tamplin & Makowski in May 1911, moving to a larger establishment in Bell Street capable of housing six buses in September 1912. Englarged to take 12 vehicles in 1914, and again in 1920 to take 36, much of the site was in Lesbourne Road which later became the registered address of London Country Bus Services Ltd when the new administrative block was opened in 1972. After the signing of the agreements with East Surrey and National, the LGOC provided these companies with bases; East Surrey worked from Dunton Green (opened April 1922 for 12 buses), Chelsham (20 January 1925, 8), Godstone (20 January 1925, 16) and Leatherhead (also January 1925, 24). Swanley, with space for 16 buses, was opened in October in the same year. National operations in the Watford and North London area were initially conducted from Watford, Leavesden Road, opened by the LGOC on 25 August 1920 and handed over to National in the following year; the base at South Street, Bishops Stortford served both National's own routes and those run on account of General. The Hatfield garage opened in premises on the south side of St Albans Road in 1922 and a much larger base was provided at High Street, Watford in 1925; this became the administrative headquarters of the Watford and North London area and the Leavesden Road garage was closed. (The LGOC reopened it in 1929 to service the new Green Line route to Golders Green.) National also worked from 1923 to 1928 from the yard of the White Hart Hotel in Romford, and from the former Wayman garage in High Bridge Street, Waltham Abbey from 1926. National, of course, was active in a number of towns on the edge of the London country agreed area, but kept its own operations entirely discrete; Castle Street depot in Luton was, however, shared as was Bishops Stortford. East Surrey opened premises of its own in Garland Road, East Grinstead in 1925 and in High Street, Crawley in 1929; both were later extended. The Thames Valley activities in the Uxbridge area were based on the LGOC-owned garage there which Thames Valley occupied from 1922 until 31 December 1928, on which date it reverted to the LGOC.

Several garages were acquired by the LGOC for use by its associates and these included the former Harvey & Burrows garage behind the Town Hall in Ware (1924) and the Road Motors base in Langley Road, Luton (1925), though this was used but briefly. Rather later Mr Fox's Woking & District

garage in St John's Road, Woking was acquired on 14 January 1931, though East Surrey moved out into the former Aldershot & District garage in Walton Road on 31 May in the same year. To facilitate operations between Erith and Dartford, the LGOC passed the small garage in London Road, Crayford to East Surrey on 1 April 1931 — this dated back to 1917 and originally housed buses provided for munitions workers. Similarly, the garage in Langley Road, Slough, opened in 1926 for the LGOC local services in Windsor and the 162B to Leatherhead, was handed over to LGCS in 1933; when acquired the Great Western Railway buses were stabled at Alpha Street, Slough.

Meanwhile, in addition to reopening Leavesden Road, Watford, several bases were set up to develop the Green Line network; these were in Guildford, Staines and Hitchin in 1930, Dorking and Addlestone in the following year. Some of these were in temporary premises or on commercial sites and permanent buildings were provided subsequently. Thus operations started from Rice and Harper's on the

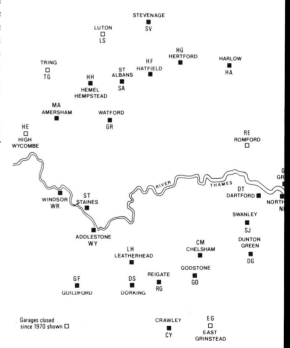

London Country Bus Services Ltd garages, 31 March 1983.

128

Top:
Hatfield garage, November 1922, not long after opening. The two single-deck buses are B types, with seats for 26 passengers in the greenhouse-like saloon; LH8478 carries the route stencil for N10 which at this time ran from St Albans to Hertford via Cole Green. The double-decker to the right is also a B; its Metropolitan Police number plate indicates that it is licensed to operate within the Metropolitan Police District, so it is probably engaged on N7 to New Barnet. All these buses had extensive slats between the wheels designed to prevent people or animals being caught under the vehicle. The bill for the Grand Palace at St Albans is of interest; Lilian Gish appears to be starring in *True Heart Susie*. *London Transport*

Above:
An impressive array of vehicles stands outside Leatherhead garage one day in October 1930. From left to right these are a single-deck K type bus, K1086, loaned by the LGOC, with seats for 24 passengers; an AEC Regal 30-seater bus with Hall Lewis bodywork, prepared for a Green Line journey; then an AEC Regent with Ransomes body, recognisable by the square cab, new in April 1930; a PS on Route 406 (Redhill to Kingston), on loan; an S type bus also on Route 406, and finally another Regent of the ST class. The East Surrey livery with generous lining is evident, as is the characteristic mounting of side-lights at roof level of single-deckers and on the canopy of double-deck vehicles. All the buses are very well-turned out. *London Transport*

London Road in Guildford and from the Weymann works in Addlestone; these Green Line garages were soon involved in bus work and ceased to be exclusively concerned with coaches. In the 1933 take-overs the LGCS acquired the Chiltern Bus Service garage in Tring on 10 May and the LPTB took possession of another seven garages; these were Dartford and the Old Dover Road base in Northfleet (the former tram sheds) from Maidstone & District on 1 July, Amersham and High Wycombe from Amersham & District (1 October, though buses carried the Amersham & District fleetname until 24 November), Harefield from Filkins & Ainsworth on 1 November, the premises of St Albans & District at the Drill Hall, Hatfield Road on 10 November, and the People's Motor Services Ltd base at Park Road, Ware on 30 November. A second garage in St Albans in Wynchlands Crescent was acquired from Flowers and Etches (City Omnibus Services) on 29 March 1934. The purchase of garages with express, later Green Line, commitments allowed some changes in the allocation of buses; thus the acquisition of the Acme base in South Street, Bishops Stortford allowed the use of the Eastern National garage nearby to lapse, and similarly London Transport bus activity in Luton was concentrated on the Park Street West premises of Strawhatter and the use of Castle Street was given up. Temporary premises were used by the Board at Bury Road, Hemel Hempstead and in the Old Brewery at Grays until the building programme got under way. One garage had been opened under the auspices of LGCS — this was at St Leonards Road, Windsor on 1 March 1933; subsequent extension of this in 1936 led to the closure of the garage at Langley Road, Slough, and of the former Premier garage on the Bath Road, though this was primarily concerned with coach work.

The operational problems of the LPTB in the early days derived in some measure from the scatter of small garages over the whole of the northern part of London country. A number of new premises was planned and opened in 1934 and 1935; these included new buildings at Addlestone, Amersham, Hemel Hempstead, St Albans, Hertford and Epping. A new garage was opened at Northfleet in 1937, replacing the Old Dover Road base, and this was then noteworthy as one of only two garages in the Country area with full canteen facilities — the other was Windsor after completion of extensions in 1936. The LPTB thus concentrated its Country bus operations on a number of strategically-placed depots across its territory; while no new garages were opened for another 15 years, many premises were extended by the addition of large administrative blocks and adjacent parking lots made necessary by the increased traffic during and after the war. The opening of Garston garage in 1952 symbolised the optimism that passenger numbers would continue to

Right:
This is a view of the former Filkins & Ainsworth premises in Harefield in October 1935, shortly before they were closed. The LPTB acquired the business on 31 October 1933, together with four ancient Crossley RAF type buses which had performed on routes to Rickmansworth and to Uxbridge. The bus in the shed is not one of these; it is a Thornycroft with Thurgood coachwork, new in 1932 and formerly with the People's Motor Services Ltd in Ware. It became NY2 in the London Transport fleet and was withdrawn in 1937 when the Leyland Cubs became available. The space for the spare wheel on the offside of the vehicle is of interest. *London Transport*

Centre right:
The forecourt of Amersham garage in May 1934. Although London Transport property since the previous year, there is no evidence of the LPTB and the enquiry office looks somewhat deserted. The vehicle on the left is a Dennis Lancet, newly delivered to the Gravesend & District Bus Service Ltd in 1933 and acquired by the LPTB on 14 October of that year. It became DT1 in the LPTB classification and was allocated to Green Line work; it lasted until 1937. The second vehicle is an AEC Regal coach with Strachan bodywork, new to Amersham & District in 1932; it became T365 in the London Transport lists, was withdrawn in 1938 and sold early in 1939. *London Transport*

Bottom right:
This is Windsor garage in January 1935. The two double-deckers are Dennis HV type buses, inherited from independents and put into a DH class by London Transport. From left to right the single-deck vehicles are a first series T type Green Line coach, a Gilford bus, GF15, inherited from the Skylark Motor Coach Co; an ADC416; and GF9, another former Skylark vehicle still with the neat oval fleet indicator in the front of the roof. These vehicles, with the sole exception of the coach, typified the heterogeneous stock that was operated in the Windsor area for some years. *London Transport*

grow, accommodation being provided for 150 buses, a number never in fact housed there. The associated problems of siting a garage with a high labour demand in an area where — at least until recently — there was attractive alternative employment available have never really been solved. Other new bases have been set up in the new towns; Stevenage became fully operational on 28 April 1959 and Hitchin, which had never been able to accommodate double-deck buses under cover, was closed; Harlow, built to the same basic plan, opened on 22 May 1963, operations ceasing at Epping the previous day. A new garage was built at Hatfield in 1959 on the opposite side of the road from the old LGOC structure which was demolished. Mention should also be made of the brief ownership by the LTE of the former Eastern National garage in Grays acquired on 30 September 1951; when services in the town were revised three months later the garage was closed.

In 1934 buses of the Country Department followed LGOC precedent and carried garage codes and running numbers. Thus DT became the code for Dartford, SJ for Swanley Junction and TG for Tring. Windsor was at first designated WC, usually explained by 'Windsor Castle' or 'Windsor Coach'; when Ware (Town Hall) closed, its WR plates were transferred to Windsor. Addlestone has always been known as WY (Weybridge) and HH very properly stands for Hemel Hempstead, though the official address was for many years Two Waters. Amersham could not carry the obvious AM because this code was being used for Plumstead; hence the use of MA; High Wycombe became HE to avoid duplication with HW for Hanwell (which is actually in Southall). The buses allocated to the Eastern National garage in Grays carried GY plates painted red; as many of the vehicles were on loan from the Central area, and hence red, the plates were almost invisible. Some plates never gained currency; by the time the BS plates were delivered Bishops Stortford had closed.

Top:
The customary obsession with wheels and tyres is demonstrated in this view of Reigate garage in July 1936. From left to right the buses are an LGOC-bodied ST (note the round cab); another ST of LGOC origin; a Reliance single-deck bus, recently rebodied; another ST; Q40; and a Dennis Lancet. All official photographs emphasise the space available in the newly-built or extended garages; the size of the engineering staff is also of note — there are 14 men working here. *London Transport*

Above:
This view of the new premises at Hatfield in April 1959 was taken shortly after they opened. The refuelling and vacuum cleaning points are by the door, while the structure in the roof is an Essex washing machine. The buses are all RTs with the single exception of the RF at the entrance. The first bus in the photograph, OLD 520, is RT4734, one of a number of similar vehicles delivered in 1954 but then held at Loughton garage in store; it did not enter service until March 1958. Its neighbour, RT3808, had had a longer run, taking up its duties in October 1953.
London Transport

With the shrinking of the operational fleet, several garages have been closed: Luton in 1976, Tring and High Wycombe in the following year. East Grinstead, after a proud and reputable history of over 50 years, closed its doors at the very end of 1981. Other garages now house many fewer vehicles than they were built for. The most recent closure, however, that of the premises in High Street, Crawley was associated with the provision of a more commodious building at Tinsley Green. This is alongside the central engineering works there, set up by London Country, which has a northern counterpart at Garston, utilising space and equipment that would otherwise be spare. A plan evolved in 1982 to move operations from Windsor garage to Slough appears well on the way to fulfilment in 1984; new premises are in process of construction in Stoke Road, just north of Slough station and part of the development costs are being defrayed by Berkshire County Council. There were once three garages in Slough concerned with bus and coach operations in

Above:

Stevenage garage in Danestreet on 4 May 1960, just a week after opening. The parked vehicles are, of course, the standard vehicles in use at this time; they are RT4167 and RF163 (which was built for and allocated to Green Line work). Service 801 for which the RT is destined was a local route from Stevenage station to Longmeadow, a part of the town now served by a batch of StevenageBus routes. The completion of this garage allowed the closure of the unpretentious shed at Fisher's Green which had been operational since 1955 and also of the long-established premises at Hitchin. *London Transport*

London country and all were closed in favour of the Windsor complex. However population changes and resultant traffic demands north of the Thames mean that the major provision of bus services has moved as well, and the positioning of a base in Slough makes good organisational sense.

4

Reorganisations

Only planners are said to enjoy reorganisations; the clients do not willingly accept change and the proprietors of the enterprise concerned shrink from the inevitable criticisms that arise from the clients and from its staff. While public reactions to changes in the services offered to it are usually unco-ordinated and limited perhaps to sporadic complaints and letters to the press, staff are institutionalised in the forms of unions, and objections from these quarters carry considerable weight. The London Passenger Transport Board was created as an agent for rationalisation and change and carried through a series of reorganisations in London country in its early years. The changes made in St Albans bus facilities on 5 December 1934 are the subject of the first section. Thereafter, either because they were so pleased by what had been achieved, or because of reluctance to open up any more hornets' nests, the Board and its successors made no major alterations, proceeding on an incremental basis with minor change following minor change in the system. Thus some 40 years passed in London country without a major reappraisal of services anywhere with the single exception of the Grays reorganisation of 2 January 1952; this was really a nettle that should have been grasped in the 1930s, but the bus passengers in Grays had to put up with 16 years of inconvenience before a rational system was implemented.

Nowhere did the organic growth style of development reveal itself more obviously than in the new towns where bus services were mounted by a series of improvisations and tacked-on additions so that the total provision became an incoherent patchwork. Only at the very end of the London Transport era in London country did the Stevenage New Town Development Corporation successfully push the London Transport Board into some recognition that the new towns needed facilities different in kind from those available elsewhere. The first result of this initiative was Blue Arrow which went through several stages before emerging as StevenageBus. London Country Bus Services Ltd therefore in 1970 inherited a time-honoured, if out-dated system which was being shocked into changed methods of working (though not of route structure) by the ill-judged Merlin and Swift rapid-transit forms, themselves a side-product of the much-heralded (and later discredited) 'Reshaping London's Bus Services' plan of 1966. When through its initial traumas, London Country has courageously and effectively carried through a programme of much-needed change; two examples are considered — the introduction of C Line in Crawley on 1 July 1978 and the Chilternlink changes that were put into effect in Amersham and High Wycombe on 13 April 1980. In the first, new town dwellers have at last a bus service tailored to their needs, marketed with confidence and helped by a large investment of new vehicles; in the second, in a more traditional environment, the interlinking of LCBS and Alder Valley route systems following the MAP report has created a flexible and logical system that appears to serve the passengers well.

St Albans

The principal services in St Albans derived from the former National routes which passed to LGCS on 2 March 1932 and to the LPTB on 1 July 1933. Operations on some roads were shared and co-ordinated, while on others there was straight competition from independent companies. National had always been handicapped in St Albans by lack of a garage there — Watford and Hatfield were the nearest operating bases in the Watford and North London area. This factor among others had allowed independent operators to initiate services in the 1920s; most of these were local routes through some destinations were a considerable distance away. The independents were acquired by the LPTB in 1933 and 1934; they were (with the number of vehicles):

1 November 1933 — Colne Services (F. Steer, 5)
9 November 1933 — Karryu Coaches (J. Kirby, 3)
10 November 1933 — St Albans & District (Charles Russet & Son, 14)
2 January 1934 — Express Motor Services (A. R. Blowers, 4)
6 February 1934 — Comfy Coaches (A. P. & P. B. Morgan, 4)
6 February 1934 — Reliance Coaches (A. Barnes, 4)
17 February 1934 — Albanian Omnibus Co (F. J. Cobb, 12)
16 March 1934 — Victoria Omnibus Service (E. A. Griffiths, 3)
29 March 1934 — City Omnibus Services (W. J. Flower & C. H. Etches, 5)

Colne Services and St Albans & District sold out voluntarily; all the others held on until they were acquired either by a refusal of consent to operate by the LPTB or by compulsory purchase. The board based its operations on the Hatfield Road premises, a former drill hall, of St Albans & District and on the small garage in Wynchlands Crescent formerly owned by City; the Comfy Coaches garage in Harpenden was mainly concerned with Green Line work.

All services in St Albans, of whatever origin, were subject to the renumbering scheme of 3 October 1934. By this date all of the former independent services had been given numbers, though otherwise they were largely unchanged; many were operated by their former owners' buses with 'General' transfers on the sides. The routes in existence at the time of reorganisation, were as follows:

Former National Routes

New Number

1: Oaklands-St Albans-Watford-West Hyde   321
(Lewis also operated over this road between Rickmansworth and St Albans)
4: St Albans-Redbourn-Dunstable   374
(Albanian also operated over this road)
5A: St Albans-Hatfield station-Welwyn Garden City (Pear Tree Village)   350
(City worked a coordinated service with National on this route; Reliance Coaches ran to Hatfield)
5B: Local service: St Albans-Fleetville   340
8: St Albans-Wheathampstead-Whitwell-Hitchin   308
8A: St Albans-Wheathampstead-Harpenden   355
8B: St Albans-Wheathampstead-Batford-Luton   365
(National had worked these under one number, 8, and they appeared as one timetable; St Albans & District also worked to Kimpton and Harpenden via Wheathampstead)
10: St Albans-Hatfield-Hertford-Bishops Stortford via Letty Green   340
11: as 10 but via Bayford Turn   341
14: St Albans-Leverstock Green-Hemel Hempstead   314
(extended to Great Gaddesden on Sundays; City and Albanian competed on this road)
51: St Albans-Harpenden-Luton   321A
(worked in co-ordination with Comfy Cars and Express)
304: St Albans-Radlett-Elstree & Borehamwood station   304
313: St Albans-Potters Bar-Enfield   313

Until the advent of LGCS the National routes, except those in the 300 series, had worked with an 'N' prefix; LGCS retained the N on the bus indicators but discarded it in the timetables.

Former Independent routes

Colne: St Albans-Napsbury-London Colney   338
Albanian: Townsend-St Albans-Welham Green   340
District: St Albans-Radlett-Shenley   given 355
Colne: Oaklands-St Albans-Shenley-Borehamwood   358
Colne and Albanian: Townsend-St Albans-London Colney   358A

Albanian: Oaklands-St Albans-Coopers Green-
  Codicote   382
Express and Victoria: St Albans-Hill End-
  Tyttenhanger   391
District: St Albans (Market Place)-Lemsford
  Road (Cricketers)-LMS station-Market
  Place (Circular)   399

The numbers allocated to these services were
unchanged in the 3 October scheme.

The reorganisation scheme instituted new route
patterns and timetables on 5 December 1934. The
principal aims were to link trunk services where this
would provide a useful passenger amenity and
economy of working, to provide co-ordinated services on roads where competition had formerly been
most intensive (or 'wasteful' in the Board's
language), to arrange for through running of services
across the city which would give cross-town facilities
and also keep the buses that formerly terminated in

the market place out of the congested city centre
altogether. In seeking to achieve these aims, Route
321 was withdrawn between St Albans and Oaklands and put through to Luton over the former 51
route, thus establishing the basis of route 321 ever
since. Alterations to secondary services included
sending Route 304 buses from Elstree over the
former 308 road to Wheathampstead, Whitwell and
Hitchin, and joining the two separate parts of 355 to

Below left:
**MBS301, new in 1968, is seen in St Albans in the last year
of London Transport operation of the Country buses there.
The slip board reads 'Autofare bus', indicating to
passengers the need to insert coins in the ticket machine in
order to gain entry. Never very popular in St Albans, the
bus had been successfully passed on by the garage by the
time LCBS came into being. Route 391 had a long history
as a local route plying to Hill End and Tyttenhanger until
the setting up of the S group of routes on 30 October
1976.** *Edward Shirras*

Below:
**Route 358 has had a long and continuous history and may
be traced back to the Colne Services route operated by
F. Steer from his garage in London Colney. This was
already numbered 358 when taken over by the LPTB on
30 October 1933 because the route entered the
Metropolitan Police District at Borehamwood. In this view
of St Peter's Street in St Albans, SMW6, complete with
AEC badge and decorative trim, is seen at work. Buses of
this type, intended for South Wales Transport, were
diverted to London Country in 1971; 11 of the class spent
their entire lives at St Albans garage, being replaced in due
time by Leyland Nationals. Currently Route 358 runs
from Borehamwood (Milton Drive) via Shenley to St
Albans, then on to Wheathampstead and Harpenden
(Church Green).** *Michael Dryhurst*

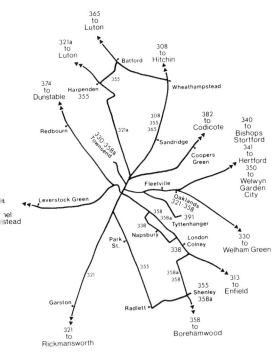

Routes in St Albans, 3 October 1934.

run from Radlett to Wheathampstead and Harpenden. (It is noteworthy that the predecessor of these routes, N8, ran through from Elstree to Kimpton for some months in 1922! The 355 looks very similar in current timetables, though its companion 304 has been diverted to Tyttenhanger.)

The classic LPTB technique of giving trunk services suburban tails was applied to the road between St Albans Market Place and Townsend; Routes 330 and 350 from Welwyn Garden City were sent over this section, as were 340 and 341 from Bishops Stortford and Hertford. Some local services were incorporated in a busy route, numbered 334,

between Oaklands and St Julians; perhaps surprisingly, the Tyttenhanger and Hill End local 391 was left unaltered, as were services to London Colney and Shenley (338 via Napsbury, 358 via the main London Road), though timetables were redrafted. The 374 was reduced to a Saturday and Sunday working, Green Line H2 offering bus fares between St Albans and Dunstable.

These changes certainly reduced the number of buses at work. If Comfy Cars is excluded, the local independent operators were using something like 50 vehicles on their services in 1932/3; by 1938, admittedly using larger buses, the LPTB was deploying some 24 Q types, Ts and Cubs on corresponding services — a 50% reduction. The services were clearly on reduced frequencies, a fact that passengers once used to buses running every few minutes found frustrating. There were subsequent changes, of course; Route 354, a circular from St Albans garage via City station, Fleetville and Marshalswick, appeared on 27 November 1935 and was a useful innovation: Townsend was served by an extension of 391A from Hill End on 9 February 1938, the trunk services to Welwyn Garden City and Hertford being withdrawn from this terminus. The postwar development of vast estates at Marshalswick, New Greens, Jersey Farm, Mile House and Cottonmill among others, has demanded augmented and altered bus facilities. The most significant of recent changes has been the introduction of the S group of routes on 30 October 1976. MBS vehicles were allocated to six routes, S1 to S6, which covered most of the former local operations, including those worked under the time-honoured numbers 354 and 391. This localisation scheme was an attempt to adapt town services to a new idiom in a changing market. While traditional bus passengers have found the new scheme difficult to cope with, it was doubtless a move in the right direction, though alterations made subsequently suggest that not all the answers have yet been found.

2 JANUARY 1952

Grays

The reorganisation in St Albans, an exercise repeated in several towns in the LPTB Country area, was — or was alleged to be — advantageous in that bus services established somewhat haphazardly were replanned and co-ordinated. In the Board's view, the new pattern was of benefit to passengers and also allowed operations to be conducted with due efficiency and economy. However, at the very edges of the Board's area, travellers in a number of towns were positively inconvenienced. Formerly useful services were severed at the Board's boundary, and where this boundary ran through a town centre passengers were required to change from London Transport buses to those of another operator. Nowhere was this inconvenience more pronounced than in Grays, which for 18 years suffered all the problems of a divided city.

The Grays and Tilbury area was initially a preserve of National which started operations there in 1921 with a route from Stanford-le-Hope to Rainham via Grays and Purfleet; this was numbered 14. A complex of services appeared during the 1920s, including local services to Tilbury, Chadwell St Mary and Aveley, together with longer routes to Brentwood, Romford and Chelmsford. Buses on these longer routes travelled through somewhat open country where the settlements were very small. There was considerable population expansion in the riverside area following rapid industrial development, and partly as a consequence independent operators set up in large numbers. At one time 27 were at work, competing with one another and with National on every road where passengers might be found. LGOC interest in the Thurrock area was surprisingly limited and at the advent of the LPTB comprised only a half share in the route from Grays to Romford via South and North Ockendon, General buses carrying G40, National — later Eastern National — 40. Route 36, referred to later, had been at one time operated on behalf of General in the Watford and North London scheme; in addition Batten's Coaches ran the Tilbury to Aldgate coach service on behalf of the LGOC.

Following the establishment of the LPTB, however, the Board took over responsibility for G40/40 and acquired Eastern National Sunday Route 31A from Grays to Rainham together with Route 36

from Grays to Aveley, Rainham and Romford. These acquisitions date from 1 September 1933; however Eastern National buses on Route 31 continued to work through to Purfleet from Tilbury until 17 April 1934 when the route was cut in half; the section from Grays to Purfleet became LT property and worked as route 372. Other operators who worked through Grays on Tilbury to Purfleet services were all acquired by the LPTB in 1934; these were Harvey's Transport Service (J. Harvey) with two vehicles on 10 March, Tilbury Coaching Services (S. J. and I. M. Skinner) with four vehicles on 24 March, and Clarke's Motor Coaches (R. Clarke) with two buses on 18 May. The Board's boundary was deemed to run through the centre of Grays; all former through services therefore divided at the War Memorial (or Queen's Hotel) and it became impossible to travel from Purfleet to Tilbury, an obvious traffic flow, without changing vehicles in Grays. The 'restricted outward runnings' to Tilbury allowed to the Board were taken up by Green Line, not the preferred mode of travel by large numbers of dock workers. It is perhaps the lack of through bus facilities that brought so much traffic to the London, Midland & Scottish Railway from Purfleet to Tilbury, though this service was not without its eccentricities, becoming in the fullness of time the last steam-operated suburban railway in the London area.

So matters remained for the next 18 years, with Grays a divided town. Of related interest is the fact that a similar situation in High Wycombe had been resolved by London Transport and Thames Valley which worked joint services 326/26 and 326A/26A from Mill End Road to Wycombe Marsh and New Bowerdean Road, very useful cross-town facilities. The formation of the British Transport Commission

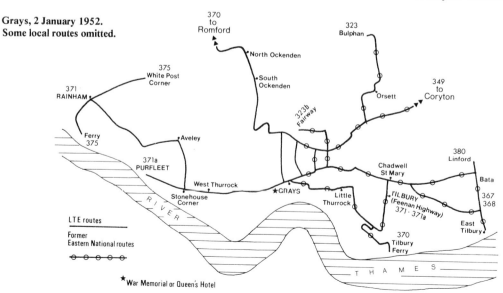

Grays, 2 January 1952.
Some local routes omitted.

138

on 1 January 1948 was instrumental in promoting change in the Thurrock area by altering the relationship between the LTE (successor to the LPTB) and Eastern National following purchase by the Commission of the Tilling interest in that company. The special problems of Grays were examined and a scheme of through running was drawn up. As a preliminary move on 30 September 1951 the LTE took over the Eastern National garage in Argent Street, Grays, together with 28 buses and responsibility for almost all the local services; Eastern National retained its routes to Brentwood, Chelmsford and Southend. London Transport maintained the existing route system, though introducing some red STL buses to work with the acquired vehicles. Services operating at this point included:

London Transport:
370: Grays-the Ockendons-Romford
370A: South Ockendon station-Grays *or* Purfleet
371: Grays-Aveley-Rainham
371A: Grays-Purfleet

Former Eastern National:
31: Grays-Tilbury (Feenan Highway) via Dock Road
37A: Grays-Tilbury Ferry via Chadwell St Mary

All these routes were rearranged on 2 January 1952 into principal through services as follows:

370: Tilbury (ferry)-Chadwell St Mary-Grays-Romford (with a peak hour service 370A between Tilbury and Purfleet)
371: Tilbury (Feenan Highway)-Dock Road-Grays-Rainham
371A: Tilbury (Feenan Highway)-Dock Road-Grays-Purfleet

The former Eastern National Routes 32 and 44 to Orsett and Bulphan were renumbered 323, and were supported by local services on 323A to Nutberry

Corner (formerly 32A shared with Our Bus, a thriving independent) and 323B to Fairway (Long Lane) (formerly 32B); a new feature was that buses on all these routes ran to and from Purfleet at peak times. London Transport also worked several services that were provided for factories and workplaces; these were:

349: Grays-Coryton or Shellhaven (formerly 35)
357: Tilbury Docks-Nutberry Corner (57)
367: Tilbury Docks-Bata Shoe Factory (81)
368: Grays-Bata Shoe Factory (82)
379: Tilbury Docks-Chadwell St Mary (37B)
380: Grays-Linford (45)

The only routes unchanged were the 374 from Grays to Aveley via the Uplands Estate (with some extensions to Rainham) and the Green Line services 723/723A)

Thus, after a long period of unsatisfactory and frustrating travelling conditions, passengers in Grays were no longer compelled to changes buses in the centre of town on transverse journeys. They had, literally, to pay for their new facilities, of course; the Eastern National fare scale which went up in half-penny steps was 'rounded off' and return tickets were abolished. However, the benefits of travelling direct from the estates to places of work in Tilbury or Purfleet were doubtless very welcome, and cross-town working has been a feature of services in the area ever since. Changes made subsequently have arisen from the development of the vast Belhus Estate and smaller housing sites. Eastern National activity in Thurrock was further reduced on 1 September 1979 when LCBS took over several services following negotiations over grant support with Essex County Council. Somewhat astonishingly, LCBS is now sole operator in Tilbury; Eastern National services in Grays are limited to routes from Chelmsford and Basildon. The special buses still run to the Bata Shoe Factory, perhaps seen to best advantage as rain sweeps over the Essex flats, but Coryton and Shellhaven are no longer served.

Crawley New Town

A glance at the 1939 Ordnance Survey map (price, on cloth 2/6 (12½p)) shows Crawley as a small, compact town, surrounded by small villages like Ifield, Oakwood and Langley Green, large estates including Milton Mount and Tilgate, and farms like Furnace Farm. All these are now entirely supplanted by vast housing developments planned on the satellite principle — ie each development has its own amenities and shopping units, though the town centre at Crawley has been greatly enlarged to provide appropriate shopping facilities. The siting of the industrial area at Manor Royal and Tinsley Green, once another tiny village, has added the travel needs of industrial workers to those of shoppers and office staff heading for the town centre. Three Bridges, once a railway station and a few residential roads, has been similarly subject to urban change; the establishment of Gatwick Airport has added another dimension to travel facilities and travel needs.

Through the years of the development of the new town, London Transport endeavoured to meet the needs of travellers, and even to anticipate them, by a series of improvisations. The basic network of bus routes, set up in the 1920s and 1930s, has survived, largely intact even today; in 1949 bus routes in Crawley included the 405 to West Croydon, the 434 between Edenbridge and Horsham, and the circular 426 running from Crawley to Three Bridges, Gatwick, Horley, Povey Cross, Charlwood and Ifield, a service on which a single Leyland Cub sufficed. There were also two Southdown routes to Haywards Heath, one via Handcross and one via Balcombe, and a connecting service from Turners Hill to Ardingly and Haywards Heath. New local services were added to the map as the housing developments advanced; they were altered as required, supplemented or withdrawn in somewhat bewildering fashion. The Board, and later the Executive, were under almost continuous fire from the people living in the new town and the Development Corporation because the services provided were almost always inadequate, especially at peak times. Providing facilities that would account for the highest level of demand at rush hours would, of course, be commercial suicide in that large numbers of staff would be running expensive vehicles for most of the day for handfuls of passengers. So, through the years, London Transport endeavoured to provide a service as near acceptability as possible and with due regard to economy.

By 1957 three separate local services were working: 426A, a somewhat distant variation of the parent route, linked Ifield with Pound Hill; 476 ran from Tilgate to Langley Green; and 483 worked from Crawley Centre to and round the Northgate Estate. In 1964 Route 476B was running to Furnace Green. In 1970 LCBS inherited a complex pattern of routes, most of them cross-town operations; some of these made loop workings in the estates, others ran in one direction only. The Southdown services, which had worked across Crawley by an agreement with LT made in 1958, became LCBS operations in April 1971; these were:

23A: Northgate-Crawley-Handcross (which had absorbed the 483 above)
76/76A: Industrial Area-Crawley-Gossops Green
79/79A: Bus Station-Gossops Green

These became 475, 474 and 479 respectively. On 30 June 1978, in addition to the historic trunk Routes 405 and 434 and their variations, the following services were operating in Crawley New Town:

405B: Crawley bus station-Gatwick Road (Rutherford Way) with some extensions to Redhill
426A: Ifield station-Crawley-Pound Hill. (The 426 still ran in very much its old form)
429: Crawley bus station-Bewbush
474/474A: Broadfield-Gossops Green-Crawley-Gatwick Road
475: Manor Royal-Crawley-Handcross
476: Ifield-Langley Green-Crawley-Furnace Green-Langley Green
476A: Ifield-Langley Green-Three Bridges-Pound Hill
478: Broadfield-Crawley-Three Bridges-Pound Hill-Broadfield
479/479A: Crawley-Gossops Green-Crawley

These services were in fact reasonably well arranged and followed established traffic flows. However, they had become suspect over the years because of unreliability arising from recurrent problems of staff and vehicle availability. The real need was to recover passengers' confidence in the services provided and in pursuance of this aim the entire existing network — the 11 routes listed above — was withdrawn. On 1 July 1978 an entirely recast pattern of local routes came into operation. Marketed as C Line, the new scheme comprised the following:

C1: ⎫ via Furnace Green and Tilgate

C2: ⎬ Industrial Area or Langley Green to Town Centre and Tilgate — via Tilgate and Furnace Green

C3: ⎪ via Haslett Avenue and Tilgate

C4: ⎭ via Tilgate and Haslett Avenue

C5: Ifield-Town Centre-Three Bridges-Pound Hill-Ifield with a loop working in Pound Hill

C6: Sundays only: Ifield-Town Centre- Pound Hill

C7: Bus Station-Gossops Green-Bewbush-Bus Station

C8: Wakehams Green-Pound Hill-Three Bridges-Crawley-Broadfield

Routes C15, C16 and C17 were peak hour services for the industrial area; C21 and C22 were schools services. All routes were allocated double-deck AN buses which worked on a flat fare principle — initially this was 20p — and at regular intervals. Community involvement was sought by putting the name of the scheme open to public competition and the selected title — C Line — was placed boldly on the vehicles together with the legend 'Crawley's own bus service'.

Public reaction has been very encouraging and in an area where civic pride has evolved the localisation

Top left:
MBS301 is a Metro-Cammell-bodied Merlin with 33 seats and space for 27 standing passengers, here working a local Crawley route in the spring of 1970. The capacity was useful at peak times when loads were heavy. This bus was among those withdrawn on 5 September 1978. The 426A has now been incorporated in the C Line routes.
Edward Shirras

Centre left:
C5 runs every 20min from Hyde Drive in Ifield to Crawley bus station and Three Bridges station, then in a loop working round Pound Hill back to Three Bridges and on to Ifield. This kind of working is one of the features of the C Line system. AN136 carries the 'Crawley's own bus service' sign that was featured at the outset.
D. M. Stuttard

Left:
A passenger waiting at the doors of Atlantean AN141 has an impressive array of notices and symbols to contemplate. from left to right they are a 'Pay as you enter please' notice; the C Line emblem with a picture of the bus; 'push to open' on the doors, twice; a notice above the door isolating switch; the garage code (CY) and running number (36); another 'Pay as you enter' notice; another large C Line poster at upper deck level; and the bus class and number. The Leyland symbol of the wheel hub is yet another attraction. *D. Trevor Rowe*

of the bus service has aided the developing sense of identity. It would appear that C Line is a successful reorganisation in that travel facilities have been simplified, regularised and improved, drivers' rosters have been rationalised — previously they had become very complicated by frequent changes of route on a single turn — and vehicles were employed more economically. Critics will wonder why it has taken over 25 years to reach this point; clearly such a reorganisation could have benefited new town dwellers at a much earlier stage. However, the evident reluctance of London Transport to contemplate radical change is highlighted by the fact that over 30 years elapsed between the reorganisations in the Country area in the 1930s and the publication of the Bus Reshaping Plan in 1966. Then another 10 years elapsed before LCBS was in the position to move confidently into a major reshaping and localisation exercise of its own; part of the delay in the final stages arose from the late arrival of the buses from Leyland, buses that were considered essential in the creation of the new C Line image. Similar schemes have now been implemented in Stevenage (StevenageBus, 26 April 1980) and Harlow (Townbus, 30 August 1980) and there have been parallel benefits to passengers and operator alike.

Below:
Atlantean AN141, resplendent in C Line insignia, arrives at Tinsley Green on the occasion of an open day. C50 is an invented number specially used for the service; it is not a designation otherwise used in the C Line scheme. This bus has Park Royal bodywork and was new in 1978.
D. M. Stuttard

Above:
Shortly after the introduction of C Line, Harlow New Town also was offered much improved services under the Townbus emblem, with Atlanteans, on and after 30 August 1978. AN72 and AN74 wait at Harlow Mill station;

AN74 is about to work a journey on T2 which will take it up to the bus station then to Staple Tye, back to the bus station and on to Old Harlow where it will terminate at Gilden Way. These buses were among the first of the type ordered by LCBS and arrived in 1972. *G. B. Wise*

Amersham and High Wycombe

The changes in bus services in Amersham and High Wycombe in 1980 were the outcome of close analysis of existing passenger needs, an analysis based on the classic tool of the social scientist, the survey. The MAP technique, originated by Midland Red, relies heavily on stated, not assumed, passenger movement, and computer projections that examine demand against resources available. The route patterns and service frequencies that will best satisfy passenger demand are also identified, together with the cost of provision in terms of vehicles and staff. At this point economic and political elements are introduced as the level of service provided depends partly on the income the bus itself generates in fares, and partly on the revenue support offered by the County Council. High Wycombe has always been a border town where the buses of London Transport (later LCBS) met those of Thames Valley (since 1972 Alder Valley). The town was fortunate in that a cross-town facility was offered by Route 326 from Micklefield Estate to Mill End Road and Sands via Wycombe Marsh, the town centre and Dashwood Avenue; this service was interworked with Alder

Below:
The old order in the Chilterns, long before passengers had to be wooed by such devices as Chilternlink, is represented by this view of a Dennis Lancet, new in 1932. This sturdy vehicle has Strachan bodywork seating 32 passengers. It became DT3 in the London Transport fleet but did not last in the Board's service beyond 1937. The hooter is of some interest as are the opening windows which appear to drop into the side of the vehicle in the manner of railway carriage door lights. *J. F. Higham*

Valley 26 and 26A, a shared operation preceding the early days of London Transport. LCBS's interest in High Wycombe itself was affected by the closure of the garage in Queen Alexandra Road in 1977, all services being worked from Amersham garage from 1 October. All LCBS services were then routed into the bus station and there was a general reshuffle of routes, route numbers and timings. In contrast, the Alder Valley services remained very much as they had been for 50 years; while LCBS was moving rapidly towards one-man-operation, Alder Valley was using some double-deck Lodekka buses (dating from the 1950s) that could only be run with a driver and a conductor. The Alder Valley garage at Wycombe Marsh until 1970 and thereafter at the bus station had suffered from shortages of staff for many years and reliability of the services was suspect. After a long period of operating an antiquated and uncertain system there was need for Alder Valley to regain public confidence; to some extent this applied to the LCBS services, though by 1980 they were on the way to recovering from the vehicular problems of the mid-1970s and the shortage of staff as the closure of the garage in High Wycombe drew near. Amersham has been affected similarly, but not to the same degree.

The surveys have shown that passengers give high priority to keeping fares down and to having bus shelters available; they also like easily-understood maps and timetables and punctuality. The planning for the new services in High Wycombe and Amersham was based on these precepts, and also on a degree of interworking between the two operators concerned which would allow improved facilities and economical use of vehicles and staff at the same time. In relating the financial aspects to the operational planning, two levels of service were identified: the basic level which could exist within its own fare income, and a 'preferred' level that would need county revenue support. At preferred level some roads retained their buses when they might have lost them altogether, and others had a higher frequency service than the income generated really justified. All operational planning was based on the needs of the area as a whole, on utilisation of the two companies' resources as appropriate, and on one-man-operation of all vehicles. Evening and Sunday services were critically evaluated and high-capacity vehicles were earmarked for weekday journeys where passenger demand was heavy, for example on school workings.

From 13 April 1980 Alder Valley and LCBS

vehicles were embellished by 'Chilternlink' stickers in white, red and green, and with the new identity passengers in the area were encouraged to think that a new era had dawned. An immediately noticeable change was the adoption by Alder Valley of numbers in the 300 series. Thus Alder Valley 303 from Totteridge interworked with LCBS 363 from Penn (Post Office) on the Bowerdean Cross Roads to Union Street, Desborough Castle Estate, Bowerdean Cross Roads circle. Joint working continued on the 326 from Micklefield Estate to Sands route, now extended to Booker (Holmer's Farm Way). A new joint service was mounted between High Wycombe and Great Missenden station, with extensions at both ends to Marlow and Amersham on Route 345 via Haslemere and Prestwood; Alder Valley retained the journeys via Cryers Hill as 346. The only trunk route altered was 362 from Chesham which was extended beyond High Wycombe to Marlow (Queens Road). In addition to the upheaval in Wycombe, there were route and timetable alterations in Amersham, most notably to the more rural services; thus 349 and 394 were recast on one timetable offering journeys from Chesham Moor to the Broadway, thence to Cholesbury and Tring via Bellingdon (349) or Hawridge (394). An interesting innovation was the initiation of express working on trunk Route 353 between Chesham Broadway and Slough on Saturdays; regrettably this proved a failure and normal working was resumed later in the year.

Thus the South Buckinghamshire area timetable was rewritten and duty rosters were recast; LCBS reduced the vehicle requirements at Amersham from 41 to 37, 10 of which were AN type buses, the first double-deckers employed there for some time; Alder Valley ran out 42 buses before the reorganisation, 31 afterwards. Hopefully, many of the declared needs of the travelling public have been met in that services are on regular-interval bases, local information abounds — the signposting at High Wycombe bus station is excellent — and buses still run to almost all the destinations previously served, if less frequently or not at all in the evenings. The 'Travelwide' weekly or monthly tickets were initially made the subject of special offers, thus going some way to containing, if not reducing, regular travellers' outgoings in fares. The reorganisation was presented in the excellent publicity made available as a new deal for the traveller. In many ways it was and it is to be hoped that public confidence will be won by the Chilternlink image. However, the background was essentially a financial one, and the operators were compelled to examine the services offered in the light of the costs involved; the County Council, too, was concerned to identify the level of subsidy that acceptable services required. If in the process improved facilities are offered to the traveller, even if incidentally, that of course is no bad thing.

Top:
RML2412 pulls in to the kerb near Penn Post Office. For many years Route 363 was in the form of an incomplete circle linking Penn, High Wycombe and Totteridge. The Penn to High Wycombe section derived from Route 1 of the Penn Bus Co Ltd which was acquired by the LPTB on 31 July 1935. Since the advent of Chilternlink Atlanteans have worked the route which has taken a rather different form, running to and from Penn with a loop working round the Desborough Castle Estate. It is supplemented over much of this road by Alder Valley Service 304 starting from Totteridge. *D. M. Stuttard*

Above:
Atlantean AN238 stands in the doorway of Amersham garage; it was one of a batch allocated to Amersham for Chilternlink duty in 1980, this one arriving in September. If worked 'in service' the buses for the 363 are scheduled for a 31min journey from the garage on 362 to take up their route in High Wycombe, a considerable distance away. *John Marsh*

5
Appendices

The General Summer Sunday Services

The early ventures of the LGOC into London country have already been surveyed. When the programme was resumed after the war, route 81, now running from Mortlake, was sent to Windsor Castle on 13 April 1919. Each year the destinations served increased in numbers; buses ran daily on some routes, only on Sundays on others. By 1924 the facilities were extensive and the LGOC published a map showing the routes operating in the summer of that year. The outer termini were as follows:

Farningham: 21B from Newington Green (daily)
Westerham Hill: 136 from Lewisham (daily)
Godstone: 59A from Camden Town (Sundays)
Reigate: 59 from Camden Town (daily)
Dorking: 107 from Clapham Common (daily)
Guildford: 115 from Kingston (daily)
Woking: 79 from Kingston (daily)
Ascot: 117A from Hounslow (Sundays)
Virginia Water: 117 from Hounslow (daily)
Windsor: 61 from Kingston via Egham (daily), and 81 from Hounslow via Slough (daily)
Beaconsfield: 98 from Ealing (Saturdays and Sundays)
Watford: 142 from Kilburn Park (daily)
St Albans: 84 from Golders Green (daily)
Hatfield: 82 from Golders Green (Sundays)
Wormley: 69A from Camberwell Green (Sundays)
Epping: 10A from Elephant and Castle (daily)
Chipping Ongar: 10 from Elephant and Castle (Sundays)
Brentwood: 26 from Stratford Broadway (daily)
Rainham: 23 from Marylebone (daily)

Below:
In its final years as a London Transport operation, Route 84 saw RTs, Merlins, Daimler Fleetlines and Swifts. This alternation of double with single-deck types was pursued to the end by the allocation of Metrobuses in the closing weeks. Here AEC Swift SMS305 is photographed near London Colney on a somewhat dismal day that does not enhance the scenery on this rather bare road. London Country has been in charge since 24 April 1982.
Michael Dryhurst

Some of these routes were very long; 59 had a running time of 148min, and 21B 132min, for example, a lengthy period to sit on a wooden seat on the top deck of a solid-tyred bus, however good the weather or the delight of the trip in prospect. Many frequencies were hourly during the week (21B, 61,

81, 115) but these were stepped up on Sundays to every 15min (69A, 81, 136) or even 10min (10A, 86, 107). The 23 was something of a mystery; a 12min service operated on Sundays all the way from Marylebone to Rainham, though how people spent their time in this little resort is entirely baffling. The 1924 leaflet identifies some expeditions in a style redolent of early Batsford books; passengers could travel to Kentish Orchards and Commons, the Surrey Hills, the Riverside (the Upper Thames, not the Essex marshes or the Kent cement works), the Beechwoods of Bucks, Hertfordshire Woods and Meadows, and Essex Woodlands. There were some stern injunctions: 'Do not leave picnic wrappers lying about; while gathering wild flowers do not pluck them up by the roots — many a woodland has been robbed of its beauty by thoughtless wild flower gatherers'. The traffic flow was almost entirely one-way, outwards from London; the buses were extremely popular and many country dwellers did not enjoy the sight of large, red double-deck buses discharging hundreds of trippers into their hitherto peaceful villages and fields. On sunny days the volume of traffic was almost overwhelming and heavy demands were made on regulating and platform staff.

Some inroads on this passenger movement were made by the charabanc — a typical 1920s conveyance — and towards the end of that decade by the coaches that took travellers further afield to Clacton, Margate and Brighton. The development of the semi-fast coaches which became Green Line also tended to reduce loadings on the buses. However, every year the programme was mounted, every year new routes or variations of the old ones were publicised. Route 98 worked all the way on Sundays from the Aldwych to Beaconsfield in 1930; in 1932 the facilities included 100C from Stratford

Broadway to Harlow, and 102 from the Aldwych to Windsor. Most of the special services began at Easter, were augmented at Whitsun and reached their peak in July and August; they were usually taken off in the first week in October when winter schedules were introduced.

The 1935 maps shows the extension of 47 to Knockholt Pound and of 69 beyond Wormley to Rye House. On Sundays the 23 now started from Wormwood Scrubs, offering buses every 6min all the way to Rainham on this somewhat unlikely route. The longer runs to Beaconsfield and Hatfield had been abandoned. The postwar maps show a steadily diminishing provision. In 1949 Farningham, Watford and St Albans had daily services; Westerham Hill and Windsor were weekend only termini; the Guildford route was cut short at Ripley. With the flight from the bus during the 1950s the Saturday and Sunday provision on Central buses withered away, and by the 1960s there were fewer buses running out of the garages than on any other day. The pleasure-seekers on the buses have departed as completely as those who used to take the Eagle boats from Tower Pier to Southend, Margate or Clacton; perhaps they were the same people.

146

The London Traffic Act 1924

The principal purpose of the Act was to limit the number of buses plying in London streets and the Metropolitan Police were given authority to regulate routes and frequencies of operation — they were already responsible for vehicle licensing. So far as operations in the London country area were concerned, these only became of interest to the Metropolitan Police if they entered the MPD (Metropolitan Police District). These were therefore numbered (as were all other London bus routes), the numbers being applied on 1 December 1924; the authorship of the scheme is always credited to Acting Chief Constable A. E. Bassom, who may — or may not — have been influenced by the fact that his son was district manager for National at Watford. The numbers are important as they form the first systematic list of bus routes in London country as a whole; some of the numbers (and the routes) are still in existence. Another provision of the Act was to establish the London & Home Counties Traffic Advisory Committee covering an extensive area well into London country as far as Gravesend, Dorking, Slough and St Albans; this provision was important in laying a political and administrative framework over the outer London area that hitherto had been managed in commercial terms by the LGOC.

The Bassom Scheme Numbers, 1 December 1924

301: Bushey-Watford-Northchurch
302: Bushey-Watford-Hemel Hempstead
303: New Barnet-Hatfield
304: Borehamwood station-St Albans
305: Bushey Heath (Alpine)-Watford
306: Waltham Cross-Enfield-Watford

306B: Waltham Cross-Epping Forest
307: Harrow Weald-Northwood-Watford
308: Havering-Romford-Aveley
309: Harefield-Watford
310: Waltham Cross-Hertford
401: Bexleyheath-Dartford-Sevenoaks
402: Bromley North-Sevenoaks
403: West Croydon-Sevenoaks
404: West Croydon-East Grinstead
405: West Croydon-Handcross
406: Kingston-Redhill
407: Sidcup-Dartford-Sidcup
408: West Croydon-Guildford
409: West Croydon-Uckfield
410: Bromley North-Reigate
411: Sidcup-Locks Bottom
412: West Croydon-Crawley-Horsham
413: West Croydon-Hartfield
414: West Croydon-Dorking-Horsham
415: West Croydon-Sanderstead
501: Uxbridge-Hounslow
502: Uxbridge-West Wycombe
503: Uxbridge-Iver-Windsor
504: Uxbridge-Amersham

Routes 301-310 were operated by National, 401-415 by East Surrey and 501-504 by Thames Valley.

Right:
One of the routes numbered in the Bassom scheme was the 410 which has therefore had a continuous history for 60 years. Here AN175, a Roe-bodied Leyland Atlantean based at Godstone, waits for time at Bromley North. This is an eminently serviceable vehicle for the route which has presented operating problems of one kind or another for much of its existence: Westerham Hill was a challenge for early engines; a low railway bridge in Oxted prevented the working of normal-height double-deckers for many years, and traffic congestion on the A25 tended to cause delays until the opening of the parallel motorway, the M25.
Michael Dryhurst

Timetables

1: East Surrey — May 1931

A study of the East Surrey timetable for Summer 1931, issued 20 May, gives some indication of the kind of service then provided. (This was the 'official timetable', price 2d.) The routes entering the London area, those in the 400 group, came first; the company's own routes, starting with 20: Reigate-Leigh-Brockham Green-Dorking, came at the end of the book. A particular feature was the absolute regularity of the services — a particular emphasis by Arthur Hawkins; thus buses ran throughout the day at intervals of 30 or 60min (occasionally more frequently) with extremely few variations or deviations from route. Many services were considerably augmented at weekends and there were additional shuttle workings on Saturdays, for example between Dunton Green and Sevenoaks on 402, between Nutfield and Redhill on 410, and between Horsham and Roffey on 34. Some of the routes were very long; a through working from West Croydon to Uckfield on 409 took 2hr 58min; Reigate to Tunbridge Wells on the 24 took 2hr 25min. There was joint working with Autocar on 24, and with Aldershot & District on Route 25: Dorking to Guildford. Two routes worked in what became the Central area; these were 411: Bromley North to Orpington and Sidcup, and 422: Eltham-Chislehurst-Orpington. These became 51 and 61 respectively and are still recognisable. The former Woking & District routes running through to Windsor were relatively new additions to the timetable.

There were some in-house advertisements: Green Line was said to 'provide safety, comfort and reliability. The best line — Green Line'. The reader was asked: 'Let us quote you for the hire of modern luxurious motorcoaches' — all quotations were said to be 'considerably reduced'. There were references to the RAF display at Hendon, an historical pageant at Rochester, The Derby at Epsom and the

Below:
The garage, in Walton Road, Woking was used by East Surrey for Routes 36, 37, 38 and 39 from 31 May 1931 after moving from the St John's Road premises formerly owned by Mr Fox of Woking & District. There was allegedly space for 20 vehicles in this garage, though doubtless most of them were small. The proximity of the billiard hall must have been a temptation to busmen going off duty, though the more youthful might have gone dancing in the hall on the extreme left. When Windsor garage opened on 1 March 1933 this garage was closed.
London Transport

Aldershot Tattoo — this last offered, at 3/6 (18p) return from Reigate, travel by 'special covered-top buses' (these must have been the STs, then almost new). Scholar's tickets, available only from head office, could be bought at 20% discount of half-price; a minimum of 50 had to be purchased. There were several exhortations 'to see the beautiful Surrey Hills' and prospective passengers were invited to travel by East Surrey to Box Hill, Crockham Hill, Ranmore Common and Newlands Corner. Passengers were warned that 'entering or leaving an omnibus whilst same is in motion' was 'entirely at their own risk'; they were also advised, if travelling on the top deck, 'to keep their seats while the bus is in motion and to beware of overhanging trees, bridges, telegraph wires, etc'. There was also a list of parcels agents — there was an 'express service' for parcels; among these were Mr W. King, Baker and Confectioner of Albury; Mr T. E. Sherlock, Draper and Outfitter, Brockham; Capt Scarle at the Halt, Effingham Junction; the Chintz Tea Rooms at Shalford, and a large number of public houses.

2: National — February 1930

The 'official' National timetable for Watford and North London, dated February 1930, was said to work to British Time. All the routes operated were listed, beginning with N1 (West Hyde to St Albans), then moving on to the 300 group, starting with 301/302 (Watford Heath to Aylesbury or Hemel Hempstead). Generally services were less intensive than East Surrey's though frequency was high on the Watford to Boxmoor road, between Watford and St Albans and between St Albans and Hatfield. Otherwise services ran half-hourly (306: Watford to New Barnet and Enfield Town), hourly or every 120min; thus the 303 ran every 2hr between Potters Bar and Hitchin, every hour on Saturday and Sunday afternoons. Many services were irregular, others ran only on certain days of the week; Saturdays and Sundays were busy days, with additional services and extensions of route — 310 ran through from Enfield to Stevenage or Royston (alternate journeys) on Sundays. The booklet includes faretables — there were single fares, some returns and some 'special return fares' available on 301/302 before 8am. Green Line services (and fares) were given in summary form. Passengers 'wishing to enter the bus' were asked 'to hail the driver when the omnibus is approaching, and *not* the conductor. Passengers wishing to alight should notify the conductor (in writing?) just before reaching the stopping place, and he will signal the driver to stop'. Enquiries, suggestions or complaints were to be sent to the District Manager, at Watford. At the very end of the book the National Omnibus & Transport Co Ltd begged 'to notify the public that this timetable is a monthly publication, and it is advisable to secure a *current* copy to avoid disappointment. The services are altered, as circumstances require, to meet the public demand'. There were few advertisements; one indicated: 'Doctors recommend Mazawattee Tea — The Tea Dyspeptics *can* enjoy!', and there was reference to a mysterious substance called 'Service Liquid Coffee'.

Route Lists

The two most substantial components of London General County Services (and later of the Country Bus & Coach Department of the London Passenger Transport Board) were the East Surrey routes and the services operated in the Watford and North London area by National. Representative route lists will give an indication of the scale of the transfers. The numbers given to the services in the LPTB numbering scheme of 3 October 1934 are indicated, though especially in the case of East Surrey some renumbering into the 400 series had taken place before this.

1: East Surrey — January 1932

LPTB numbers
3 October 1934

20: Reigate-Brockham Green-Dorking-Holmwood	439
21: Reigate-Redhill-South Merstham	460
22: Dorking-Holmbury St Mary-Sutton	422
23: Dartford-Leyton Cross-Swanley	423
24: Reigate-East Grinstead-Tunbridge Wells*	424
25: Dorking-Gomshall-Guildford†	425

* Joint with Autocar Services
† Joint with Aldershot & District

2: National — December 1930
'General Index to Services at a Glance'

Above:
Route 403 retained its identity on the local service to Warlingham Park Hospital after the parent route for Sevenoaks and Tonbridge became 483. RT3147 waits at the stands in West Croydon. It was new in May 1950 and has therefore seen continuous service for over 20 years. It was withdrawn in 1976. *Edward Shirras*

N64: Luton-Tea Green†	364
301: Watford Heath-Aylesbury	301
302: Watford Heath-Hemel Hempstead	302
303: New Barnet-Hitchin Market	303
304: St Albans-Elstree	304
306e: Watford-Enfield Town	306
309: Watford-Harefield	309
310: Hertford-Enfield	310A
310a: Stevenage-Hertford-Enfield	310
311: Watford-Shenley	311
313: St Albans-Enfield Town	313
316: Enfield-Ware-Royston	—

These routes were Eastern National property but LGCS ran them until 30 June 1933.

† *Though listed with the N prefix this was not always applied.*

Large additions to the LPTB Country Bus network came from Maidstone & District Motor Services on 1 July 1933 and from Amersham & District Motor Bus & Haulage Co Ltd on 24 November 1933.

Routes taken over from Maidstone & District, 1 July 1933

M&D No	LPTB No
1: Gravesend Clock Tower-Swanscombe (Craylands Lane)	487
1: Gravesend Clock Tower-Swanscombe (Eglinton Road)	488
3: Northfleet (Leather Bottel)-King's Farm Estate	495
4: Northfleet (Dover Road Schools)-Gypsy Corner	497
22: Gravesend-Northumberland Bottom (Tollgate Inn)	492
23: Gravesend-Singlewell	493
25: Farningham-Wrotham	485
26: Dartford-Gravesend-Denton	486
27: Gravesend-Betsham-Longfield-Ash	489
27: Gravesend-Southfleet-Longfield-Ash	490
42: Dartford-Longfield-Meopham (Hook Green)	491
44: Gravesend-King's Farm Estate	496

Note: Maidstone and District services 1, 3 and 4 were derived from those taken over for bus operation from the Gravesend & Northfleet Electric Tramways Ltd on 29 February 1929. Most of the M&D routes continued to run, though in truncated form; 26 continued from Gravesend to Faversham, for example, and 25 from Wrotham to Maidstone. The LT Routes 492 and 493 were really boundary markers which compelled M&D which operated over the same roads to charge a minimum fare; they were later absorbed into other routes, but still offered minimal services. Though 76 vehicles were scheduled in the Act, the LPTB appeared content with 55 (43 buses and 12 coaches).

Routes taken over from Amersham & District, 23 November 1933

A&D No	LPTB No
1: Ley Hill-Chesham-Amersham-Hazlemere-High Wycombe	362
2: Ley Hill-Chesham-Amersham (Crescent)	362
3: Ley Hill-Chesham-Amersham-Gerrards Cross-Windsor	353
4: Chesham Moor-Chesham-Chartridge-Great Missenden	394
5: Chesham-Amersham-Great Missenden	369A
6: Gerrards Cross-The Chalfonts via Gold Hill or Kingsway	305
7: Chesham-Cholesbury-Wigginton-Tring	397
8: Chesham-Hivings Hill-Bellingdon	348
9: Chesham-Fullers Hill-Hyde Heath	359
10: Gerrards Cross-The Chalfonts-High Wycombe	305
11: Wycombe Marsh (George V)-Mill End Road	326
11: High Wycombe (New Bowerdean Road)-Mill End Road	326A
12: High Wycombe-Holmer Green (The Common)	362A
13: High Wycombe-Penn-Beaconsfield (White Hart)	373
14: High Wycombe-Beaconsfield-Farnham-Slough-Windsor	441
15: High Wycombe-Four Ashes-Widmer End	366
16: Chesham-Bovingdon-Boxmoor-Hemel Hempstead	316
17: (This was the Chesham-Amersham-Uxbridge-Oxford Circus coach service, part of the Green Line network; it became route R)	
18: High Wycombe-Loudwater-Wooburn Common	502A
19: Great Missenden-Amersham-Windsor	369
23: Chesham-Amersham-Coleshill-Penn-Beaconsfield	396
502: West Wycombe-High Wycombe-Beaconsfield-Uxbridge	502

Note: Routes 4, 7, 16 and 23 were acquired from Chesham & District Bus Co Ltd on 8 December 1932, together with a local route from Chesham Broadway to Pond Park. The LPTB numbers were applied from 3 October 1934, though the 502 was subsequently changed to 455 on 1 December 1934 (and 502A to 455A). The Amersham & District network was subjected to very few changes in the 1930s; indeed the existence of many of the route numbers in the LCBS timetable shows a remarkable survival ability among these services. Forty-three buses were acquired by the LPTB; there were five coaches as well, but these were originally LGOC-owned and supplied for the Chesham-Oxford Circus coach service.

Bus Companies adjoining London Country

Maidstone & District Motor Services Ltd
Company registered 22 March 1911. LPTB acquired services in the Dartford and Gravesend areas 1 July 1933 and passed management of Autocar Services Ltd to M&D on the same day. M&D absorbed Autocar and Redcar Services Ltd in 1935. There were border exchanges with LCBS at Sevenoaks and Gravesend in 1976 and 1978. The company has a common management with East Kent Road Car Co Ltd, and East Kent buses now serve Sevenoaks on the long route from Folkestone.

Southdown Motor Services Ltd
Company registered 2 June 1915. LPTB passed certain services beyond its boundaries at Forest Row and Crawley to the Southern Railway, which passed them to Southdown, 1 July 1933. Local services in Crawley were surrendered to LCBS in 1971. There have been joint operations with Green Line since 11 May 1981, the starting date of 773: Gatwick to Brighton.

Aldershot & District Traction Co Ltd
Company registered 24 July 1912. Surrendered routes in the Guildford area to LPTB 2 August 1933. Merged with Thames Valley to form Thames Valley & Aldershot Bus Co Ltd (Alder Valley) 1 January 1972. Involved in Weyfarer. Thamesline and Chilternlink, with some boundary adjustments, in 1980. Joint coach operations with Green Line date from 16 May 1982.

Below:
Former Maidstone & District Leyland Titan, TD143, stands somewhat forlornly in the Langley Road, Slough garage. Delivered in 1928, it had an open-top body seating 24 passengers 'outside' and another 24 in the saloon. After acquisition by the LPTB the bus was fitted with a roof from a discarded NS in November 1935 and assumed its current appearance. The vehicle was sold out of service in the following year and subsequently worked for Liverpool Corporation until September 1946. *London Transport*

Above:
A familiar sight in Thames Valley, later Alder Valley, territory was for many years the Bristol vehicles of this type, eminently reliable and pleasing to travel in. This bus, built in 1952, lasted until the late 1960s and is seen here on the Henley to High Wycombe route. *B. C. Coward*

Right:
The section of Route 337 between Hemel Hempstead and Dunstable via Gaddesden Row and Studham was abandoned by London Country in 1972 and Court Line mounted a replacement service. However, Court Line became bankrupt and from 9 December 1974 United Counties took over operation and later extended the route into Luton as 43. Here United Counties 198, a Ford with Plaxton bodywork, once owned by Court Line, is seen in Dunstable. *Kevin Lane*

Thames Valley Traction Co Ltd

Registered 12 May 1897. Operated routes from Uxbridge on behalf of LGOC 1922 to 1928. Surrendered the Staines to Windsor road to LGCS 10 June 1933. Merged with Aldershot & District (above).

United Counties Omnibus Co Ltd

This area was originally the Midland Area of Eastern National (and before that of National), the change being made on 1 May 1952. There have been boundary adjustments with LCBS in the Luton area in 1976 and at Hitchin. Joint operation with Green Line of 760: Northampton to Heathrow began 27 March 1982.

Eastern Counties Omnibus Co Ltd

Company formed 14 July 1931. Made contact at Hitchin until 1933 and at Royston until 1935. Since 25 April 1981 has worked with Green Line on routes from Cambridge to Victoria.

Eastern National Omnibus Co Ltd

Company registered 28 February 1929, a descendant of the National Omnibus & Transport Co Ltd which continued to have legal responsibility for operations in the Watford and North London area until the formation of LGCS which took them over 1 March 1932. Eastern National lost some routes in Grays in 1933 and 1934, and the bulk of the Grays activities, 30 September 1951. There have been further border exchanges with London Country Bus Services on 1 September 1979. Curiously there are few joint workings with Green Line, though the Eastern National route 402: Southend to Victoria via Dartford would appear to be an obvious candidate.

Note: Green Line and Oxford/South Midland have worked routes to Oxford since 20 July 1980. All the companies listed are, of course, constituent members of the National Bus Co, formed 1 January 1969.

Above:
Eastern National extended Route 402 from Southend to run on from Dartford to Victoria, Eccleston Bridge on 23 November 1980. Subsequently fare restrictions were removed and the service effectively replaces Green Line 701 which disappeared in 1975. The 402 also runs over former London Transport roads from Grays to Dartford, the only bus route to do so apart from Thames Weald's Tunnel service. Seven return journeys are offered daily in the current timetable, and the service has become both ambitious and useful. Here the brand new Bristol seen at Southend has just returned from the very first journey in 1969. *T. Coughton*

Garages in London Country

The following garages have been maintained as operational bases in London country; their relative importance may be judged by the figures given for three separate dates of the vehicle 'run-out' — ie the maximum number of vehicles allocated to cover timetabled and other regular workings. The garage codes derived from long-established LGOC practice, though the code plates were not put on to the buses or coaches until 1934.

154

Code	Garage	June 1938		October 1969		16 May 1981	
		Buses	*Coaches*	*Buses*	*Coaches*	*Buses*	*Coaches*
CM	Chelsham	16	7	25	10	22	—
CY	Crawley	7	3	36	—	36	4
DG	Dunton Green	18	6	36	10	19	6
DS	Dorking	15	9	16	9	13	6
DT	Dartford	19	—	25	7	15	5
EG	East Grinstead	18	8	16	4	16	—
EP	Epping	4	24	—	—	—	—
GD	Godstone	25	5	25	3	23	—
GF	Guildford	21	12	12	7	14	10
GR	Garston*	—	—	72	6	58	4
GY	Grays	15	20	51	9	32	10
HA	Harlow	—	—	35	12	33	12
HE	High Wycombe	18	4	18	10	—	—
HF	Hatfield	10	7	28	5	30	4
HG	Hertford	39	18	47	8	31	10
HH	Hemel Hempstead	26	3	51	6	49	9
HN	Hitchin	—	4	—	—	—	—
LH	Leatherhead	27	7	59	—	35	—
LS	Luton	11	12	21	4	—	—
MA	Amersham	26	16	34	4	41	4
NF	Northfleet	43	6	40	11	36	7
RE	Romford (London Rd)	—	80	—	19	—	—
RF	Romford (North St)	—	12	—	—	—	—
RG	Reigate	29	9	40	12	33	9
SA	St Albans	44	3	55	13	39	14
SJ	Swanley	18	3	25	3	19	—
ST	Staines	7	13	8	10	10	17
SV	Stevenage	—	—	29	4	41	4
TG	Tring	6	5	10	7	—	—
TW	Tunbridge Wells	—	9	—	—	—	—
WA	Watford (High St)	58	—	—	—	—	—
WT	Watford (Leavesden Rd)	11	18	—	—	—	—
WR	Windsor	52	25	46	16	26	13
WY	Addlestone	17	11	28	7	15	7

Totals allocated for service:

Double-deck buses		300		558		267	
Single-deck buses		289		341		421	
Coaches		359		224		153	
Total		948 (Saturday)		1123 (Wed.)		841 (Wed.)	

Note *Garston was renamed Watford on 31 March 1979 in connection with the Watfordwide scheme; the GR plates were retained.

Garages closed during this period
RF: Romford (North Street) — 29 September 1942
WT: Watford (Leavesden Road) — 17 June 1952
WA: Watford (High Street) — 28 April 1959
HN: Hitchin — 27 April 1959
EP: Epping — 21 May 1963
TW: Tunbridge Wells — 2 December 1967
LS: Luton — 29 January 1977
TG: Tring — 2 April 1977
RE: Romford (London Road) — 2 July 1977
HE: High Wycombe — 30 September 1977
EG: East Grinstead — 31 December 1981

Garages opened during this period
GR: Garston — 18 June 1952
SV: Stevenage — 28 April 1959 (though a temporary shed had been in use since 1955)

New premises have been provided for Hatfield (opened 18 February 1959) and for Crawley (opened 21 November 1982)

Additional codes in current use by LCBS include:

CP: Central Pool (ie buses or coaches overhauled and awaiting allocation)

CW: Central Works (Tinsley Green)

NW: Northern Works (Garston)

Below:

Two RTs allocated to Route 477 (Dartford to Orpington) stand at the entrance of Swanley garage in September 1955. The shed is very much an East Surrey structure, though it was built by the LGOC; similarly the office accommodation and enquiry bureau on the left could only have been designed by the LPTB. The buses are RT3434 and RT3597; the first was allocated to Swanley in February 1952 and the second in October of the same year. Only RT3434 survived to enter LCBS service in 1970. *London Transport*

Certain codes fell out of use at an early stage; these included:

BL: Slough (Alpha Street) — opened by LGOC 20 April 1930 for Express Department, later Green Line. Closed 1933

BS: Bishop's Stortford — former Acme garage, closed 1934 (before the code plates arrived!)

CR: Crayford — LGOC, transferred to LGCS. Closed 1934

HA: Harefield — former Filkins and Ainsworth; out of use by 1934. (This was the only 'Country' garage in Middlesex)

SL: Slough (Langley Road) — LGOC, transferred to LGCS; closed 1937

SU: Slough (Bath Road) — former Premier Line garage, used for Green Line; closed 1936 on completion of extensions at Windsor

WE: Ware (Park Road) — former People's Motor Services; closed 1935

WR: Ware (Town Hall) — originally Harvey & Burrows; closed on opening of Hertford 2 January 1935

Note: The closure dates are those on which buses or coaches were reallocated; the premises were sometimes retained for storage or other purposes.

Buses and Coaches Fleet Lists

June 1938: Fleet List

Double-deckers:

LT   AEC Renown — 1
ST   AEC Regent — 124
STL   AEC Regent — 151
Q   AEC — 5
TD   Leyland Titan — 52 (inherited)

Single-deckers:

T   AEC Regal — 408
Q   AEC — 180
R   AEC Reliance — 43
TF   Prototype — 1
LT   AEC Renown — 3
TD   Leyland Titan — 14 (inherited)
TR   Leyland Tiger — 24 (inherited)
C   Leyland Cub — 75
CR   Leyland Cub — 1 (rear-engined)
BD   Bedford — 19 (inherited)
DC   Dennis — 3 (inherited)

Note: The inherited vehicles, mainly Leylands, were of limited life expectancy as London Transport brought in more standardised buses and coaches including the STLs. The number of small, mainly one-man-operated buses, the C, CR, BD and DC classes, is interesting — the total is 98.

1 July 1962:

Buses and Coaches allocated for service

Ruthless standardisation reduced the 'Country' fleet to the following categories:

Double-deckers:

RT   AEC Regent — 787 (for bus and Green Line)
RLH   Lowbridge and AEC Regent — 38
RMC   Routemaster coach — 1

Single-deckers:

RF   AEC Regal — 290 (for bus and Green line)
T   AEC Regal — 1 (sole survivor at CY)
RW   AEC Reliance — 3 (experimental)
GS   Guy Special — 53

1 January 1970: London Country Fleet List

Double-deckers:

RT   AEC Regent — 462
RML   Long Routemaster — 100
RLH   Lowbridge Regent — 17
RMC   Routemaster coach — 69
RCL   Long Routemaster coach — 43
XA   Leyland Atlantean — 3
XF   Daimler Fleetline — 8

Above:
Both buses and routes have long passed into history. The vehicles are Leyland Cubs, C7 and C63, photographed at Swanley garage in 1950. New in 1935, they were replaced by the Guy Specials in 1953. Route 478 was initially a replacement for Green Line Route B when it was withdrawn on 31 August 1939; it continued to run alongside 703 between Swanley and Wrotham after the war, though the timetable steadily withered and the only remnant now is operated as 423 as far as West Kingsdown. The 479 was a 'back road' working between Dartford and Farningham, routed via the Chequers Inn at Darenth and Horton Kirby. It was a postwar venture, put on when traffic was buoyant; when the decline set in it was an early casualty, being withdrawn on introduction of the winter schedules in 1958. The vehicles were sturdy and reliable, though the bumpers are conspicuously fragile.
Michael Dryhurst

Single-deckers:

RF   Regal — 430
GS   Guy Special — 10
RC   Reliance coach — 14
XMB   AEC Merlin — 1
MB   AEC Merlin — 33
MBS   AEC Merlin — 75

Note: Towards the end of its time London Transport was experimenting with high-capacity single-deck vehicles, of which the XMB, MB and MBS were to bring LCBS some years of trouble. The small bus, the GS, was in very limited use at this time.

Above:

Among the horrors of travel in the 1970s is the all-over advertisement bus. Here RMC1490, photographed at Northfleet garage, puts on a show for London & Manchester Assurance in June 1973. The vehicle started life as a dignified Green Line coach in 1962; in going the rounds as a mobile display it was allocated to several garages in turn so that the local populace could have the benefit of seeing it. *Edward Shirras*

Below:

Modern double-deck buses are not so alike as is sometimes assumed. From left to right are AF2, a Daimler Fleetline, and two Leyland Atlanteans, AN78 and AN120. All were built in 1972. The bodywork is respectively by Northern Counties, Park Royal and Metropolitan-Cammell-Weymann; the differences in frontal styling are interesting and repay close study. *London Country*

31 December 1982: London Country Bus Fleet

Double-deckers:

AN	Leyland Atlantean — 291	
LR	Leyland Olympian — 30	
AF	Daimler Fleetline — 7 (out-of-use)	
DMS	Daimler Fleetline — 2 (out-of-use)	
RMC	Routemaster coach — 1	
	(RMC4, much treasured)	

Single-deckers:

SNB	Leyland National — 486	
LNB	Leyland National — 36	
LN	Leyland National — 1	
BN	Bristol LHS — 32 (25 out-of-use)	
BL	Bristol LHS — 5 (all out-of-use)	
RP	AEC Reliance — 44 (18 out-of-use)	
RN	AEC Reliance — 10	
SMA	AEC Swift — 2 (both out-of-use)	
RF	AEC Regal — 1 (another treasure)	

Coaches:

RS	AEC Reliance — 45	
RP	AEC Reliance — 75	
TL	Leyland Tiger — 42	
DL	Leyland Leopard — 17	
PL	Leyland Leopard — 15	
D	AEC Reliance — 5	
P	AEC Reliance — 12	
DV	Volvo — 2	

Fleet list totals:	Double-deck buses	331
	Single-deck buses	599
	Coaches	213
	Total	1,143

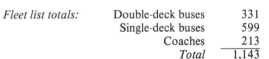

Bibliography

General background to bus and coach services is provided in two books by John Hibbs: *The History of British Bus Services* (David & Charles, 1968) and *The Bus and Coach Industry*, sub-titled *Its Economics and Organisation* (Dent, 1975). An earlier book by L. A. G. Strong, *The Rolling Road*, is less specialist and somewhat romantic and sets out to be 'the story of travel on the roads of Britain'; it was published by Hutchinson in 1956. Background specific to London Transport is authoritatively covered in two volumes by T. C. Barker and M. Robbins: *A History of London Transport* (Allen & Unwin, 1963 and 1974); bus activity in London country is dealt with in outline, and of great interest are the appendices which include lists of all the firms taken over by London Transport and its predecessors. Apart from chapters in this work there is very little material specific to the London General Omnibus Co except a monograph published by London Transport in 1955 to celebrate the centenary of the company.

East Surrey by Bell Street (H. J. Publications, 1974) has all the virtues of a scholarly treatise — it is thorough, detailed and painstaking; it does not make easy reading but there is nothing to equal it. National activities are covered admirably by R. J. Crawley, D. R. McGregor and F. D. Simpson in *The Years Between (1909-1969)*, Vol 1 (published by D. R. McGregor, 1979); the countrywide operations are included, together with detailed reference to the Watford and North London area; there is no comparable book. John Cummings has produced two excellent studies: *Railway Motor Buses and Bus Services in the British Isles, 1902-1933* (Oxford Publishing Co, Vol 1, 1978, Vol 2, 1980). Very detailed, very thorough, this writer describes the services based on Slough by the GWR and on Watford by the LNWR, later LMS.

There are two very general books concerned with LPTB; V. Sommerfield's *London Transport, a Record and a Survey* (LPTB) is an entirely uncritical brief monograph dealing with the early years of the Board; Charles Graves' *London Transport Carried On* (LPTB, 1947) explores the wartime period but has little to say about London country. In *The London Country Bus* (Oakwood Press, 1968) J. S. Wagstaff gives a chatty survey of a great deal of ground. Green Line affairs are dealt with by Albert McCall in his splendidly detailed account of the development of the coach services, *Green Line* (New Cavendish Books, 1980); D. W. K. Jones and Bernard Davis celebrated the 50th anniversary of Green Line in *Green Line, 1930 to 1980*, published by London Country, 1980. There is also my own book on the subject, *Fifty Years of the Green Line* (Ian Allan, 1980). Published just in time for inclusion here is a definitive work on independent operators: *Country Independents 1919-1939*, part 1 (H. J. Publications, 1983). It surveys London Country from Grays round to St Albans in detail.

Photographic studies include three books by John Gray, all published by Ian Allan: *London's Buses in Camera 1933-1969*, *London's Country Buses* and *London's Suburban Buses*. All are rewarding, as is Terence Cooper's *London and its Buses* published by London Transport in 1979 to mark the 150th anniversary of George Shillibeer's first horsebus of 1829. *The Kaleidoscope of London Buses Between the Wars* by George Robbins and Alan Thomas (published by Marshall, Harris and Baldwin Ltd) has some fascinating photographs and much telling detail in text and captions.

Vehicles have an extensive literature of their own. I have found most useful and informative *The London Motorbus — Its Origins and Development* by J. Graeme Bruce and Colin H. Curtis (London Transport, 1973) and Colin Curtis's *Buses of London* (London Transport, 1977) which gives a brief historical review of every type of bus purchased by LT or its successors since 1908. Two books published by the Oakwood Press are J. S. Wagstaff's *The London Single-deck Bus of the Fifties* (RF and GS buses mainly) and *The London Routemaster Bus*; both are pleasingly detailed. Ken Blacker's *RT — The Story of a London Bus* (Capital Transport, 1979) is exceptional in the quality of its information and range of photographs. Also most interesting is Richard Clark's *In Shades of Green — the Story of the Country Routemasters* (Regent Transport Publishing, 1980). There is much detailed reference material in the LOTS (London Omnibus Traction Society) publications including *The London Bus*, available monthly to members, and the quarterly *London Bus Magazine*; most useful to general reader and enthusiast alike are the annual *Reviews*, available since 1973. Successive *ABC of London Transport* books have been published by Ian Allan since the first, by Barrington Tatford, appeared in 1945. Recently Capital Transport has produced handbooks on *London Country Buses and Green Line Coaches*.

Magazines and periodicals studied include *Buses*,

Above:
Country bus work is not always — not even often! — like this. Bristol BL34 approaches the stop on Ranmore Common to collect walkers returning to Dorking one summer Sunday in 1980. Cow parsley and tall grasses, rising to the sun, almost engulf the stop sign opposite.
B. J. Garrard

formerly under the redoubtable editorship of John Parke, now in the capable hands of Stephen Morris. It is hard to realise, now that there is so much material on buses and coaches about, how much a pioneer this magazine was. House magazines have also been of the greatest interest; the LGOC's *Penny Fare* became the rather more formal *London Trans-port Magazine. Country Bus News*, with some delightful editorial material by Albert McCall dates from 1956; *The Bulletin*, started in 1963, also concerned with events in London country, makes somewhat melancholy reading. LCBS affairs were first covered in the *London Country Magazine* which appeared between June 1970 and Christmas 1972. They are now the subject of *London Country Matters*, a very well produced broadsheet.

Much of the material cited, though not all, is held in the library attached to the London Transport Museum in Covent Garden. This is an admirable resource not widely known and includes a very rich store of reports, magazines, books and periodicals associated with all aspects of London Transport. There is no admission charge — a phone call on 01-379 6344 to the Librarian will allow access to a transport researcher's treasure trove.